C Programming for Microcontrollers

Featuring ATMEL's AVR Butterfly and the Free WinAVR Compiler

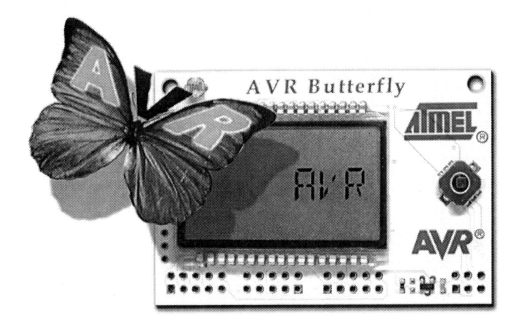

Joe Pardue

SmileyMicros.com

Smiley Micros
5601 Timbercrest Trail
Knoxville, TN 37909
Email: book@SmileyMicros.com
Web: http://www.SmileyMicros.com

ISBN 0-9766822-0-6

For Marcia

God only knows what I'd be without you...

Table of Contents:

Chapter 1: Introduction 11
  Why C? 12
  Why AVR? 12
  Goals 14
Chapter 2: Quick Start Guide 17
  Software 19
    WinAVR – Oh, Whenever… 19
    Programmers Notepad 19
    AVRStudio – FREE and darn well worth it. 20
    Br@y++ Terminal: 20
  Hardware 21
    Constructing Your Development Platform 21
  Blinking LEDs – Your First C Program 27
    Write it in Programmers Notepad 27
    Download to the Butterfly with AVRStudio 31
    Blinky Goes Live 33
    Simulation with AVRStudio 35
  GOOD GRIEF! 37
Chapter 3: A Brief Introduction to C – What Makes Blinky Blink? 39
  Comments 39
  Include Files 39
  Expressions, Statements, and Blocks 39
  Operators 40
  Flow Control 40
  Functions 41
  The Main() Thing 42
Chapter 4: C Types, Operators, and Expressions 45
  Data Types and Sizes 45
  Variable Names 49
  Constants 49
  Declarations 50
  Arithmetic Operators 50
  Relational and Logical Operators 52
  Bitwise Operators 53
  Assignment Operators and Expressions 61
  Conditional Expressions 62

Precedence and Order of Evaluation...62
Projects...65
   Port Input and Output..65
   Cylon Eye Speed and Polarity Control 70
Chapter 5: C Control Flow...73
Statements and Blocks 73
If-Else and Else-If...74
Switch...75
Loops – While, For and Do-while..78
Break and Continue...79
Goto and Labels 80
A few practical examples: strlen, atoi, itoa, reverse...............................81
Chapter 6: C Functions and Program Structures.....................................87
Function Basics...87
Returns 89
Variables External, Static, and Register 90
Scope..91
Headers...92
Blocks...92
Initialization 92
Recursion 93
Preprocessor 94
Projects...98
   Is anybody out there? Communicating with a PC 98
Chapter 7: Microcontroller Interrupts and Timers 109
Interrupts 109
   Projects..114
   Grab your joystick – and test your interrupts..................................114
Timers/Counters..119
Calibrating the Butterfly oscillator: 121
   Projects..128
   Precision Blinking..128
   Pulse Width Modulation – LED Brightness Control 133
   Pulse Width Modulation - Motor Speed Control 137
   Speedometer..144
Chapter 8: C Pointers and Arrays 153
Addresses of variables 153

Function Arguments 157
Arrays 159
FIFOs and LIFOs: Stacks and Queues (Circular Buffers) 167
Function Pointers 169
Complex Pointer and Array Algorithms 170
Projects 171
   Messenger 171
   Does anybody know what time it is? A Real Time Clock 178
   Music to my ears. "Play it again Sam." 189
Chapter 9 – Digital Meets Analog – ADC and DAC 207
   But First - A Debugging Tale 207
   Analog to Digital Conversion 210
   Projects 216
      DAC and ADC - Function Generator / Digital Oscilloscope ... 227
Chapter 10: C Structures 241
   Structure Basics 241
   Structures and Functions 243
   Structure Arrays 246
   Typedef 246
   Unions 247
   Bit-fields 247
   Projects 251
      Finite State Machine 251
Chapter 11 The Butterfly LCD 261
   PC to LCD test program 262
   Conclusion 270
Appendix 1: Project Kits 273
Appendix 2: Soldering Tutorial 275
Appendix 3: Debugging Tale 279
Appendix 4: ASCII Table 283
Appendix 5: Decimal, Hexadecimal, and Binary 285
Appendix 6: Motor Speed Control Wheel 287
Appendix 7: HyperTerminal 289
Index 295

Table of Figures:

Figure 1: C being invented 11
Figure 2: The Butterfly front 21
Figure 3: RS-232 connections. 22
Figure 4: Battery holder, switch, and batteries. 23
Figure 5: External battery connection to Butterfly 23
Figure 6: Butterfly hooked up to RS-232 24
Figure 7: Bray's Terminal 25
Figure 8: Enter name to send to the Butterfly 25
Figure 9: Blinky wiring diagram and photo of wired board 26
Figure 10: Hardware setup for Blinky 27
Figure 11: From the cover of the Battlestar Galactica comic *Red Cylon* 34
Figure 12: from page 92 of the ATMega169 data book 58
Figure 13 ATMega169 Block Diagram 65
Figure 14: Port I/O switch input and LED output 69
Figure 15: Bit 7 high   Figure 16: Bit 7 low 71
Figure 17: Pulse Width Modulation Duty Cycle 134
Figure 18: Motor Speed Control Schematic and Parts 137
Figure 19: Motor Speed Control Breadboard Labeled 138
Figure 20: Motor Speed Control Hardware 138
Figure 21: Motor Base 139
Figure 22: Motor Wheel Stationary and Spinning 139
Figure 23: Opto Interrupt Switch - H21A1 145
Figure 24: Opto Interrupter Glued on Motor Base 145
Figure 25: Speedometer 146
Figure 26: PDP-11 153
Figure 27: 10-bit successive approximation ADC Figure 211
Figure 28: Potentiometer Schematic 225
Figure 29: Voltage measurement 226
Figure 30: R-2R resistor ladder 228
Figure 31: Breadboard of R-2R DAC 228
Figure 32: Breadboard R-2R DAC wiring 229
Figure 33: R-2R DAC with Oscilloscope 229
Figure 34: Function Generator / Digital Oscilloscope on HyperTerminal 230
Figure 35: Sine Wave   Figure 36: Square Wave 230
Figure 37: Triangle Wave   Figure 38: Sawtooth Wave 231

Figure 39 Butterfly Menu...253
Figure 40: Cheap soldering iron, solder and wick from JAMECO.....................276
Figure 41: Seasoning the tip...276

Chapter 1: Introduction

C Programming and microcontrollers are two big topics, practically continental in size, and like continents, are easy to get lost in. Combining the two is a little like traipsing from Alaska to Tierra del Fuego. Chances are you'll get totally lost and if the natives don't eat you, your infected blisters will make you want to sit and pout. I've been down this road so much that I probably have my own personal rut etched in the metaphorical soil, and I can point to all the sharp rocks I've stepped on, all the branches that have whacked me in the face, and the bushes from which the predators leapt. If you get the image of a raggedy bum stumbling through the jungle, you've got me right. Consider this book a combination roadmap, guidebook, and emergency first aid kit for your journey into this fascinating, but sometimes dangerous world.

I highly recommend that you get the book, 'The C Programming Language – second edition' by Kernighan and Ritchie, here after referred to as K&R. Dennis Ritchie, Figure 1, wrote C, and his book is the definitive source on all things C.

Figure 1: C being invented

In Figure 1, Dennis Ritchie, inventor of the C programming language stands next to Ken Thompson, original inventor of Unix, designing the original Unix operating system at Bell Labs on a PDP-11

I have chosen to follow that book's organization in this book's structure. The main difference is that their book is machine independent and gives lots of examples based on manipulating text, while this book is machine dependent, specifically based on the AVR microcontroller, and the examples are as microcontroller oriented as I can make them.

Why C?

Back in the dark ages of microprocessors, software development was done exclusively in the specific assembly language of the specific device. These assembly languages were character based 'mnemonic' substitutions for the numerical machine language codes. Instead of writing something like: 0x12 0x07 0xA4 0x8F to get the device to load a value into a memory location, you could write something like: MOV 22 MYBUFFER+7. The assembler would translate that statement into the machine language for you. I've written code in machine language (as a learning experiment) and believe me when I tell you that assembly language is a major step up in productivity. But a device's assembly language is tied to the device and the way the device works. They are hard to master, and become obsolete for you the moment you change microcontroller families. They are specific purpose languages that work only on specific microprocessors. C is a general-purpose programming language that can work on any microprocessor that has a C compiler written for it. C abstracts the concepts of what a computer does and provides a text based logical and readable way to get computers to do what computers do. Once you learn C, you can move easily between microcontroller families, write software much faster, and create code that is much easier to understand and maintain.

Why AVR?

As microprocessors evolved, devices increased in complexity with new hardware and new instructions to accomplish new tasks. These microprocessors became known as CISC or Complex Instruction Set Computers. Complex is often an understatement; some of the CISCs that I've worked with have mind-numbingly complex instruction sets. Some of the devices have so many instructions that it becomes difficult to figure out the most efficient way to do anything that isn't built into the hardware.

Then somebody figured that if they designed a very simple core processor that only did a few things but did them very fast and efficiently, they could make a much cheaper and easier to program computer. Thus was born the RISC, Reduced Instruction Set Computers. The downside was that you had to write additional assembly language software to do all the things that the CISC computer had built in. For instance, instead of calling a divide instruction in a CISC device, you would have to do a series of subtractions to accomplish a division using a RISC device. This 'disadvantage' was offset by price and speed, and is completely irrelevant when you program with C since the complier generates the assembly code for you.

Although I'll admit that 'CISC versus RISC' and 'C versus assembly language' arguments often seem more like religious warfare than logical discourse, I have come to believe that the AVR, a RISC device, programmed in C is the best way to microcontroller salvation (halleluiah brother).

The folks that designed the AVR as a RISC architecture and instruction set while keeping C programming language in mind. In fact they worked with C compiler designers from IAR to help them with the hardware design to help optimize it for C programming.

Since this is an introductory text I won't go into all the detailed reasons I've chosen the AVR, I'll just state that I have a lot of experience with other microcontrollers such as Intel's 8051, Motorola's 68xxxes, Zilog's Z's, and Microchip's PIC's and I'm done with them (unless adequately paid – hey, I'm no zealot). These devices are all good, but they require expensive development boards, expensive programming boards, and expensive software development tools (don't believe them about the 'free' software, in most cases the 'free' is for code size or time limited versions).

The AVR is fast, cheap, in-circuit programmable, and development software can be had for FREE (really free, not crippled or limited in any way). I've paid thousands of dollars for development boards, programming boards, and C compilers for the other devices, but never again -- I like free. The hardware used in this text, the ATMEL Butterfly Evaluation Board can be modified with a few components to turn it into a decent development system and the Butterfly and needed components can be had for less than $40.00 (See Appendix 1 Project Kits). You can't get a better development system for 10 times this price and you can pay 100 times this and not get as good.

Okay, maybe I am a zealot.

Goals

What I hope to accomplish is to help you learn **some** C programming on **a specific** microcontroller and provide you with enough foundation knowledge that you can go off on your own somewhat prepared to tackle the plethora (don't you just love that word, say it 10 times real quick) of microcontrollers and C programming systems that infest the planet.

Both C programming and microcontrollers are best learned while doing projects. I've tried to provide projects that are both useful and enhance the learning process, but I've got to admit that many of the early projects are pretty lame and are put in mainly to help you learn C syntax and methods.

Suggested Prerequisites:
- You should be able to use Windows applications.
- You should have an elementary knowledge of electronics, or at least be willing to study some tutorials as you go along so that you'll know things like why you need to use a resistor when you light up an LED.
- I've received lots of suggestions about what needs to be in this book. Some folks are adamant that one must first learn assembly language and microcrocontroller architecture and basic electronics and digital logic and bla bla bla before even attempting C on microcontrollers. I politely disagree and say that you should just jump right in and learn what's fun for you. You'll run across lots of stuff that you will want to learn about, but I won't cover in the book so you should be able to bracket your ignorance (and mine) making a note when you hit something you don't know but would like to. Then you can learn it later. I'm using lots of things that aren't directly relevant to C programming (like communicating with a microcontroller from a PC using a serial port or like what the heck is that transistor motor driver thingee…). If you get really curious, then GOOGLE for a tutorial on the topic.

By the time you complete the text and projects you will:

- Have an intermediate understanding of the C programming language.
- Have a elementary understanding microcontroller architecture.
- Be able to use the WinAVR and AVR Studio tools to build programs.
- Be able to use C to develop microcontroller functions such as:
  - Port Inputs and Outputs
  - Read a joystick
  - Use timers
  - Program a Real Time Clock
  - Communicate with a PC
  - Conduct analog to digital and digital to analog conversions
  - Measure temperature, light, and voltage
  - Control motors
  - Make music
  - Control the LCD
  - Flash LEDs like crazy

On the CD you will find the ATMEL ATMEGA169 data book. At 364 pages, it is the comprehensive source of information for the microcontroller used on the AVR Butterfly board. Open it on your PC with Adobe Acrobat and look around a bit: intimidating isn't it? But don't worry; one of the purposes of this text is to give you enough knowledge so that you can winnow the wheat from the chaff in the data book and pull out what you need for your C based control applications.

I know how easy it is to get bogged down in all the detail and lose momentum on this journey, so we'll begin with the 'Quick Start' chapter by learning only enough to make something interesting happen: kind of a jet plane ride over the territory. Then we will proceed at a comfortable pace from the simple to the complex using as interesting examples as I can come up with. I'm partial to LEDs so you are going to see a lot of flashing lights before we are through, and hopefully the lights won't be from you passing out from boredom and boinking your head on the keyboard.

Chapter 2: Quick Start Guide

The purpose of this quick start guide is to help you modify the Butterfly hardware so you can use it as a development board and to show you how to use the FREE software for writing and compiling C code and downloading it from your PC to the Butterfly.

The AVR Butterfly is an evaluation kit for the ATMEGA169 microcontroller that was custom designed with an AVR core and peripherals to make it both a general-purpose microcontroller and an LCD controller. This little board is by far (at this writing) the lowest cost system for learning and developing that I've ever seen. I don't know how much these things cost them to make, but Digi-Key (www.digikey.com) sells them for $19.99 (Spring 2005), which has to be a real loss leader for ATMEL (www.ATMEL.com). But their loss is our gain, and I'm sure they are happy to prime-the-pump a little, knowing that we'll get hooked on the AVR and buy lots of their product.

It is simply amazing what the Butterfly has built in:

- 100 segment LCD display
- 4 Mbit (that's 512,000 bytes!) dataflash memory
- Real Time Clock 32.768 kHz oscillator
- 4-way joystick, with center push button
- Light sensor
- Temperature sensor
- ADC voltage reading, 0-5V
- Piezo speaker for sound generation
- Header connector pads for access to peripherals
- RS-232 level converter for PC communications
- Bootloader for PC based programming without special hardware
- Pre-programmed demos with source code
- Built-in safety pin for hanging from your shirt (GEEK POWER!)
- Kitchen sink.

I mean this thing has everything (except a kitchen sink... sorry). If anyone can find a development platform with anywhere near this much for this price, I want to hear about it. And, no, I don't own stock in ATMEL, or work for them, I just couldn't find anything that comes close to this system for my goal of teaching C programming for AVR microcontrollers (or any microcontrollers for that matter). If I seem to be raving a bit, get used to it, I do that a lot.

There are sufficient instructions on the AVR Butterfly box to show you how to use all the built-in functions. Play with it now before you risk destroying it in the next step. Don't say I didn't warn you. If you break it, you'll have to order a new one from Digi-Key (www.digikey.com). I shudder to think how many of these things will get burned up, blown up, stepped on, and drenched in coffee. And that's just me this morning.

Note: in order to save you money, rather than selling you the Butterfly and the experiments kits, you will find a parts list (Appendix 1) so that you can buy this stuff directly from the vendors. But check my website: www.smileymicros.com, no telling what you'll find. (Hopefully, not a 'going out of business' sale.)

If you purchased the e-book, you can download the WinAVR software from http://sourceforge.net/projects/winavr (this book uses version 20040404) and the AVRStudio software from the http://www.atmel.com web site. On the ATMEL website search for the AVRStudio version 4.11 (later versions may not correlate to this book). If, for some reason, these sites are not available (I can't guarantee what they'll do to their sites) look on the http://www.smileymicros.com website for updated information on how to get the software. If you purchased a hard copy of the book, you will find the software on the accompanying CD.

Don't get bogged down in all the installation choices given, just accept suggested defaults so your installation will match this book. And, as an aside, by the time you install all this software, the WinAVR and the AVRStudio will have new and improved versions available on their web sites. DON'T USE THEM! This text is based on the versions on the CD or on the SmileyMicros.com web site and using the new and improved software may only confuse things. Of course, by the time you finish this text, you will be encouraged to get the latest and greatest, by then you'll know all you need to use it wisely.

Software

We will use three FREE software packages, the WinAVR compiler from sourceforge.net, the AVRStudio 4 from ATMEL, and Br@y++'s Terminal.

WinAVR – Oh, Whenever…

WinAVR is a set of tools for C programming the AVR microcontroller family. A bunch of folks have volunteered their time to write this software and give it away as part of the free software movement (www.sourceforge.net). These folks generously giving their time to help others is almost enough to change my cynical opinion of humanity. You can spend thousands on C compilers for microcontrollers and before WinAVR you had to spend several hundred even for a crappy compiler. This software is FREE, but SourceForge has expenses so send them some money at www.sourceforge.net/donate.

At http://sourceforge.net/projects/winavr/ you see the summary:

"WinAVR (pronounced "whenever") is a suite of executable, open source software development tools for the ATMEL AVR series of RISC microprocessors hosted on the Windows platform. Includes the GNU GCC compiler for C and C++."

Go to: http://winavr.sourceforge.net/index.html and check out their homepage.

But don't get too distracted with all that yet, just use the tools as shown here, and once you reach the end of this book, then you'll have the skills to fully exploit those web sites.

Programmers Notepad

We'll be writing our software using the most excellent Programmers Notepad, another FREE program available at sourceforge.net and included in the WinAVR distribution package. Imagine what Microsoft would charge for this FREE software. Be a good guy or gal and send them some money at http://www.pnotepad.org.

AVRStudio – <u>FREE</u> and darn well worth it.

AVR Studio is provided free by the good folks at ATMEL Corporation, who seem to understand that the more help they give developers, the more they will sell their microcontrollers. Actually, this too could cost hundreds and still be darn well worth it, but unless you just really like Norway, don't send them any money, they'll get theirs on the backend when you start buying thousands of AVRs for your next great invention.

The AVR Studio will be used for two things: first, to download your software to the AVR Butterfly, and second, to simulate the ATMEGA169 running your software.

Br@y++ Terminal:

The original Quick Start Guide chapter used HyperTerminal, which is hard to setup, clunky, and hated by so many folks on the AVRFreaks.net forum that I contacted Br@y++ and he gave me permission to use and distribute his highly recommended and easy to use and understand terminal package. You can get it at http://bray.velenje.cx/avr/terminal or http://www.smileymicros.com. It is shown in Figure 7: Bray's Terminal. The examples in the text still show the HyperTerminal, but it shouldn't be a problem substituting Bray's. If you want to use HyperTerminal, the introduction to it is in Appendix 1.

Hardware

Constructing Your Development Platform

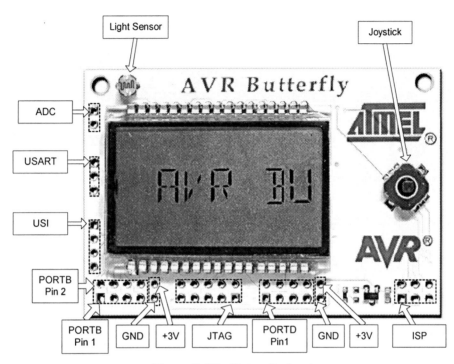

Figure 2: The Butterfly front

Solder the female headers to the ADC, PORTB, and PORTD lands. Note that the square pads are pin1 and that PORTB and PORTD seem to have 10 pins, but they don't, pins 9 and 10 are ground and power respectively (see Figure 2).

The RS-232 Connection:
Communication with the PC requires three lines: TXD, RXD, and GND. The TXD is the transmit line (data from the PC to the Butterfly), RXD is the receive line (data from the microcontroller to the PC) and GND is the common ground. Notice that there is a bit of relativity in this equation, the microcontroller's RXD wire is the PC's TXD wire and vice versa. I can't count the number of times I've

done stupid things like connecting the microcontroller's RXD pin to the DB-9 RXD pin, because I didn't think 'RXD – receive - relative to what?'

The parts list has a DB-9 female solder cup RS-232 connector. Follow the illustrations in Figure 3.

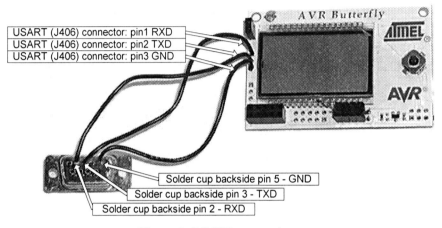

USART (J406) connector: pin1 RXD
USART (J406) connector: pin2 TXD
USART (J406) connector: pin3 GND

Solder cup backside pin 5 - GND
Solder cup backside pin 3 - TXD
Solder cup backside pin 2 - RXD

Figure 3: RS-232 connections.

NOTICE HOW THE RXD AND TXD LINES CROSS OVER – PAY CAREFUL ATTENTION AS IT IS EASY TO GET THESE REVERSED.

Constructing the power supply:

The Butterfly comes with a CR2450 coin battery that will power the LCD for a long time, but will be used up quickly by the RS-232 connection and our experiments. Remove the coin battery and construct a battery pack with parts from the JAMECO parts list (Appendix 7) using the following pictures. Be sure and get the power, red wire, and ground, black wire, correct: as shown in Figure 4 and Figure 5.

NOTE: ALL THE ILLUSTRATIONS SHOW PORTD WITH AN 8-PIN HEADER AND THE POWER WIRES SOLDERED IN PLACE. THE PARTS KIT SPECIFIES 10-PIN CONNECTORS FOR BOTH PORTS B AND D. USE THE 10-PIN HEADER ON PORTD AND INSERT RATHER THAN SOLDER THE POWER WIRES.

Figure 4: Battery holder, switch, and batteries.

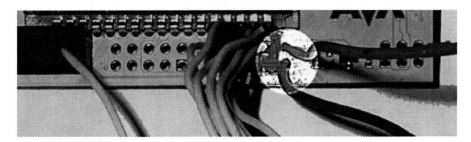

Figure 5: External battery connection to Butterfly

A few days after making the power supply I left it on all night, so I added an LED (Figure 4) to the switch so that I'd know that it was on. You can solder the long leg of an LED to the rightmost pin on the switch, where the +3V goes to the Butterfly, and then solder a 150 resistor to the short leg and the resistor to the rivet at the base of the battery on the right. The LED is lit when the switch is to +3V.

Test your Connection using Brays Terminal:

Hook your RS-232 cable to the Butterfly as in Figure 6. Then run Bray's Terminal, (well, Br@y++'s to be exact – available at http://bray.velenje.cx/avr/terminal and http://www.smileymicros.com) and configure it as in Figure 7 with the radio buttons set to select your COM port, 19200 Baud rate, 8 Data bits, parity of none, 1 Stop bits, and no handshaking.

Click the connect button. Turn on your Butterfly power supply, then with the joystick button centered press it and watch the stream of ?????? question marks that should be coming from the Butterfly. This is the Bootloader telling you that it is alive and ready to be boot loaded, or perhaps it is just curious as to what's going on?

Figure 6: Butterfly hooked up to RS-232

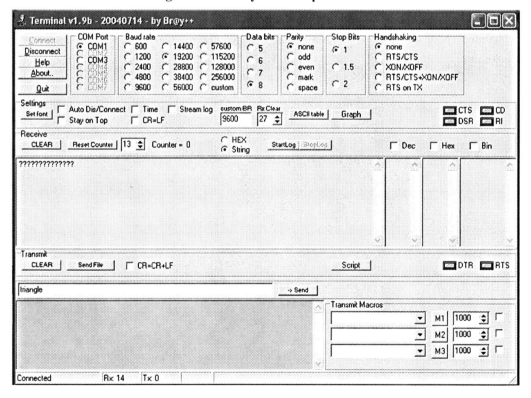

Figure 7: Bray's Terminal

If you don't get the string of question marks, then try the other COM ports (in Figure 7 only COM1 and COM3 are shown for my machine, yours may be different. Press disconnect then connect and try again. If it still doesn't work, carefully check that the RS-232 cable is connected. Try again. Still no? Recheck that you've got the DB-9 soldered correctly to your Butterfly. Try again. Still no? Is it turned on? If you move the joystick upward do you get the LCD scrolling message? Yes? Turn it off and on and press the center again. Still no? If its not working by this point go back and meticulously retry everything you can think of, including passing a dead chicken over the setup while chanting voodoo hymns. It took me a while to get all this running and I supposedly know what I'm doing, so don't feel bad if this is a little harder than you might hope. (You get what you pay for).

In a moment you will scoop out the Butterfly's brains, toss them aside, and stick in some brains that Igor got from a garage sale, so let's do one final test on the Butterfly as it came out of the package. If all goes well, you will eventually be able to reload the Butterfly's original brains, but all seldom goes will, as Igor will readily attest.

With the Butterfly hooked up to the RS-232 port and the Br@y++ Terminal running, turn the Butterfly on and click the joystick up to get the LCD scrolling. Move the joystick straight down three times till you see 'Name' then move the joystick to the right twice till you see 'Enter name' then move the joystick straight down once and you will see 'Download name' then push down the joystick center for a moment until you see 'Waiting for input'. Now write a name in the bottom text panel of the Br@y++ Terminal (Figure 8) and hit enter (or push it gently if you prefer). The name you entered should be scrolling across the LCD as shown in Figure 6.

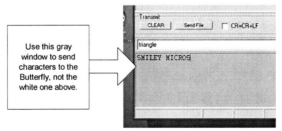

Figure 8: Enter name to send to the Butterfly

Let's Blink Some LED's:

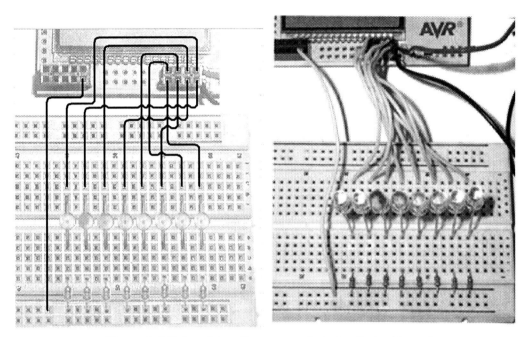

Figure 9: Blinky wiring diagram and photo of wired board

All the parts are listed in the JAMECO parts list Appendix 1. Put the LEDs in the breadboard with the short leg on the resistor side. Use the 150-Ohm resistors to jumper to the ground strip. You'll need to make a bunch of jumper wires, cut 9 pieces about 4 inches long and strip each end about 3/8 inch, then connect them to the breadboard as shown in Figure 9, with the right most LED connected to pin 1 of PORTD (Figure 2) and subsequent pins connected sequentially. The pins are numbered with the odd pins on the bottom of the PORTD land and the even pins on the top. Cut a 6" wire and use it to connect the ground strip to the ground pin of PORTB as shown.

Now connect your RS-232 cable between the computer and the RS-232 connector you soldered to the Butterfly. Your hardware should look like Figure 10.

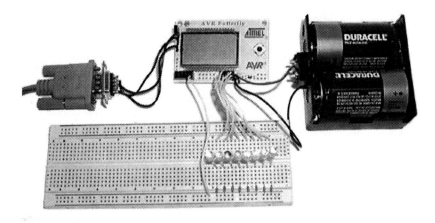

Figure 10: Hardware setup for Blinky.

Blinking LEDs – Your First C Program

You might wonder why blinking an LED is the first project, when traditional C programming texts start with the classic "Hello, world" program. It certainly seems that since the Butterfly has an LCD that can show the words it would be easy. But the reality is that controlling the LCD is much more complex than blinking an LED, so we'll save the LCD for later when we've gotten a better handle on things.

- Make a directory called Blinky for this project.
- Copy '…/WinAVR/Samples/makefile' (notice that it has no extension) to the Blinky directory.

Write it in Programmers Notepad

- Find Programmers Notepad that was installed as part of WinAVR (you should have an icon for it on your desktop) and open it. You will need to add a tool, which will let you use the AVR Studio simulator.
- Open the Tools menu and click on Options.

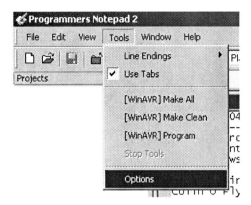

- In the Options window select Tools:

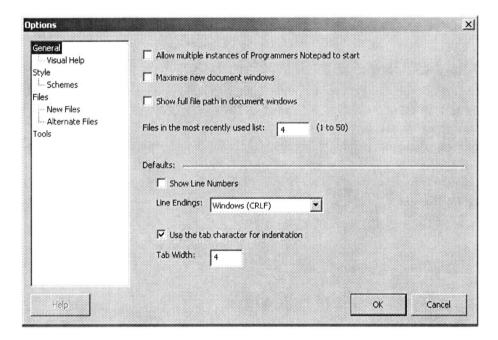

- Then select Add:

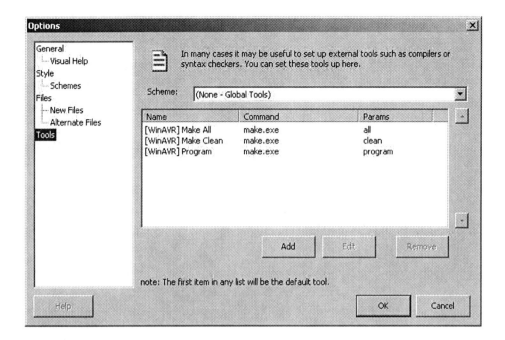

- Change the check box to look like:

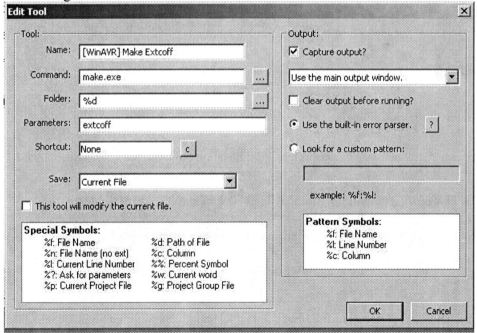

- Click OK.
- Click File, then New, then C/C++, and name it Blinky.c.
- Save in Blinky directory and CAREFULLY TYPE exactly as shown:

```c
// Blinky.c
#include <avr/io.h>
#include <avr/delay.h>

int main (void)
{
   // set PORTD for output
   DDRD = 0xFF;

     while(1) {

          for(int i = 1; i < 128; i = i*2)

          {
             PORTD = i;
             _delay_loop_2(30000);
          }

          for(int i = 128; i > 1; i -= i/2)

          {
             PORTD = i;
             _delay_loop_2(30000);
          }
       }
       return 1;

}
```

- Open File and again save 'Blinky.c' to your Blinky directory
- NOTE: YOU MUST ADD THE EXTENSION '.c' TO THE NAME
- Open the file 'makefile' in your Blinky directory.
- Change these lines:

```
MCU = atmega128

# Output format. (can be srec, ihex, binary)
FORMAT = ihex
```

```
# Target file name (without extension).
TARGET = main
```

- To:

```
MCU = atmega169

# Output format. (can be srec, ihex, binary)
FORMAT = ihex

# Target file name (without extension).
TARGET = Blinky
```

- Close and save changes to makefile to the Blinky directory.
- Open Tools and click [WinAVR] Make All to make your Blinky.hex file
- Open Tools and click [WinAVR] Make Extcoff to make your Blinky_coff file.

Download to the Butterfly with AVRStudio

- Find AVR Studio (you should have an icon for it on your desktop) and open it.
- In the File menu Open '…\Blinky\Blinky.cof
- Select the AVR Simulator and the ATMEGA169 as:

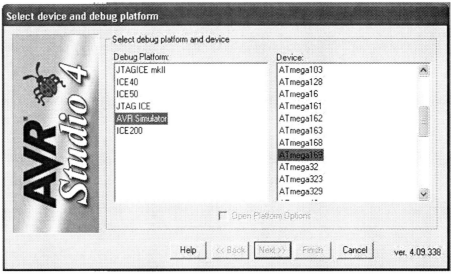

- Select Finish
- DO NOT try to run the simulation; the delay loop will take forever to run. We'll use the simulator later.
- Turn the Butterfly off, then back on.
- Press and **hold down** the joystick button.
- Back to the AVR Studio, open the Tools menu and WHILE HOLDING DOWN THE JOYSTICK BUTTON click the AVR Prog menu item. Then wait until you see:

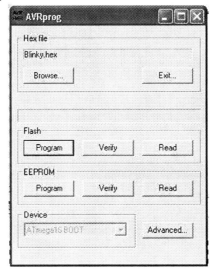

- Release the joystick button. Your finger hurts doesn't it? Enter Blinky.hex in the 'Hex file' box. Press the program button and the program should magically flow from your PC into the AVR Butterfly Flash memory.
- AVR Prog will say: Erasing Programming Verifying OK.
- WHEN YOU WANT TO DOWNLOAD A DIFFERENT HEX FILE, DON'T FORGET TO CHANGE THE HEX FILE NAME. DON'T SAY I DIDN'T WARN YOU AFTER YOU WASTE TIME SCRATCHING YOUR HEAD OVER WHY YOUR NEW PROGRAM SEEMS TO RUN EXACTLY LIKE THE LAST ONE YOU DOWNLOADED. I make this mistake a lot.
- If instead of the above window you get:

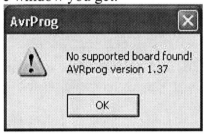

- Go back a few steps and try again. You probably left Bray's Terminal running so it has locked the port. Then maybe not.

Blinky Goes Live

- Turn the power supply off and then back on, the LCD will be blank, click the joystick up (maybe a couple of times) and:

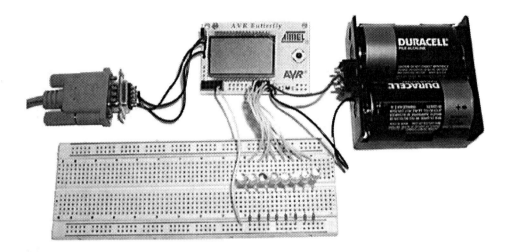

- Your LEDs should be making like a Cylon with the light bouncing back and forth. If you don't know what a Cylon is, try Googling Battlestar Galactica, not that I'm recommending the series, but the bad guys had great eyes:

Figure 11: From the cover of the Battlestar Galactica comic *Red Cylon*.

When you compiled Blinky.c you may have suspected that a lot of stuff was going on in the background, and you would have been right. The compiler does a lot of things, and fortunately for us, we don't really need to know how it does what it does. We only need to know how to coax it to do what we need it to do, which in our case is convert Blinky.c into Blinky.hex that we can download to the Butterfly. If you raise the hood on WinAVR you would see a massively complex set of software that has been created over the years by folks involved in the open software movement. When you get a little extra time check out www.sourceforge.net.

When you have questions about WinAVR, and you will, check out the forums on www.AVRFreaks.net, especially the gcc forum, since WinAVR uses gcc to compile the C software. Try searching the forums before asking questions since someone has probably already asked your question and received good responses. Forum helpers tend to get annoyed with newbies who don't do sufficient background research before asking questions.

Simulation with AVRStudio

Now that you've gone to the trouble to construct the hardware, and have the burned fingers to prove it... guess what? You didn't need to do any of that to test Blinky or get an introduction to C programming for microcontrollers. With a minor modification you can run Blinky in the AVR Studio simulator and learn the introductory C programming ideas in the next chapter without any of the hardware. I decided to do things the hard way, ummm... hardware way because our goal is to control 'real' things like LEDs, not virtual things like little boxes on your PC screen. Theoretically, we could have a whole slew of virtual things to control, from LEDs to motors to full blown Cylon robots wreaking havoc on your screen, which actually sounds kind of fun, but not nearly so much fun as having a real Cylon robot stomping around your neighborhood scaring the noodles out of your enemies. Fun aside, it is often more practical to simulate software before running it in the real world. You wouldn't want your Cylon to mistake you, the imperious leader, for an enemy, would you?

The simulator runs your program in a virtual environment that is MUCH slower than the real microcontroller. Most of your code will run plenty fast to simulate, but some things, such as the delay functions take too long to simulate. In Blinky we call _delay_loop_2(30000); We don't know yet how this function works, but we can guess that we are telling it to do something 30000 times. If we simulate the delay, the simulated LEDs will move at geologic speeds, making glaciers seem fast, so we remove the delay before simulation.

- Open Blinky.c in Programmers Notepad and save it to a new directory, SimBlinky, as SimBlinky.c.
- Put comment lines in front of **both** of the _delay_loop_2() function calls in main():
- // _delay_loop_2(30000);
- Open the makefile in the Blinky directory
- Change the target: TARGET = SimBlinky
- Save the makefile to the SimBlinky directory
- Run the Make All, then Make Extcoff.
- In the AVRStudio open the SimBlinky.coff file.
- In the AVRStudio Workspace window click the I/O ATmega169, then the PORTD, you should see: (the following image shows PORTB instead of PORTD, -- live with it)

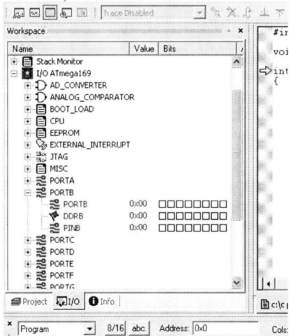

- In the toolbar click the AutoStep button:

- The simulator will run showing the LED scan as a scan of the PORTD and PIND items in the Workspace window:(this shows PORTB but you'll actually see PORTD)

- See, I told you it wasn't as much fun as watching real LEDs blink.
- Spend some time with the AVR Studio simulator and associated help files; you'll find the effort well worth it in the long run.

GOOD GRIEF!

That was a 'Quick Start'???? Well, maybe things would go quicker if you wanted to pay a fortune for a software and hardware development system, but for **FREE** software, and unbelievably cheap hardware, you've got to expect to do a little more of the work yourself. Besides, you couldn't pay for all the debugging education I bet you got just trying to follow what I was telling you. If you think the 'Quick Start' section was confusing, you should try reading all the stuff it's based on.

Chapter 3: A Brief Introduction to C – What Makes Blinky Blink?

This section takes a very brief look at Blinky.c to help begin understanding what each line means. Later, these items will be covered in greater detail in context of programs written specifically to aid in learning the C programming language as it is used for common microcontroller applications.

Comments

You can add comments (text the compiler ignores) to your code two ways.

For a single line of comments use double back slashes as in

```
// Blinky.c
```

For multiline comments, begin them with /* and end them with */ as in:

```
/*
Blinky.c is a really great first program for microcontrollers
it causes eight LEDs to scan back and forth like a Cylon's eyes
*/
```

Include Files

```
#include <avr/io.h>
#include <avr/delay.h>
```

The '#include' is a preprocessor directive that instructs the compiler to find the file in the <> brackets and tack it on at the head of the file you are about to compile. The io.h provides data for the port we use, and the delay.h provides the definitions for the delay function we call.

Expressions, Statements, and Blocks

Expressions are combinations of variables, operators, and function calls that produce a single value. For example:

```
PORTD = 0xFF - counter++
```

This is an expression that sets the voltage on pins on Port D to +3V or 0V based on the value of the variable 'counter' subtracted from 0xFF (a hex number - we'll learn about these and ports later). Afterwards the counter is incremented.

Statements control the program flow and consist of keywords, expressions, and other statements. A semicolon ends a statement. For example:

```
TempInCelsius = 5 * (TempInFahrenheit-32)/9;
```

This is a statement that could prove useful if the Butterfly's temperature readings are derived in Fahrenheit, but the user wants to report them in Celsius.

Blocks are compound statements grouped by open and close braces: { }. For example:

```
for(int i = 1; i < 128; i = i*2)

{
        PORTD = ~i;
        _delay_loop_2(30000);
}
```

This groups the two inner statements to be run depending on the condition of the 'for' statement.

Operators

Operators are symbols that tell the compiler to do things such as set one variable equal to another, the '=' operator, as in 'DDRB = 0xFF' or the '++' operator for adding 1, as in 'counter++'.

Flow Control

Flow control statements dictate the order in which a series of actions are performed. For example: 'for' causes the program to repeat a block. In Blinky we have:

```
for(int i = 1; i < 128; i = i*2)
{
        // Do something
}
```

On the first pass, the compiler evaluates the 'for' statement, notes that 'i' is equal to 1 which is less than 128, so it runs the block of 'Do something' code. After running the block the 'for' expression is reevaluated with 'i' now equal to the previous 'i' multiplied by 2 'i = i*2' which is 2 and 2 < 128 is true, so the block is run again. Next loop, i = 4, and so on till i = 128, and '128 < 128' is no longer true, so the program stops running the loop and goes to the next statement following the closing bracket.

Quick now, how many times does this loop run? The series of 'i' values evaluated against the '< 128' is '1,2,4,8,16,32,64,128' and since it takes the 128 as the cue to quit, the loop runs 8 times.

The while('expression') statement tests the 'expression' to see if it is true and allows the block to run if it is, then it retests the expression, looping thru the block each time it finds the expression true. The program skips the block and proceeds to the next statement when the expression is false. The while(1) will run the loop forever because '1' is the definition of true (false is defined as 0).

Functions

A function encapsulates a computation. Think of them as building material for C programming. A house might be built of studs, nails, and panels. The architect is assured that all 2x4 studs are the same, as are each of the nails and each of the panels, so there is no need to worry about how to make a 2x4 or a nail or a panel, you just stick them where needed and don't worry how they were made. In the Blinky program, the main() function twice uses the _delay_loop_2() function. The writer of the main() function doesn't need to know **how** the _delay_loop_2(30000) function does its job, he only needs to know **what** it does and what parameters to use, in this case 30000, will cause a delay of about 1/8 second.

The _delay_loop_2() function is declared in the header delay.h and the makefile is set up so that the compiler knows where to look for it.

Encapsulation of code in functions is a key idea in C programming and helps make chunks of code more convenient to use. And just as important, it provides a way to make tested code reusable without having to rewrite it. The idea of function encapsulation is so important in software engineering that the C++

language was developed primarily to formalize these and related concepts and force their use.

The Main() Thing

All C programs must have a 'main' function that contains the code that is first run when the program begins.

```
int main (void)

{
    // Do something

}
```

Blinky has:

```
int main (void)

{

        // set PORTD for output
        DDRD= 0xFF;

        while(1)

        {
                for(int i = 1; i < 128; i = i*2)

                {
                    PORTD = ~i;
                    _delay_loop_2(30000);
                }

                for(int i = 128; i > 1; i -= i/2)

                {
                    PORTD = ~i;
                    _delay_loop_2(30000);
                }

        }

}
```

In this function we leave C for a moment and look at things that are specific to the AVR microcontroller. The line:

```
DDRD = 0xFF;
```

Sets the microcontroller Data Direction Register D to equal 255. This tells the microcontroller that Port D pins, which are hooked up to our LEDs, are to be used to output voltage states (which we use to turn the LEDs on and off). We use the hexadecimal version, 0xFF, of 255 here because it is easier to understand what's happening. You disagree? Well, by the time you finish this text, you'll be using hexadecimal numbers like a pro and understand they do make working with microcontrollers easier, but for now, just humor me.

The program tests the while(1) and finding it true, proceeds to the 'for' statement, which is also true and passes to the line:

```
PORTD = ~i;
```

Which causes the microcontroller to set the Port D pins to light up the LEDs with the value of ~i. The '~' inverts the value of i , we'll learn more about this later.

Say what? Okay, 'i' starts off equal to 1, which in binary is 00000001 (like hexadecimal, you'll grow to love binary). This provides +3V on the rightmost LED, lighting it up and leaves the other LEDs unlit at 0V.

The first 'for' loop runs eight times, each time moving the lit LED to the left, then it exits. In the next 'for' loop the -= operator subtracts i/2 from i and sets i equal to the results causing the LED to move to the right. When it is finished the loop runs again… for how long? Right… forever. Or at least until either the universe ends or you unplug the Butterfly.

NOTE: the Butterfly LCD dances like crazy with each LED pass, because some of the Port D pins are also tied to the LCD. It's a bug in our design, but in the world of marketing it would be called a free bonus feature available exclusively to you for an unheard of low price if you act immediately. Will it harm the LCD? Probably not, but I don't know for sure, so don't leave Blinky running overnight.

That's enough for a quickie introduction. We skimmed over a lot that you'll see in detail later. You now know just enough to be dangerous and I hope the learning process hasn't caused your forehead to do too much damage to your keyboard.

Chapter 4: C Types, Operators, and Expressions

Data Types and Sizes

Seen on a shirt at a Robothon event:

There are exactly 10 types of people in the world.
Those who understand binary numbers and those who don't.

If this doesn't make sense to you now, it will in a minute.

Bits

The first computers were people with quill pens who spent their lives calculating tables of things like cannonball trajectories to help soldiers more accurately slaughter their enemies. Later mechanical computers, with brass gears and cams, were developed to make the slaughter cheaper, quicker, and easier. Then one day a genius figured that you could do all this computing even easier if you used switches. Switches can be off or on, and the fundamental datum is the 'bit' with exactly two 'binary', states. We variously refer to these states as '0 and 1' or 'on and off' or 'true and false'. It's the latter that allows us to use bits to automate Boolean logic and thus the modern binary logic computer entered the world and now slaughter is so cheap, quick and easy to compute that anybody can do it. Maybe this is skimming the topic a bit (har!) but a full explanation would begin with the first sentence of Genesis and only hit its stride about the time Alan Turing offed himself as his unjust reward for saving the free world, and while fascinating, it won't get us blinking LEDs any quicker, so Let's move on.

Each of our LEDs is connected to a microcontroller pin that can have two voltage states: ground or +3v, which can be manipulated as a data bit.

Bytes

The AVR and many other microcontrollers physically handle data in 8-bit units called bytes, a data type that can have 256 states, 0 thru 255. This is shown in the following sequence of states, (leaving out 9 thru 247, see Appendix 5 to see them all, and be sure to take a magnifying glass):

00000000 = 0		11111000 = 248
00000001 = 1		11111001 = 249
00000010 = 2		11111010 = 250
00000011 = 3	(9 thru 247)	11111011 = 251
00000100 = 4		11111100 = 252
00000101 = 5		11111101 = 253
00000110 = 6		11111110 = 254
00000111 = 7		11111111 = 255
00001000 = 8		

Look at our Cylon eye and notice that we have 8 LEDs with one lit at a time scrolling back and forth. What you are seeing is 8 of the 256 possible states being presented in a sequence that fools us into thinking we are seeing a back and forth scrolling motion. If the presentation sequence were random, we'd just see the light blinking on and off chaotically. Using binary numbers where the lit LED is represented by 1 shown next to the hexadecimal and decimal equivalent, what we are seeing is:

```
00000001 = 0x01 = 1
00000010 = 0x02 = 2
00000100 = 0x04 = 4
00001000 = 0x08 = 8
00010000 = 0x10 = 16
00100000 = 0x20 = 32
01000000 = 0x40 = 64
10000000 = 0x80 = 128
01000000 = 0x40 = 64
00100000 = 0x20 = 32
00010000 = 0x10 = 16
00001000 = 0x08 = 8
00000100 = 0x04 = 4
00000010 = 0x02 = 2
00000001 = 0x01 = 1
```

In microcontroller applications, we will often be dealing with the states of byte-sized ports, like Port D. A port is a place where ships come and go, or in the case of a microcontroller it is a place where outside voltages (0V or 3V) can be read or set.

We use binary and hexadecimal numbers for ports because it is cumbersome and non-intuitive to think of port data as decimal numbers, Quick, what will 66 look like on our LEDs? Quick, what will 01000010 look like on our LEDs? Since 01000010 = 66, you see my point? And I bet you get the joke at the beginning of this section.

The hexadecimal system is another commonly seen number system used in microcontrollers. It has a base of 16, that is 16 states per digit:

0, 1, 2, 3, 4, 5, 6, 7, 8, 9, A, B, C, D, E, and F.

Since we use numbers to the base 10 because we have ten digits, fingers if you count the thumb as a finger, to count with. It might help to imagine an alien with 16 fingers, or better yet: 4 hands with three fingers and one thumb on each. In C, a hexadecimal number is preceded by 0x. The hex byte representation of the decimal number 129 is 0x81. The decimal and binary equivalents of the hex numbers are:

$$0 = 0000 = 0x0$$
$$1 = 0001 = 0x1$$
$$2 = 0010 = 0x2$$
$$3 = 0011 = 0x3$$
$$4 = 0100 = 0x4$$
$$5 = 0101 = 0x5$$
$$6 = 0110 = 0x6$$
$$7 = 0111 = 0x7$$
$$8 = 1000 = 0x8$$
$$9 = 1001 = 0x9$$
$$10 = 1010 = 0xA$$
$$11 = 1011 = 0xB$$
$$12 = 1100 = 0xC$$
$$13 = 1101 = 0xD$$
$$14 = 1110 = 0xE$$
$$15 = 1111 = 0xF$$

It is very common for new users of hex numbers to make the mistake of saying, 'Well there are 16 hex integers, so 0xF, the last one, is 16.' We make this mistake because we think of counting beginning with 1, but for most computer use you'll see counting beginning with 0. 0 is the first integer and 15 is the 16th integer. When you count like a computer your first digit (left thumb?) is 0 not 1. If a computer had those alien hands to count on, the first thumb would be 0 and the last would be 15 (0xF if it was speaking hex instead of dec). Try to keep this in mind because it will bite you later.

Experienced microcontroller programmers memorize the binary equivalent of hex digits and find hex numbers very useful. For instance, given 0xA9, what would the LEDs (or the voltage states of an 8-bit register) look like? If you memorize the table, you come up with 0xA = 1010 and 0x9 = 1001, so the LEDs (voltage states) will look like: 10101001. As pointed out earlier, ask the same question in decimal, what will 169 look like on the LEDs and good luck on doing that in your head. Look at Appendix 5 to see all the byte states in decimal, hexadecimal, and binary. Finally, all jokes equating byte to bite are prohibited.

char
The name of this data type is short for character, and is typically used to represent a character in the ASCII character set (Appendix 4 – ASCII Table). Originally, there were 127 ASCII characters used by Teletype machines to transmit and receive data. You will note that in Figure 1, you see Dennis Ritchie, who wrote C, standing next to Ken Thompson, who wrote UNIX, working on a Teletype machine. Clunky as they were (the Teletype, not Ritchie and Thompson), Teletypes were light years ahead of entering data by individual switches representing each bit of data. Teletypes send and receive characters so a lot of C, especially the standard library, is character oriented. The number of bits in a char is machine dependent, but in all machines I've encountered including the AVR, a char is an 8-bit byte which can have 256 bit states. The computer uses this byte of data as representing a signed value from −128 to + 127.

The ASCII code was extended to include characters for 128 to 255 primarily to do weird European characters, math symbols, and character graphics on early PCs.

unsigned

If the modifier unsigned is used in the definition of a char variable: 'unsigned char', the value is from 0 to 255. Many C compilers will have 'byte' or 'Byte' defined as equaling 'unsigned char'. The 'byte' keyword is not part of C, but it is very convenient, since in microcontrollers we usually use a lot of numbers, but not a lot of 'char'acters.

int

On AVR microcontrollers int declares a 16 bit data variable as having values from –32768 to +32767. A variable declared with 'unsigned int' will have a value from 0 to 65535.

The long and short of it

Everybody else makes that dumb joke at this point, so why be different?

You can declare variables as 'short int' and 'long int'. For C the size is machine dependent, but on many systems a short int is the same as an int, 16 bits, while a long int is 32 bits.

Variable Names

The changeable data you are processing is stored in bytes of RAM, Random Access Memory, at specific addresses. Variables are names that provide an alias for the address being used. We'll look at the gory details in the 'Variables External, Static, and Register' section of Chapter 6.

Constants

Constants are data that cannot be changed by the program and are usually stored in ROM, Read Only Memory. We could just type in the constant value wherever needed, but that will get old quick, so we alias the value with a name. We usually do this in a header file or at the start of the software module, which adds the advantage that if we ever want to change the constant we can do it once in the definition instead of at each occurrence in the code. By convention, constant names are all caps. For example we might want to use pi in calculation (pi contains a decimal so we use the float data type) so we define as follows:

```
#define PI 3.1415926
```

We can then use PI anywhere in our software and the compiler will automatically substitute the numerical value for it:

```
float pieCircumference = 0.0; // we don't know yet
float piePanRadius = 2.2; // this we measured
```

```
// sometimes you just gotta have pie.
pieCircumference = PI * ( piePanRadius * 2 );
```

Declarations

A declaration is a text statement that declares to the complier how your words are to be used. When you declare 'unsigned char counter = 0' you are telling the compiler that when it encounters the word 'counter' to consider it as data stored at some specific location with the alias name 'counter' that can have values from 0 to 255, but in this case initially has a value of 0.

Arithmetic Operators

Operators seem like ordinary arithmetic or algebra symbols, and they mostly are. But they are different from arithmetic or algebra often enough that you need to pay attention when operations don't act like you think they should. The compiler might just be doing what you told it to do, rather than what you wanted it to do. An example of the kind of confusion you can run into when you use the '=' assignment operator and the '==' 'is equal to' operator:

```
x = y;
if(x==y) _delay_loop_2(30000);
```

The first statement assigns x the value of y. The second statement calls the _delay_loop_2(30000) function if x is equal to y. What about:

```
if(x=y) _delay_loop_2(30000); //BAD STATEMENT
```

This will set x equal to y, and then call the _delay_loop_2(30000) function. The 'if' becomes meaningless because the condition, x=y, is always true, so the delay will always run. The WinAVR compiler will think something is strange and issue this warning:

Warning: suggest parentheses around assignment used as truth value

Which will scroll by so fast you won't see it, so you'll assume the compile was good. Notice how clear (NOT) this warning was? Most complier warnings are even more cryptic. Not all compilers will flag this error with a warning. It is a very easy mistake to make, and you will feel really dumb after an hour of debugging, looking for something obscure, only to find a lousy missing '=' character. I do this all the time.

Note: Some of these operators may seem strange at this point, but they are explained fully in later sections. Then they'll seem really strange.

Table 1: Arithmetic Operators

Operator	Name	Example	Defined
*	Multiplication	x*y	Multiply x times y
/	Division	x/y	Divide x by y
%	Modulo	x%y	Provide the remainder of x divided by y
+	Addition	x+y	Add x and y
-	Subtraction	x-y	Subtract y from x
++	Increment	x++	Increment x after using it
--	Decrement	--x	Decrement x before using it
-	Negation	-x	Multiply x by −1
+	Unary Plus	+x	Show x is positive (not really needed)

Table 2: Data Access and Size Operators

Operator	Name	Example	Defined
[]	Array element	x[6]	Seventh element of array x
.	Member selection	PORTD.2	Bit 2 of Port D
->	Member selection	pStruct->x	Member x of the structure pointed to by pStruct
*	Indirection	*p	Contents of memory located at address p
&	Address of	&x	Address of the variable x

Table 3: Miscellaneous Operators

Operator	Name	Example	Defined
()	Function	wait(10)	call wait with an argument of 10
(type)	Type cast	(double)x	x converted to a double
?:	Conditional	x?y:z	If x is not 0 evaluate y, otherwise evaluate z
,	Sequential evaluation	x++,y++	Increment x first, then increment y

Relational and Logical Operators

Table 4: Logical and Relational Operators

Operator	Name	Example	Defined
>	Greater than	x>y	1 if x is greater than y, otherwise 0
>=	Greater than or equal to	x>=y	1 if x is greater than or equal to y, otherwise 0
<	Less than	x<y	1 if x is less than y, otherwise 0
<=	Less than or equal to	x<=y	1 if x is less than or equal to y, otherwise 0
==	Equal to	x==y	1 if x equals y, otherwise 0
!=	Not equal to	x!=y	1 if x is not equal to y, otherwise 0
!	Logical NOT	!x	1 if x is 0, otherwise 0
&&	Logical AND	x&&y	0 if either x or y is 0, otherwise 1
||	Logical OR	x||y	0 if both x and y are 0, otherwise 1

Bitwise Operators

Table 5: Bitwise Operators

Operator	Name	Example	Defined
~	Bitwise complement NOT	~x	Changes 1 bits to 0 and 0 bits to 1
&	Bitwise AND	x&y	Bitwise AND of x and y
|	Bitwise OR	x|y	Bitwise OR of x and y
^	Bitwise exclusive OR	x^y	Bitwise XOR of x and y
<<	Left shift	x<<2	Bits in x shifted left 2 bit positions
>>	Right shift	x>>3	Bits in x shifted right 3 bit positions

Bitwise operators are critically important in microcontroller software. They allow us to do many things in C that can be directly and efficiently translated into microcontroller machine operations. Keep in mind that these operators work on **bits** but are similar enough to the logical operators that you will get confused. Let's look at the truth tables for &, |, and ^:

```
   AND          OR          XOR
0 & 0 = 0    0 | 0 = 0    0 ^ 0 = 0
0 & 1 = 0    0 | 1 = 1    0 ^ 1 = 1
1 & 0 = 0    1 | 0 = 1    1 ^ 0 = 1
1 & 1 = 1    1 | 1 = 1    1 ^ 1 = 0
```

Let's create a variable, myByte and do some bitwise operations on it:

    unsigned char myByte = 0;

We can set bit 3 (numbering from the right starting with 0):

    myByte = myByte | 0x08;

To see what's happening Let's look at these in binary:

```
myByte = 00000000 = 0x00
  0x08 = 00001000 = 0x08
-----------------------
    OR = 00001000 = 0x08
```

Suppose myByte = 0xFF:

```
myByte = 11111111 = 0xFF
  0x08 = 00001000 = 0x08
-----------------------
    OR = 11111111 = 0xFF
```

Or maybe myByte = 0x55:

```
myByte = 01010101 = 0x55
  0x08 = 00001000 = 0x08
-----------------
    OR = 01011101 = 0x5D
```

This all shows that only the 3rd bit of myByte is affected by the OR operation, since it is the only bit equal to 1 in 0x08.

Now let's do the same thing with the & operator:

unsigned char myByte = 0;

We can set bit 3 with:

myByte = myByte & 0x08;

To see what's happening Let's look at these in binary:

```
myByte = 00000000 = 0x00
  0x08 = 00001000 = 0x08
-----------------------
   AND = 00000000 = 0x00
```

Suppose myByte = 0xFF:

```
myByte = 11111111 = 0xFF
  0x08 = 00001000 = 0x08
-----------------------
   AND = 00001000 = 0x08
```

Or maybe myByte = 0x55:

```
myByte = 01010101 = 0x55
  0x08 = 00001000 = 0x08
-----------------------
   AND = 00000000 = 0x00
```

And maybe myByte = 0xAA:

```
myByte = 10101011 = 0xAA
  0x08 = 00001000 = 0x08
-----------------------
   AND = 00001000 = 0x08
```

In each of the above cases we are only dealing with a single bit, but we might be interested in any or all of the bits. One of the most important features of using masks with bitwise operators is that it allows us to set or clear a specific bit or set of bits in a byte without knowing or affecting the bits we aren't interested in. For example, suppose we are only interested in bits 0, 2, and 6. Let's set bit 6, regardless of its present value, then clear bits 0 and 2, also regardless of their present value and, here's the trick, leave bits 1, 2, 4, 5, and 7 as they were when we began. Let's have myByte starting equal to the secret to life the universe and everything, which according to Douglas Adams is 42, but remember that the start value doesn't matter to us since we are going to force 3 bits to values regardless of the start value.

NOTE:
```
     myByte =  myByte | 0x08;
```
is the same as
```
     myByte |= 0x08;
```
which we will use from now on.

At the beginning myByte is equal to 42 = 0x2B = 00101011. We set bit 6 with:

```
     myByte |= 0x40;
```

which does the following:

```
myByte = 00101011 = 0x2B
  0x40 = 01000000 = 0x40
-----------------------
    OR = 01101011 = 0x6B
```

Next we want to clear bits 0 and 2:

```
myByte &= 0xFA;
```

which does the following:

```
myByte = 01101011 = 0x6B
  0xFA = 11111010 = 0xFA
-----------------------
   AND = 01101010 = 0x6A
```

So in summary we set bits with '|' and clear bits with '&'.

The Butterfly Software has a clever snippet in LCD_driver.c where the '&' and '~' operators are used to convert a lowercase letter to a capital:

```
// c is a letter
if (c >= 'a')    // Convert to upper case
    c &= ~0x20; // if necessary
```

This statement first checks to see if the character c is greater than or equal to 'a' and uses the convenient fact that in ASCII the letters are sequential with the capitals beginning at 0x41 ('A') and the lowercase beginning at 0x61 ('a'). So if the character is >= 0x61 (which is 'a') then it is lowercase and we can derive the uppercase version by subtracting 0x20. So why do we use 'c &= ~0x20' instead of subtracting as in 'c -= 0x20'? Well, it is more efficient for the machine to take the inverse of the minuend and then AND it with the subtrahend (this by the way, is the first time since grammar school that I've actually used minuend and subtrahend, I'm amazed that these terms actually stuck. Maybe it was the teachers steely glare and the dangerous looking pointer she held.) Let's look at it shall we?

```
0x20 = 00100000
~0x20 = 11011111

'a' = 0x61 = 01100001
     ~0x20 = 11011111
     -------------------
         AND = 01000001 = 0x41 = 'A'
```

This is a lot harder for us than ordinary subtraction, but much easier for the machine.

While using &= and/or |= is acceptable, the Butterfly code generally does this a little differently, not to make your life harder, but to make the code a little clearer, though it won't seem that way at first. When we create masks to set or clear bits, we will name the bits so for instance the first bit in port D is named PD0 and we can guess that the eighth bit is named PD7. That's simple, but it gets hairy when we give complicated names to all the bits in the dozens of registers. For instance in the Timer0 register: TCCR0A, Timer/Counter Control Register A we have the following bits named (page 90 ATMEGA169 databook):

Timer/Counter Control
Register A – TCCR0A

Bit	7	6	5	4	3	2	1	0
	FOC0A	WGM00	COM0A1	COM0A0	WGM01	CS02	CS01	CS00
Read/Write	W	R/W	R/W	R/W	R/W	R/W	R/W	R/W
Initial Value	0	0	0	0	0	0	0	0

Bit 7 = FOC0A – Force Output Compare A
Bit 6 = WGM00 – Waveform Generation Mode 0
Bit 5 = COM0A1 – Compare Match Output Mode 1
Bit 4 = COM0A0 – Compare Match Output Mode 0
Bit 3 = WGM01 – Waveform Generation Mode 1
Bit 2 = CS02 – Clock Select Bit 2
Bit 1 = CS01 – Clock Select Bit 1
Bit 0 = CS00 – Clock Select Bit 0

Bits 0, 1, and 2 the Clock Select Bits are defined as:

Table 53. Clock Select Bit Description

CS02	CS01	CS00	Description
0	0	0	No clock source (Timer/Counter stopped)
0	0	1	$clk_{I/O}$/(No prescaling)
0	1	0	$clk_{I/O}$/8 (From prescaler)
0	1	1	$clk_{I/O}$/64 (From prescaler)
1	0	0	$clk_{I/O}$/256 (From prescaler)
1	0	1	$clk_{I/O}$/1024 (From prescaler)
1	1	0	External clock source on T0 pin. Clock on falling edge.
1	1	1	External clock source on T0 pin. Clock on rising edge.

Figure 12: from page 92 of the ATMega169 data book

Let's initialize the timer with:

```
// Set Fast PWM mode and CLK/256 prescaler
TCCR0A |= (1<<WGM01)|(1<<WGM00)|(4<<CS00);
```

We use the left shift operator '<<' to shift the number before the operand to the numeric position in the byte specified by the number following the operand. In the case of (1<<WGM01) we shift a 1 to the left by WGM01 bit positions, and we see from iom169.h:

```
/* TCCR0A */
#define  FOC0A     7
#define  WGM00     6
#define  COM0A1    5
#define  COM0A0    4
#define  WGM01     3
#define  CS02      2
#define  CS01      1
#define  CS00      0
```

WGM01 = 3, so (1<<WGM01) is the same as (1<<3) and means to shift 0000001 three places left to 00001000. Now look at The TCCR0A register and notice where the WGM01 bit is located. Ah ha! Like I said, we have a way of dealing with a bit by a name.

But wait, wouldn't that mean that (4<<CS00) means we are setting the CS00 bit to 4? But a bit can only be 0 or 1 so how the heck do we set a bit to 4?. Well, or course we don't. The CS00 = 0, so we are left shifting the number 4 by 0 meaning we aren't doing any shifting of the 4, we are just ORing it with the other two values:

```
TCCR0A |= (1<<WGM01)|(1<<WGM00)|(4<<CS00);
```

Since 4 = 00000100, we will be setting the CS02 bit, not the CS00 bit. So why didn't we say (1<<CS02) instead of (4<<CS00)? And the answer is 'because'. Actually the answer is that the lower three bytes of the TCC0RA register can be considered a three bit field for a number used to select the clock. The number 4 selects the clock/256 prescaler (see the Clock Select Bit table in Figure 12 above). Now we can see that (5<<CS00) would mean set the clock to clk/1024 and so forth. We will often think in terms of multi-bit fields.

Our goal was to 'Set Fast PWM mode, CLK/256 prescaler' (this will be explained later in the timer section) so we want to set bits 6, 3, and 2 (01001100 = 0x4C) without affecting the other bits. If we OR it like before we would:

```
TCC0RA |= 0x4C;
```

Which is:

```
TCC0RA = xxxxxxxx = we don't know, or need too.
  0x4C = 01001100
  ----------------------
    OR  = x1xx11xx = our bits are set the rest are not
changed.
```

The only problem is what does it mean to setup the timer with 0x4C? When you see TCC0RA |= 0x4C; you don't know what it is doing and you have to derive the binary and look in the data book to figure it out. But using:

```
TCCR0A |= (1<<WGM01)|(1<<WGM00)|(4<<CS00);
```

The (1<<WGM01)|(1<<WGM00)|(4<<CS00) is the same as 0x4C except that we can read that we are setting both the Waveform Generation bits and we are setting

the clock prescaler to 4, we may still have to use the data book to look at the Waveform generator and Clock Select tables, but it is still clearer isn't it?

Which gives you a better chance at knowing what is going on?

```
        TCC0RA |=  0x4C;
```
Versus:
```
        TCCR0A |= (1<<WGM01)|(1<<WGM00)|(4<<CS00);
```

Heck, I don't know, but it is how the guys in Norway do it so we'll give them the benefit of the doubt and do it the Norway way and be able to steal all that cool Butterfly code.

Testing Bits
Now we have our timer setup, but suppose there is a function that needs to know how the Waveform Generator is set so that it can choose among several alternative actions? We can test a bit by using the AND operator, but not assigning any values. For example:

Waveform Generator Modes:

WGM01	WGM00	Mode
0	0	Normal
0	1	PWM, phase correct
1	0	CTC
1	1	Fast PWM

```
if(  !(TCC0RA & WGM01) && !(TCC0RA & WGM00) )
{
        // do this only if in the normal mode
}
else if(  !(TCC0RA & WGM01) && (TCC0RA & WGM00) )
{
        // do this only if in the PWM, phase correct mode
}
else if(  (TCC0RA & WGM01) && !(TCC0RA & WGM00) )
{
        // do this only if in the CTC mode
}
```

```
else if(  (TCC0RA & WGM01) && (TCC0RA & WGM00) )
{
        // do this only if in the Fast PWM mode
}
```

The (TCC0RA & WGM01) test will be 1, true, only if the WGM01 bit is 1, likewise for the (TCC0RA & WGM00) statement. The !(TCC0RA & WGM01), adding the '!' or NOT to the statement means that it is true only if the innards of the () are false. The 'if' statement will only be true if both the first and (logical AND = &&) the second are true. So we've used two bitwise ANDs and a logical AND in this statement.

AND I hope it is clear. It isn't, so get out the pencil and paper computer and work through it till it is. Seriously, when I was editing and reread this section I had a 'good grief' moment. But this is critical since we will be doing lots of clearing and setting control register bits. And it is as simple as I can make it, so do carefully walk through the example, pencil and paper in hand and work each example.

Assignment Operators and Expressions

Table 6: Assignment Operators

Operator	Name	Example	Defined
=	Assignment	x=y	Put the value of y into x
+= -= *= /= %= <<= >>= &= ^= |=	Compound assignment	x += y	This provides a short cut way to write an expression, the example: x += y; is the same as x = x + y;

Conditional Expressions

You will frequently need to make decisions based on external conditions. For example, if the temperature is above 150° F, turn the fan on, if it is under 100° F, turn the fan off. You could write this as:

```
if( temp > 150)
        Fan(ON);
else if( temp < 100)
        Fan(OFF);
```

Or, if you want to use above 150° F to turn on the fan, and below 150° F to turn off the fan, you could use the C conditional operator ?: (Table 3) as below:

```
temp > 150 ? Fan(ON)  :  Fan(OFF);
```

The operation has the form: expresson1 ? expression2 : expression3, and follows the rule that if expression1 is true (non-zero value) then use expression2, otherwise use expression3. This operator seems a little gee-wiz-impress-your-friends and not as clear as the if-else expression, but you'll see this expression a lot, so get used to it.

Precedence and Order of Evaluation

When a statement has a sequence of operators such as:

```
x = 50 + 10 / 2 - 20 * 4;
```

The compiler follows an order of calculation based on operator precedence (Table 7). But what the compiler does, may not be what you intended. Calculate the value of x. Did you get 40? If you performed the calculations sequentially as listed you get:

```
x = 50 + 10 / 2 - 20 * 4
x = 60 / 2 - 20 * 4
x = 30 - 20 * 4
x = 10 * 4
x = 40
```

So the answer is 40, right? Wrong, according to C it is –25. The compiler does the division and multiplication first, then the addition and subtraction:

```
x = 50 + 10 / 2 - 20 * 4
x = 50 + 10 / 2 - 80
x = 50 + 5 - 80
x = 55 - 80
x = -25
```

Some C gurus will memorize the precedence and associativity table and actually write statements like x = 50 + 10 / 2 – 20 * 4. Such clever programmers are dangerous and should be avoided when possible. The Germans have a word for clever: kluge, and in programming 'kluge' is a well-deserved insult. Don't be clever be clear. Clever programming is difficult to read and understand. If the clever programmer gets run over by a truck (hopefully) his code will be inherited by some poor guy who will have to figure things out. **_DO NOT_ memorize the Table of Operator Precedence and Associativity in C. _DO_ use '(' and ')' to make your program clear!**

Which is clearer:
```
x = 50 + 10 / 2 - 20 * 4;
```
or:
```
x = 50 + (10 / 2) - (20 * 4);
```

The second adds nothing for the compiler, but tells the reader what was intended. But what if you really meant to have the operations performed in the order listed? Then you would write:
```
x = ((((50 + 10) / 2) - 20) * 4);
```

Which would make x = 40. The parentheses can get mighty confusing, but not nearly as confusing as their absence.

Table 7: Operator Precedence and Associativity in C

Operator Type	Operators	Associativity
Expression	() [] . ->	Left to right
Unary	- + ~ ! * & ++ -- sizeof(type)	Right to left
Multiplicative	* / %	Left to right
Additive	+ -	Left to right
Shift	<< >>	Left to right
Relational (inequality)	< <= > >=	Left to right

Relational (equality)	== !=	Left to right
Bitwise AND	&	Left to right
Bitwise XOR	^	Left to right
Bitwise OR	|	Left to right
Logical AND	&&	Left to right
Logical OR	||	Left to right
Conditional	?:	Right to left
Assignment	= *= /= %= += -= <<= >>= &= |= ^=	Right to left
Sequential evaluation	,	Left to right

Projects

Port Input and Output

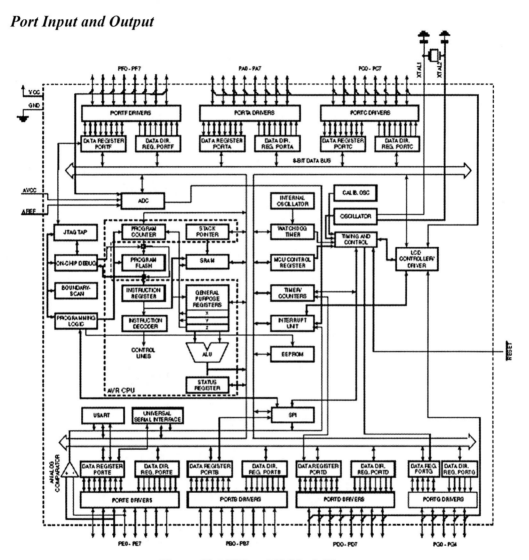

Figure 13 ATMega169 Block Diagram

We skimmed over a lot in Chapter 2 so that we could get some LEDs blinking. Let's now take a more detailed look at I/O ports.

When this book was written, Digi-Key listed AVRs with as few as 6 I/O pins on the ATTINY11 ($0.54) to as many as 54 on the ATMEGA169 ($8.60), the microcontroller used on the Butterfly. Most of these pins are organized into ports, collections of pins that are setup and used with port specific access and control registers. Many of the pins have more than one possible function: they can be used to input or output digital logic data or they might be used for detecting external interrupts or as input for clocks or for analog to digital conversions and so on. In this section we'll be looking at digital I/O.

The ATMEGA169 on the Butterfly has six 8-bit and one 4-bit general purpose I/O ports as shown in Figure 13 ATMega169 Block Diagram (copied from the ATMega169 data book page 3, Figure 2.) Looks mighty complex doesn't it? Well this is a simplified block diagram of a circuit that is vastly more complex. When you see a photomicrograph of these chips they resemble aerial photos of a vast ancient city with streets laid out in a grid surrounded by a wall. The ports are the gates to the city where the ancient electrons riding their very tiny ancient donkeys enter and leave the city. I'd continue in this vein but then I'd probably win a prize in the awful metaphor competition so I'll stop.

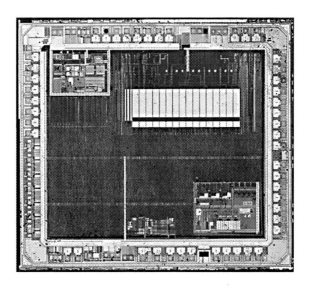

ATmega169 Silicon Die Curtesty of Christopher Tarnovsky from Flylogic.net

Each port has three associated I/O memory locations, that act as guards determining who shall pass (guess I won't stop):

1. Data Direction Register - DDRx – Read/Write
2. Data Register – PORTx – Read/Write
3. Port Input Pins – PINx – Read Only

For example port A has: PORTA, DDRA, and PINA.

When used for general purpose I/O the port Data Direction Register must be set to tell the micro whether a pin will be used for input or output. To use a pin for input, set the associated DDRx bit to 0; to use it as output set it to 1. For example, to use the upper 4 bits of PORTD as inputs and the lower 4 bits as output, set the bits to 00001111, which, as we've seen, in hex is 0x0F:

```
DDRD = 0x0F;
```

In this project we will set port B to input data from switches and port D to output +3V to drive LEDs. We use the PINB register to read the switches from port B and write the value to port D using the PORTD register.

First we set the DDRB register so that all the pins are used as inputs:

```
DDRB = 0x00.
```

Next we set the DDRD register so that all the pins are used as outputs:

```
DDRD = 0xFF.
```

Then we write an infinite loop that gets the switch data from port B using PINB and equates it to PORTD that will light the LEDs.

Open a new C/C++ file in Programmers Notepad and write the following program. Save it as PortIO.c in a new directory PortIO.

```
// PortIO.c
#include <avr/io.h>
```

```
int main (void)
{
        // Init port pins
        DDRB = 0x00; // set port B for input
        DDRD = 0xFF; // set port D for output

        while(1)
        {
                PORTD = PINB;
        }
}
```

Open the makefile in the Blinky directory and save it to the PortIO directory then change:

```
TARGET = PortIO.
```

Follow the Blinky example to write, compile, and download this little program. Remember to turn the Butterfly off and back on, then hold down the center joystick button before and while clicking on the 'AVR prog…' menu item in AVRStudio. Also remember to browse to the PortIO.hex file in AVRStudio (I often forget to change the hex file and end up programming the Butterfly with an earlier hex file). And finally after the code downloads, remember to turn the Butterfly off and back on then click the joystick to the upper position to start the program.

If everything goes as planned, the LEDs will display the state of the switches as shown below. I told you we'd have some lame examples.

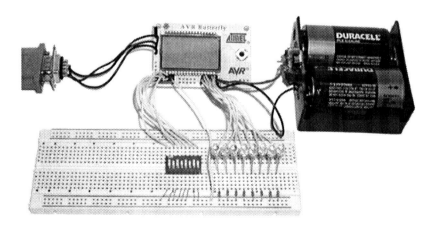

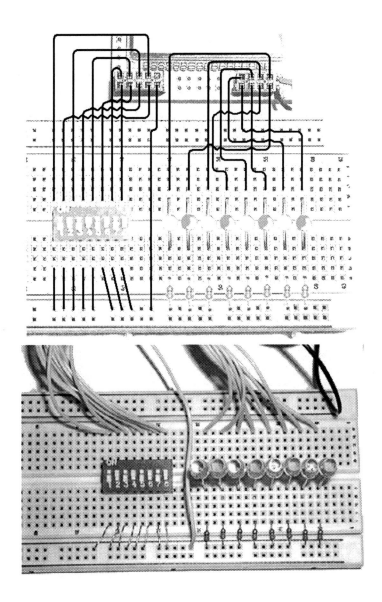

Figure 14: Port I/O switch input and LED output

Cylon Eye Speed and Polarity Control

In this example we will use port B to input data that we will use to control the Cylon eye movement rate and the LED polarity. By polarity I mean that we will set either all the LEDs on except the sweep LED which will be off, or all the LEDs off and the sweep LED on. We will control the polarity with the switch connected to the port B pin 7, leaving the lower pins to allow us to set the speed increase factor from 0 to 127.

In this example we will use the ~ bitwise operator to invert the LEDs on port D.

Open PortIO.c in Personal Notepad and save it as CylonEyes.c in a new directory CylonEyes. Make the following changes to the main() function

```c
// CylonEyes.c
#include <avr/io.h>
#include <avr/delay.h>

int main (void)
{
        // declare and initialize the scroll delay_count
        unsigned long delay_count = 10000;

        // declare a variable for the speed increase
        unsigned long increase = 0;

        // declare a variable for the polarity
        unsigned char polarity = 0;

        // Init port pins
        DDRB = 0x00; // set port B for input
        DDRD = 0xFF; // set port D for output

        while(1)
        {
                // read the switches
                increase = PINB;

                // set the polarity
                if(increase > 127)
                {
                        increase -= 127;
                        polarity = 1;
```

```
        }
        else polarity = 0;

        // set the delay count
        delay_count = 5000 + (increase * 500);

        // scroll those eyes
        for(int i = 1; i <= 128; i = i*2)
        {
                if(polarity) PORTD = ~i;
                else PORTD = i;
                _delay_loop_2(delay_count);
        }

        for(int i = 128; i > 1; i -= i/2)
        {
                if(polarity) PORTD = ~i;
                else PORTD = i;
                _delay_loop_2(delay_count);
        }
    }
}
```

Open the makefile in the Blinky directory and change TARGET = CylonEyes then save it to the CylonEyes directory. Compile, load, and play.

Figure 15: Bit 7 high

Figure 16: Bit 7 low

71

Chapter 5: C Control Flow

We specify the order in which computations are performed with control statements. We've already peeked at some of these concepts, now Let's jerk open the kimono and take a good hard look.

Statements and Blocks

Expressions such as PORTD = ~i or _delay_loop_2(30000) or i -= 128 become statements when they are followed by a semicolon:

```
PORTD = ~i;
_delay_loop_2(30000);
i -= 128;
```

The semicolon terminates the **statement**.

Compound statements are made by enclosing a group of statements or declarations in a block delimited by braces '{' and '}'. This causes the compiler to handle the block as a unit.

Tale of a bug:
I wrote the following statement:

```
while(QuarterSecondCount < 17600);
QuarterSecondCount = 0;
```

Then decided that the 17600 wait count was too long so I changed it to 2200:

```
while(QuarterSecondCount < 2200)//17600);
QuarterSecondCount = 0;
```

But I wanted to leave the 17600 in case I ever needed it again, so I commented it out. Do you see a problem here?

Well, what I meant to say was:

```
while(QuarterSecondCount < 2200);
QuarterSecondCount = 0;
```

73

Which is two statements, the first waits while an interrupt (Chapter 7) increments QuarterSecondCount in the background, and once that is finished the QuarterSecondCount is set to zero. What the compiler saw was:

```
while(QuarterSecondCount < 2200)
QuarterSecondCount = 0;
```

because the compiler doesn't see the comments – the //17600;. See the problem yet?

Well how about the equivalent statement:

```
while(QuarterSecondCount < 2200) QuarterSecondCount = 0;
```

The compiler also doesn't know about the line break, all it sees is the last statement, which says that while QuarterSecondCount is less than 2200, set QuarterSecondCount to 0. So each time the interrupt incremented QuarterSecondCount, this statement set it back to zero.

This is the kind of bug, that after spending X amount of time locating, you carefully hide it from your boss lest she think you are stupid or careless or both. Fortunately, I am my own boss, so I've learned to live with my stupid and careless employee. (I fired myself once, but that just didn't work out.)

If-Else and Else-If

We can make decisions using the if-else statement:

```
if (expression)
      statement1
else
      statement2
```

If the expression has a non-zero result (it is true), then we do statement 1, if the expression has a 0 result (it is false) we do statement 2. We can make a list of related decisions using else if:

```
if (expression1)
        statement1
else if (expression2)
        statement2
else if (expression3)
        statement3
else
        statement4
```

In this case each expression will be evaluated sequentially looking for the first non-zero (true) expression and if they all equal 0 (false) we do statement 4. You can omit the final else statement if you want to do nothing if all the expressions are 0 (false). We will use an example of this construction later when we write a program for using the joystick interrupts:

```
if(input == KEY_PLUS)PORTD= ~0x01;
else if(input == KEY_NEXT)PORTD = ~0x02;
else if(input == KEY_PREV)PORTD = ~0x04;
else if(input == KEY_MINUS)PORTD = ~0x08;
else if(input == KEY_ENTER)PORTD = ~0x10;
```

Which may be read as: if the input is equal to KEY_PLUS then set port D equal to the inverse of a byte equal to 1 (a byte of 1 is binary 00000001, the inverse is 11111110 and since we output a 0 to a pin to light an LED, this statement lights the LED). If the first line is true then the rest of the statements are skipped. If the first line isn't true, then each line is evaluated sequentially until a true expression is found or it drops out the bottom and does nothing.

Switch

The 'if else' construction limits us to expressions that are either true or false. If we want to make decisions using expressions that can have any numeric result we use the switch statement that selects an expression with results equal to a specified constant.

```
switch (expression) {
      case constant expression1 : statements
      case constant expression2 : statements
      case constant expression3 : statements
      default: statements
}
```

We can redo the if else if block used in the joystick interrupt example using a switch statement as follows:

```
switch(input){
      case KEY_PLUS :
            PORTD = ~0x01;
            break:
      case KEY_NEXT :
            PORTD = ~0x02;
            break;
      case KEY_PREV :
            PORTD = ~0x04;
            break;
      case KEY_MINUS :
            PORTD = ~0x08;
            break;
      case KEY_ENTER :
            PORTD = ~0x10;
            break;
      default:
}
```

So if the 'input' is equal to KEY_NEXT, then PORTD = ~0x01. The 'break' statement causes an immediate exit from the switch block - there is no need to check the rest as we have found our case. If you want to continue evaluating cases against the input, leave out the break and the next statements will be looked at.

You can let cases fall through, which can be handy in circumstances such as evaluating character input where you don't care if the character is a capital or lower case letter, or perhaps you want the same response for a range of integers:

```
switch( input){
      case 'a' :
      case 'A' :
            DoaA();
            break;
      case 'b' :
```

```
                case 'B' :
                        DobB();
                        break;
                case '0' :
                case '1' :
                case '2' :
                case '3' :
                        Gofer0123();
                        break;
                case '4' :
                case '5' :
                case '6' :
                case '7' :
                        Gofer4567();
                        break;
                default:
                        DoDefault();
                        break;
        }
```

This can be compacted as:

```
        switch( input){

                case 'a' : case 'A' :
                        DoaA();
                        break;

                case 'b' : case 'B' :
                        DobB();
                        break;
                case '0' : case '1' : case '2' : case '3' :
                        Gofer0123();
                        break;
                case '4' : case '5' : case '6' : case '7' :
                        Gofer4567();
                        break;
                default:
                        DoDefault();
                        break;
        }
```

Switch statements are error prone and a frequent source of head boinking bugs (one where you boink your head for being dumb enough to leave out a break statement). The break after default: isn't even necessary, but is recommended (by K&R) as a good practice to help you remember to use it when you add a statement to the end of the list.

Loops – While, For, and Do-while

We've been using while for a while (har!).

```
while(expression)
{
        // Do stuff while expression is true
}
```

While will repeat the associated statement or block as long as the expression is true.

The code fragment:

```
int i;
while( i < 128)
{
        PORTD = i;
        _delay_loop_2(30000);
        i = i*2;
}
```

This does exactly the same thing as the for loop in our first example program:

```
for(int i = 1; i < 128; i = i*2)

{
        PORTD = i;
        _delay_loop_2(30000);
}
```

The for loop is constructed as follows:

```
for(expresson1; expression2; expresson3)

{
        // Do stuff
}
```

Usually *expression1* and *expression3* are assignments or function calls and *expression2* is a test of some sort. The expressions can be any expression including the empty expression which is nothing followed by a semicolon:

```
for(;;)
{
        // Do stuff forever
}
```

This is an alternative way to do the while(1) eternal loop.

You can usually accomplish the same goal using either while or for statements. Generally it is clearer to use for loops with a simple initialization and incrementing such as:

```
for(int i = 1; i < 128; i = i*2)
{
        // Do stuff while I less than or equal 128
}
```

But it's really a matter of personal preference though most C dudes will want to smack you around a little if you don't do it their way.

While and for loops test for the termination condition before running the block, 'do while' runs the block first insuring that the block will be run at least once:

```
do
{
        // Do stuff at least once
}
while(expression);
```

Break and Continue

A break statement throws you out of the loop immediately and without regard for the terminating *expression*. It only throws you out of the innermost loop in nested loops.

79

A continue statement causes the loop to skip the following statements in the block and start the loop over again. You won't see this often, but it can come in handy for amazingly complex decision loops. Gurus use it a lot for job security.

Goto and Labels

There are those who would burn you at the stake for using 'goto'. I'm not one of those, but I won't throw water on you when some other C dude sets you on fire for this heresy. The goto statement is probably the laziest, most unnecessary, confusing, and potentially harmful thing you can stick in your code. It allows you to jump all over the place without regard to logic or common sense, creating the infamous 'spaghetti code'. But I have used it on occasion to escape a deeply nested loop as a quick fix for a bug when I didn't have time to rewrite the code like it should have been written in the first place. But I have never shown anyone such code; I have my pride you know. Anyway, the goto statement causes a jump to a label as follows:

```
while(expression){
     for(expression;expression;expression){
          do{
               if(expression){
                    switch(expression){
                         case expression:
                             if(expression) expression;
                             else goto GETMEOUTOFHERE!;
                             break;
                         case expression:
                              expression;
                              break;
                         default:
                    break;
                    }
               }
          }while(expression)
     }
}

GETMEOUTOFHERE!:
// Put more code here, or better yet, rewrite the nested loops above.
```

A few practical examples: strlen, atoi, itoa, reverse

In a serial communications project that we'll get to later, we will want to convert numbers into character strings to use in communicating with the PC. There are functions in the Standard Library, stdlib.h, that do everything we need; however, to help us learn Let's write them ourselves (with some help from K&R).

```
int strLen(char s[])
{
        int i;

        i = 0;

        while(s[i] != '\0') ++i;

        return i;
}
```

In strlen, we accept a pointer to a string (we'll talk about pointers later). The string is an array of characters with a terminal character '\0' (we'll talk about arrays later). The while statement evaluates each character, incrementing the index, i, until the terminal character is found. The return value is the number of characters, not including the terminal character.

In C the single and double quotes have specific meaning for defining characters: when you see 'x' the compiler sees the ASCII number for the single character x, when you see "x" the compiler sees a string with the character x followed by the string termination character '\0'. Whenever you see two characters a backslash and a following character like '\0', the C compiler sees this as a single nonprintable character called an 'escape sequence'.

In the serial communications project we will use several escape sequences, for example '\r' is a non-printable character that tells the Teletype machine to return the print head to the left of the platen and roll the paper one line. What? You aren't using a Teletype machine? Maybe not, but you are using a direct ancestor of one, and C was written on one, so thou shouldest get thyself used to anachronisms.

We define non-printable characters using escape sequences and I guess this is just about as good a place as any to show them all:

Table 8: Escape Sequences

\a	alert (bell)
\b	backspace
\f	formfeed
\n	newline
\r	carriage return
\t	horizontal tab
\v	vertical tab
\\	backslash
\?	question mark
\'	single quote
\"	double quote
\000	octal number
\xhh	hexadecimal number
\0	null

Before you look at the next function, take out your paper and pencil computer and come up with an algorithm for converting an ASCII character string of numerals into an integer, for example convert the string of char data types: "1234" to the int 1234. Give this some thought and see what you come up with. I'm serious now, do it or the rest of the ink in the book will fade away and you'll have an expensive drawing pad. Need a hint? Look at Table 9: ASCII Table (in appendixes) and note that the characters for 1, 2, 3, and 4 are sequential integer numerals, 0x31, 0x32, 0x33, and 0x34.

```
//NOTE: stolen from K&R p. 43 atoi function
int atoi(char s[])
{
    int i, n;

    n = 0;
    for(i = 0; s[i] >= '0' && s[i] <= '9'; ++i)
        n = 10 * n + (s[i] - '0');
    return n;
}
```

The atoi, ASCII to integer, function converts a string of ASCII characters representing the integers 0 thru 9 into an integer number equivalent to the string. If you didn't figure this one out yourself then use your paper and pencil computer to run the function with char s[] equaling '1,2,3,4,\0' to see how it works. Note the condition in the 'for' statement will cause the loop to bail if one of the characters is not equal to or between '0' and '9'. This gets us out of the loop, but not out of trouble. In a robust function, we would have some kind of error reporting mechanism so that code calling atoi could know that it sent a bad string and so the calling function could build in some way to recover. We'll get into all that later and be careful not to make mistakes now. (Famous last words)

The conversion algorithm relies on the convenient fact that the ASCII characters for integers are represented by a sequence of numbers. '0' is 0x30 in ASCII, '1' is 0x31, and so on. So if s[i] = '1', the character, we get (s[i] – '0') = 1, the integer. That is, we subtract the character '0' which has a value of 0x30 from the character '1' which has a value of 0x31, leaving us with the number 1. Voila: ASCII to integer.

We start with n = 0, so the first time thru the 10*n = 0 and the character is converted to the 1's position in the integer. For each subsequent pass, the n has a value so it gets multiplied by 10 providing the 10's, 100's, and so forth.

You were asked to think about this algorithm before looking at the atoi function. Don't be concerned if yours wasn't as simple and elegant as this one. Mine wasn't. It takes a while to start thinking like a computer. Then your brain turns to silicon and people avoid you.

Now think about the problem of reversing the characters in an array. How would you do this? Try it on the pencil and paper computer, then look at the reverse function.

```
//NOTE: stolen from K&R p. 62 reverse function
// reverse: reverse a string s in place
void reverse(char s[])
{
        int c, i, j;

        for (i = 0, j = strLen(s)-1; i < j; i++, j--){
                c = s[i];
```

```
                    s[i] = s[j];
                    s[j] = c;
            }
      }
```

This is pretty straightforward. Put the first char from the array in a box, then put the last character in the array in the position of the first character, then take the stored character and put it in the last position in the array. Move your index in one position on both ends and repeat.

Now try to develop an algorithm for converting an integer to an ASCII string. Mine worked, but wasn't even close in the quality of the actual function in K&R. Oh, well.

```
//NOTE: stolen from K&R p. 64 itoa function
void itoa(int n, char s[])
{
      int i, sign;

      if ((sign = n) < 0) // record sign
            n = -n;                     // make n positive
      i = 0;
      do {  // generate digits in reverse order
            s[i++] = n % 10 + '0'; // get next digit
      } while ((n /= 10) > 0); // delete it
      if (sign < 0)
            s[i++] = '-';
      s[i] = '\0'; // add null terminator for string
      reverse(s);
}
```

In my attempt at this, I never thought to do it backwards then reverse the string. First store the integer in the 'sign' variable and we get the sign of the integer by using the 'if' statement to see if the integer is less than 0, if so, we multiple it by – 1 to make it positive. Then we use do while, because we want to have at least one digit. Now get out your paper and pencil computer and run the number 1234 through the do while loop, since no amount of explaining will be as effective as running the numbers yourself. Don't be tempted to succumb to boredom and blow this off, you must be able to understand this at this point in the book. And it will be on the test.

Chapter 5: C Control Flow

Chapter 6: C Functions and Program Structures

Function Basics

About now you are probably wondering why you bought the Butterfly and all that cool hardware. Where are the projects? Let's blow something up! Patience grasshopper, we'll have a project at the end of this chapter and many more later. It will be worth it, I promise.

We've been using functions enough that by now you probably have a good intuitive feel for them, but Let's be formal and define some things. First a 'reuse' of what was said earlier:

Encapsulation is a key idea in C programming and provides the possibility of making chunks of code convenient to use. And just as important, it provides a way to make tested code reusable while not allowing the programmer to mess with it and chance breaking something. These ideas are so important in software engineering that the C++ language was developed primarily to formalize these concepts and force their use.

One of the main functions of functions (har!) is to break computations up into logical chunks and separate them to help clarify the code. A function should do one thing, and if you find yourself writing a function that seems to be doing two separable things, try separating it into two functions.

A function must be declared before it is defined somewhere, usually in a header file or before the main() function. For example:

```
void sendChar(char ) ;
```

Which tells the compiler that the sendChar() function takes a char as an argument and doesn't return anything when finished. The compiler can use this information to make sure you are using it correctly when you make calls to the function.
A function definition is the function text as:

```
void sendChar(char myData)
{
    // Do stuff with the variable 'data'
}
```

Note that the argument now not only has the type 'char' but a specific variable 'myData'. It doesn't matter what you name the argument in the calling function, as long as the type matches, so:

```
sendChar(myByte);
```

This is just fine, since the sendchar function will use the data in 'myByte' as the data in 'myData' in the function definition. An important consideration is that the data in 'myByte' is copied to sendchar(myByte), but the variable 'myByte' is not sent. Think about this. In the calling function, 'myByte' is an alias for the address of some data, in this case a char. The called function takes that char and puts in memory at another address aliased, in this case, with the name 'myData'. 'myByte' and 'myData' have the same value but are not stored in the same place. The function only sees a copy of 'myByte' not the actual 'myByte' itself. If the function chages the 'myData' variable, that change is not reflected in the calling functions 'myByte' variable. This is a source of a surprising number of bugs among novice C programmers. To clarify let's make a function named adder that adds two numbers.

```
void adder(unsigned char a1, unsigned char a2, unsigned char r)
{
    r = a1 + a2;

    if(r == 2) getrewarded();
    else getboinked();
}
```

Let's call it in main()

```
int main()
{
        unsigned char add1 = 1;
        unsigned char add2 = 1;
        unsigned char results = 0;

        adder(add1,add2,results);
```

88

```
        if(results == 2) getrewarded();
        else getboinked();
}
```

If you think 1 + 1 = 2 prepare to get boinked. You'll getrewarded() in adder() and getboinked() in main(). In the adder function, r = 2, but this doesn't change the 'results' in the parameter list in the function call to adder in the main() function.

Returns

Ouch! Boinking hurts, so Let's make adder work right, we change the return type from void to char and declare r as an unsigned char:

```
char adder(unsigned char a1, unsigned char a2)
{
        unsigned char r;

        r = a1 + a2;

        if(r == 2) getrewarded();
        else getboinked();

        return r;
}
```

And in main we set 'results' equal to adder so it gets set to the data returned by adder:

```
int main()
{
        unsigned char add1 = 1;
        unsigned char add2 = 1;
        unsigned char results = 0;

        results = adder(add1,add2);

        if(results == 2) getrewarded();
        else getboinked();
}
```

Now we get two rewards. If we want to skip the reward we could write adder:

```
char adder(unsigned char a1, unsigned char a2)
{
        return a1 + a2;
}
```

And we have a concise and totally useless function. If we want to add 1 and 1, we just add them.

External Variables

Another way to do the adder() thing would be to use and external variable (global). These are variables defined outside any function, usually in a header or before main() and are available for any function to use. We could have written:

```
void adder(unsigned char, unsigned char);
unsigned char results = 0;

int main()
{
        unsigned char add1 = 1;
        unsigned char add2 = 1;

        adder(add1,add2);

        if(results == 2) getrewarded();
        else getboinked();
}

void adder(unsigned char ad1, unsigned char a1)
{
        results = a1 + a2;
}
```

Which would work fine. Unless of course an interrupt triggered right after we set results in adder() and changed it to 3. Then when the interrupt finishes and we look at results in main() we get boinked again. This is a good reason to avoid external variables. You never know where they've been or what kind of nasty stuff they might track in. Also they permanently occupy memory, while defining 'results' in adder would only use memory when adder is called, and release the memory when finished.

Scope

Variable names have scope, meaning the sections of code where they are recognized, that determine how they can be used.

Variable names declared in a function are recognized only in that particular function. For example, you can have multiple functions with the int i declared local to that function and they won't interfere with each other. Likewise, a variable declared within a block remains local to that block.

External variables have scope from the point they are declared to the end of the text file. If you compile a file, you can call functions in it from other files, but you cannot use an external variable declared in another file.

There is a difference in the definition and the declaration of an external variable. If you use the extern keyword as in:

```
extern int tramp;
```

you have declared that tramp will be an int, but you have not defined it. To use tramp you must define it in each file that will use it. Something like:

```
int tramp = NULL;
```

This must appear in a source file that uses it. For example:

In file1:
```
extern double gadabout;
extern char harlot;
```

In file2:
```
double gadabout = 0;
char harlot = '?';
```

In this case changes to gadabout and harlot in file1 will also appear in file2 and visa versa. Maybe I'm being harsh calling them tramp, gadabout, and harlot, but externs are even more prone to being who-knows-where and doing who-knows-what than regular external variables so they are bug prone.

An example bug comes when you create an extern:

```
extern int upcount;
```

in file1 and declare it in files 1 and 2 and put your code aside for a few months, then get busy on file3 and decide that you need an external variable to do some up counting, so you declare it int upcount = 0; forgetting that it has already been declared as an extern in file1 which you have stuck in a library and no longer look at. Then you start getting weird bugs where the seemingly impossible event occurs that your upcount is getting changed unpredictably. This kind of error is so common that it was one of the reasons C++ was invented. Use externs if absolutely necessary (sometimes nothing else will do) but use them with extreme caution.

Headers

Header files are a convenient place to stick all the stuff that you put before the main() function. They are files with a suffix of .h and are declared as:

```
#include <LEDblinker.h>
#include "PCcomm.h"
```

If the declaration uses angle brackets <filename> the compiler looks in an implementation defined location, usually an 'include' directory. If it uses quotes "filename" the compiler looks in the same directory that the source program was located. The choice will depend on how you've decided to organize your development file system.

Blocks

Initialization

If you don't explicitly set a variable equal to some value, external and static variables are guaranteed to be initialized to zero; automatic and register variables are guaranteed to be initialized to random garbage. It's good practice to always initialize a variable.

External and static variables must be initialized with a constant expression, but you can use other variables in the initialization of automatic and register variables:

```
int dosomething(int x, int y, int z)
{
        int a = 0;
        int b = x + y + z - 12;
        // do stuff
}
```

Recursion

Recursion happens when a function calls itself. I've never called myself. I'm afraid that I might answer the phone and then have to deal with the philosophical or psychiatric implications. However, C has no problems with functions calling themselves, other than the psychiatric problems it tends to cause programmers when confronted with a recursive function and the task of figuring out what's going on. C Gurus love recursive functions.

```
void recursivefunc(double data)
{
        double mess;
        // Do some stuff
        recursivefunc(mess); // calls itself
        // Do more stuff
}
```

You'll find recursion used quite appropriately in some standard library functions and in many data sorting applications. But recursion can be very problematic in microcontrollers where we are usually limited in RAM memory. Each time you call a function some data is put on the stack using RAM that isn't released until the function returns. Each function you call within a function puts more data on the stack locking up more RAM. Recursive functions look like a good way to quickly and unpredictably fill the stack leading to the often-fatal condition known as blowing your stack. Your stack usually starts at the end of RAM and builds downward. Your variables usually start at the beginning of RAM and build upward. So putting too much on the stack may push it down far enough overwrite variables. That may kill your code immediately or only occasionally, like at the worse possible moment. Maybe I'm just not smart enough, but I've never written a recursive function for a microcontroller and I don't plan on it.

Preprocessor

The preprocessor runs before the compiler as a separate first step.

#include

We have already discussed a little about #include but now would be a good time to mention how to use them to prevent name conflicts. We saw in the discussion on 'extern' that it is possible to forget that you have declared a variable name as an extern in one file then define a variable using a name in another file causing potentially fun results: that is if you consider it fun to stay up all night to find a stupid bug. One way to lessen the likelihood of such a bug is to keep a single header file for all the C source files in a program. For instance, if we decide to build a Killer Cylon Robot, we might want to write different C sources files for the various components we need:

> CylonEyes.c
> CylonLegs.c
> CylonArms.c
> CylonBlaster.c
> CylonEnemyDiscriminator.c
> and so forth…

We could create a header file CylonKillerRobot.h, include it in each of the project files and use it for all of our variable and function declarations. By putting all the definitions in this file we lessen the likelihood of creating a name conflict that causes the code in CylonEnemyDiscriminator.c to substititute 'theProgrammer' for 'theEnemy' leading to the programmer learning that bugs yield extreme boinking.

#define

The #define directive tells the preprocessor to substitute a specified arbitrary sequence of characters anywhere it sees a specific token:

```
#define token arb1 arb2 arb3
```

Which causes the complier to substitute 'arb1 arb2 arb2' everywhere it sees 'token'.

One possible source of problems occurs when you reuse a token. You might write:

```
#define Up 0
```

And come back a month later, when your header file has 500 lines and forget that you have already defined Up and add:

```
#define Up 1
```

The preprocessor uses the last #define and you won't get any warnings, other than the one I'm giving you. But you probably will get some mysterious bugs that you'll blame on the hardware until much later you finally see what you've done and apply a well-deserved boink to your own head.

Macro Substitution

We can use #define to make a simple token that replaces a complex, or frequently used expression. For example we may want to determine the larger of two variables:

```
#define larger( x, y)   ( (x)>(y) ? (x) : (y) )
```

Which we would use as:

```
int a = 9;
int b = 7;
int c = 0;

c = larger( a, b);
```

The preprocessor replaces the last statement with:

```
c = ( (a)>(b) ? (a) : (b) );
```

Which is what the compiler sees.

The expression larger(a, b) looks like a function but isn't. A macro is substituted in the code anywhere that it is used, while a function is located in only one place and is called each time it is used. The big difference from a microcontroller perspective is that nothing is pushed on the stack when a macro is used, unlike functions, which use extra RAM. Also macros create in-line code that can be faster than function calls (no processor overhead). And finally, macros don't require formally declared data types:

```
double da = 12;
double db = 14;
double dc = 7;
double dd = 0;

dd = larger( (db-da), dc);
```

If larger() was a function, the parameters require a data type such as int or double, but couldn't use both (okay, there is casting, but that's another topic).

Conditional Inclusion

Often microcontrollers come in families that differ only in a few features, pinouts, memory size, and register locations. You can write C code for the entire family if you substitute aliases for the things that differ. Let's say that SuprMic16 uses pins 12 and 13 for USART transmit and receive, while SuprMic8 uses pins 6 and 14, and SuprMic4 uses pins 1 and 2. We put the following in our SuprMic.h file:

```
#if SuprMicX == 16
#       define TXD 12
#       define RXD 13
#elif SuprMicX == 8
#       define TXD 6
#       define RXD 14
#elif SuprMicX = 4
#       define TXD 1
#       define RXD 2
#else
#       error "No definition for SuprMicX TXD and RXD pins."
#endif
```

If we are using the SuprMic8 in our Killer Cylon Robot project we should put the following in our CylonKillerRobot.h file:

```
#ifndef SuprMicX
#       define SuprMicX = 8
#       include <SuprMic.h>
#endif
```

The ifndef means 'if not defined' so that the preprocessor will use the #define SuprMicX = 8 and #include <SuprMic.h> lines only the first time it sees the #ifndef SuprMicX line. This prevents the preprocessor from attaching the contents of SuprMic.h in each file that uses CylonKillerRobot.h

As a matter of standard practice, always begin a header file with an #ifndef statement and a #define so that the preprocessor will only use that header's data once in a project. If you put the header data in more than once you may get a lot of compiler errors about multiple declarations.

Projects

Is anybody out there? Communicating with a PC

Most microcontrollers are buried deep in some device where they run in merry isolation from the rest of the world. Their programs are burned into them and never change. But there are many instances when we might want to communicate with a microcontroller. The Butterfly uses a joystick and an LCD, which is fine for its built-in applications. For anything more complex, like changing the microcontroller software, nothing beats using the PC's RS232 serial communications port to communicate with the microcontroller through its Universal Synchronous Asynchronous Receiver Transmitter, USART, peripheral. The microcontroller and the PC must agree on the transmission speed in data bits per second, Baud rate, the number of bits per data unit, Data Bits, the parity of the data, Parity, the number of stop bits, Stop Bits, and Flow Control. (Refer to Constructing Your Development System section of Chapter 2 for the required settings) All this information is somewhat arcane and is legacy from the days of Teletype machines. Fortunately the USART takes care of most of this stuff for you, so you don't need to understand it. If you are really interested, get Jan Axelson's book *Serial Port Complete* (www.lvr.com).

What we need is a method to send commands and data from the PC and receive responses from the Butterfly. In this section we will develop a generic command interpreter skeleton that we will reuse in later programs. In this project we will use this skeleton to build a demonstration that let's the PC send a command name and a number to the Butterfly. The Butterfly will respond with text.

We will put this software in four files:
    PC_Comm.h
    PC_Comm.c
    Demonstrator.h
    Demonstrator.C

The PC_Comm files have many things in them that are well beyond our C training at this point, so just copy them and don't think too hard about it yet. We will revisit each function later as we increase our knowledge. You should have no trouble understanding anything in the Demonstrator files. If you do, review. In future projects we will only need to make changes to Demonstrator.h and Demonstrator.c.

Demonstrator

Create a new PC Comm directory and in Programmer's Notepad open a new C/C++ file and write:

```
// Demonstrator.h CommDemo version

        void initializer(void);

        void parseInput(char *);

        void Comm1(char *);
        void Comm2(char *);
        void Comm3(char *);
        void Comm4(char *);

        void responder(char *, char );
```

Save this file as Demonstrator.h.

In Programmer's Notepad open a new C/C++ file and write:

```
// Demonstrator.c PC Comm version

#include "PC_Comm.h"

void initializer()
{
        // Calibrate the oscillator:
        OSCCAL_calibration();
        // Initialize the USART
        USARTinit();

        // say hello
        sendString("\rPC_Comm.c ready to communicate.\r");
        // identify yourself specifically
        sendString("\rYou are talking to the PC_Comm demo.\r");

}
```

```c
void parseInput(char s[])
{
 // parse first character
 switch (s[0])
 {
  case 'c':
   if( (s[1] == 'o') && (s[2] == 'm') && (s[3] == 'm') )
       switch (s[4]) // parse the fifth character
       {
         case 'a':
               Comm1(s);
               break;
         case 'b':
               Comm2(s);
               break;
               case 'c':
               Comm3(s);
               break;
         case 'd':
               Comm4(s);
               break;
               default:
               sendString("\rYou sent: '");
               sendChar(s[0]);
               sendString("' - I don't understand.\r");
         }
         break;
  case 'd':
   if( (s[1] == 'e') && (s[2] == 'm') && (s[3] == 'o') && (s[4] == '?') )
       sendString("You are talking to the PC_Comm demo.\r");
       break;
  case 'h':
   if( (s[1] == 'e') && (s[2] == 'l') && (s[3] == 'l') && (s[4] == 'o') )
       sendString("Hello yourself\r");
       break;
       default:
         sendString("\rYou sent: '");
         sendChar(s[0]);
         sendString("' - I don't understand.\r");
         break;
       }
       s[0] = '\0';
}

void Comm1(char s[])
{
       responder(s,s[4]);
}
```

```
void Comm2(char s[])
{
        responder(s,s[4]);
}

void Comm3(char s[])
{
        responder(s,s[4]);
}

void Comm4(char s[])
{
        responder(s,s[4]);
}

void responder(char s[], char c)
{
        char sComm[11];
        unsigned char i = 5, j = 0;

        while( (s[i] != '\0') && (j <= 11) )
        {

                if( (s[i] >= '0') && (s[i] <= '9') )
                {
                        sComm[j++] = s[i++];
                }
                else
                {
                        sendString("Error - Comm");
                        sendChar(c);
                        sendString(" received a non integer: ");
                        sendChar(s[i]);
                        sendChar('\r');
                }
        }

        sComm[j] = '\0';

        if(j>11)
        {
                sendString("Error - Comm");
                sendChar(c);
                sendString(" number too large\r");
                sendChar('\r');
        }
        else
        {
                sendString("\rThank you for sending the number: ");
                sendString(sComm);
```

```
                sendChar('\r');
        }
}
```

Save this file as Demonstrator.c.

PC_Comm

The next two programs, PC_Comm.h and PC_Comm.c can be copied from the CD to the CommDemo directory, or if you want a preview of coming attractions, you can open a new C/C++ file in Programmer's Notepad and write:

```
// PC_Comm.h
#include <avr/io.h>
#include <avr/interrupt.h>
#include <avr/delay.h>

#include <stdlib.h>

#include "Demonstrator.h"

void OSCCAL_calibration(void) ;
void USARTinit(void);
char isCharAvailable(void);
char receiveChar(void);
void sendChar(char ) ;
void sendString(char *);

Save this file as PC_Comm.h.

In Programmer's Notepad open a new C/C++ file and write:

// PC_Comm.c

#include "PC_Comm.h"


int main(void)
{
        char string[64];
        unsigned char count = 0;

        // run the initialization routine
        initializer();

         //Begin forever chatting with the PC
         for(;;)
         {
                // Check to see if a character is waiting
                if( isCharAvailable() == 1 )
                {
```

```c
                        // If a new character is received, get it
                        string[count++] = receiveChar();

                        // receive a packet up to 64 bytes long
                        if(string[count-1] == '\n')// HyperTerminal string ends with \r\n
                        {
                                string[count-2] = '\0'; //convert to a string
                                parseInput(string);
                                string[0] = '\0';
                                count = 0;
                        }
                        else if(count > 64)
                        {
                                count = 0;
                                string[0] = '\0';
                                sendString("Error - received > 64 characters");

                        }
                }
        }
        return 0;
}


char isCharAvailable()
{
        // Does the RX0 bit of the USART Status and Control Register
        // indicate a char has been received?
        if ( (UCSR0A & (0x80)) ) return 1;
        else return 0;
}

char receiveChar()
{
        // Return the char in the UDR0 register
        return UDR0;
}

void sendChar(char data)
{
    int i = 0;

    // To send data with the USART put the data in the USART data register
    UDR0 = data;

    // Check to see if the global interrupts are enabled
    if(SREG & 0x80)
    {
        // Wait until the byte is sent or we count out
                while ( !(UCSR0A&0x40) && (i<10000) )
                {
                        i++;
                }
    }
    else  // Wait until the byte is sent
        while( !(UCSR0A&0x40) );
```

```
        // Clear the TXCflag
        UCSR0A=UCSR0A|0x40;
}

void sendString(char s[])
{
        int i = 0;

        while(i < 64) // don't get stuck if it is a bad string
        {
                if( s[i] == '\0' ) break; // quit on string terminator
                sendChar(s[i++]);
        }
}

void USARTinit()
{
    // Increase the oscillator to 2 MHz for the 19200 baudrate:
    CLKPR = (1<<CLKPCE);          // set Clock Prescaler Change Enable
    // set prescaler = 4, Inter RC 8MHz / 4 = 2MHz
    CLKPR = (1<<CLKPS1);

    // Set the USART baudrate registers for 19200
    UBRR0H = 0;//(unsigned char)(baudrate>>8);
    UBRR0L = 12;//(unsigned char)baudrate;

    // Enable 2x speed change
    UCSR0A = (1<<U2X0);

    // Enable receiver and transmitter
    UCSR0B = (1<<RXEN0)|(1<<TXEN0)|(0<<RXCIE0)|(0<<UDRIE0);

    // Set the USART to asynchronous at 8 bits no parity and 1 stop bit
    UCSR0C = (0<<UMSEL0)|(0<<UPM00)|(0<<USBS0)|(3<<UCSZ00)|(0<<UCPOL0);
}


//Calibrate the internal OSCCAL byte, using the external
//32,768 kHz crystal as reference
void OSCCAL_calibration(void)
{
    unsigned char calibrate = 0;//FALSE;
    int temp;
    unsigned char tempL;

    CLKPR = (1<<CLKPCE);          // set Clock Prescaler Change Enable
    // set prescaler = 8, Inter RC 8MHz / 8 = 1MHz
    CLKPR = (1<<CLKPS1) | (1<<CLKPS0);

    TIMSK2 = 0;              //disable OCIE2A and TOIE2

    ASSR = (1<<AS2);         //select asynchronous operation of timer2 (32,768kHz)

    OCR2A = 200;            // set timer2 compare value

    TIMSK0 = 0;             // delete any interrupt sources
```

104

```
    TCCR1B = (1<<CS10);     // start timer1 with no prescaling
    TCCR2A = (1<<CS20);     // start timer2 with no prescaling

    //wait for TCN2UB and TCR2UB to be cleared
    while((ASSR & 0x01) | (ASSR & 0x04));

    // wait for external crystal to stabilise
    for(int i = 0; i < 10; i++)
        _delay_loop_2(30000);

    while(!calibrate)
    {
        cli(); // mt __disable_interrupt();  // disable global interrupt

        TIFR1 = 0xFF;    // delete TIFR1 flags
        TIFR2 = 0xFF;    // delete TIFR2 flags

        TCNT1H = 0;      // clear timer1 counter
        TCNT1L = 0;
        TCNT2 = 0;       // clear timer2 counter

        while ( !(TIFR2 && (1<<OCF2A)) );   // wait for timer2 compareflag

        TCCR1B = 0; // stop timer1

        sei(); // __enable_interrupt();  // enable global interrupt

        if ( (TIFR1 && (1<<TOV1)) )
        {
            temp = 0xFFFF;       // if timer1 overflows, set the temp to 0xFFFF
        }
        else
        {   // read out the timer1 counter value
            tempL = TCNT1L;
            temp = TCNT1H;
            temp = (temp << 8);
            temp += tempL;
        }

        if (temp > 6250)
        {
            OSCCAL--; // the internRC oscillator runs to fast, decrease the OSCCAL
        }
        else if (temp < 6120)
        {
            OSCCAL++; // the internRC oscillator runs to slow, increase the OSCCAL
        }
        else
            calibrate = 1;//TRUE;    // the interRC is correct

        TCCR1B = (1<<CS10); // start timer1
    }
}
```

Save this file as PC_Comm.c.

Finally make these changes to the makefile:

```
# Target file name (without extension).
TARGET = PC_Comm

# List C source files here. (C dependencies are automatically
generated.)
SRC = $(TARGET).c

SRC += Demonstrator.c
```

Using PC_Comm:

Download the code to the Butterfly.
Open HyperTerminal
Start the program.

In HyperTerminal you should see:

PC_Comm.c ready to communicate.
You are talking to the PC_Comm demo.

Type in:
demo?
You should receive:
You are talking to the PC_Comm demo.

Type in:
hello
You should receive:
Hello yourself

Type in:
coo
You should receive:
You sent: " - I don't understand.

Type in:
comma123
You should receive:

Thank you for sending the number: 123

Type in:
commb4567
You should receive:
Thank you for sending the number: 4567

Type in:
commc123456789012
You should receive:
Error - Commc number too large

Type in:
commd890
You should receive:
Thank you for sending the number: 890

This is a lot of software. Don't worry about he PC_Comm yet, but you should fully understand the demonstrator.c and demonstrator.h files by now. If not, carefully review.

Chapter 7: Microcontroller Interrupts and Timers

Interrupts and Timers are critical to microcontroller applications, but they have nothing to do with the C programming language. I can't think of a good way to progressively discuss C and smoothly mix in these topics so we will stop with the C for a while and look at our hardware. Interrupts and timers will be helpful in making later projects more useful.

C knows nothing about interrupts or timers. These things are machine dependent and specific. While the general concepts will apply to other microcontroller families, the specifics are for the AVR family and more specifically for the ATmega169.

Interrupts

We usually use one of two methods in microcontroller software to check to see if an event has occurred: polling and interrupts. Polling occurs when a section of code, usually an infinite loop in main(), looks to see if an event has happened. For instance, it may check pin 6 to see if the voltage is +3 or 0 (logic true or false), and if +3 do one thing and if 0 do another. If the microcontroller hardware is designed so that pin 6 can be used to interrupt the program, then we don't have to poll the pin, we can set up the software so that when the pin state we are interested in, say falling from +3V to 0v, an interrupt function will be called.

Interrupts on microcontrollers are much like interrupts in daily life. The telephone, for instance, interrupts your activities by its insistent ringing. But imagine how it would be if you had to poll the telephone to receive calls. Periodically, you'd pick up the receiver and say 'Hello, anybody out there?' and your caller would shriek, "I've been waiting for an hour! Why don't you check your phone every five minutes like a normal person?" The ringing interrupting workflow might be annoying, but if someone is calling you to tell you that your garage is on fire, you want to know about it immediately.

Microcontrollers respond to interrupts much like you would. Maybe you are reading a book and the phone rings. You use you fingernail to scratch a mark next to the line you were reading and dog-ear the page before closing the book. (Librarians everywhere groan) Then you answer the phone and when the call is finished and you've put out the fire in your garage, you can refer to the desecrations to your book and go right back to where you left off your reading.

From the hardware perspective an interrupt causes the microcontroller to stop what it is doing, store sufficient data so that later it can get back to what it was doing, look to see which interrupt happened, run the interrupt code, and when finished restore the machine to its state before the interrupt occurred using the previously stored data.

Interrupts are great, but they provide an avenue for some particularly pernicious bugs. For example when your code is reading an integer from memory and since an integer is made of two bytes the code gets the first byte, then is stopped by an interrupt that changes the value of the integer before returning control to the part of the code that was reading the integer which then gets the second byte of the integer. The integer will be wrong because it will be made half from the pre-interrupt value and half from the post-interrupt value. The crazy making debugging problem is that the interrupt can happen at any time, maybe only very rarely during the integer read. Your system can run like a champ and then locks up for no apparent reason. You don't want this kind of bug in your pacemaker. You prevent this bug by disabling interrupts before reading variables that can be changed by interrupts then enabling them after you've got the correct number.

We'll study interrupts by using some fairly intense code based on the Butterfly software used to read the joystick. If you compare the software used in this example to the Butterfly software you might think I stole some of it. And you'd be correct. That is one of the central principles of software engineering: **if it ain't nailed down - steal it**. Heck, if it is nailed down, get a crowbar and rip it up. It's also called 'code reuse' and you'd be stupid to reinvent the wheel by trying to write something from scratch when you have perfectly good code already available. There are only two reasons to write stuff you can steal, one is that you want to learn by doing, and the other is to avoid a lawsuit - if the software doesn't specifically state that it can be used, then it is copyrighted. Hopefully, I won't get sued.

Some of this code will have concepts that will be explained later. Expect a little confusion. Now may be a good time for a nap.

The Atmega169 data book lists 23 interrupts in Table 22 on page 47. Two of these interrupts, the Pin Change Interrupts: PCI0 and PCI1 are triggered by changes on some of the port pins. Pins on Port E can be configured to trigger a PCI0 interrupt and pins on Port B can be configured to trigger a PCI1 interrupt.

The joystick just happens to be attached to pins on both Port B and Port E making it an ideal candidate to study interrupts with the added benefit that when we get though, we'll be able to use the joystick like it was intended. The joystick pins map as follows:

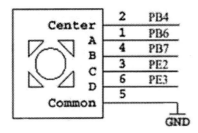

```
Bit                 7   6   5   4   3   2   1   0
-------------------------------------------------
PORTB               B   A       O
PORTE                               D   C
-------------------------------------------------
PORTB | PORTE       B   A       O   D   C
=================================================
```

Where:

        A = up
        B = down
        O = center push
        D = left
        C = right

The PCMSK1 register controls which pins contribute to the interrupt. If a bit is set to 1 the corresponding bit in Port B is enabled to trigger the PCI1 interrupt. A 0 disables the interrupt for a pin. To enable the buttons of interest:

Port B bit position	7	6	5	4	3	2	1	0
PCMSK1 bit	1	1	x	1	x	x	x	x

We use 'x' to indicate that we don't care what that bit is. Since some other part of the software might be using that bit, we want to leave it as is. The statement:

```
PCMSK1 |= ((1<<PINB4)|(1<<PINB6)|(1<<PINB7))
```

Changes bits 4, 6, and 7 to 1 and leaves the rest of the bits as they were. As a review, remember what the '|' does: 1|1=1, 1|0=1, 0|1=1, and 0|0=0. So the 1 bits will set to one no matter what they were in PCMSK1 and the 0 bits will set the PCMSK1 bit to 1 if it was already 1 and to 0 if it was already 0. If this is still obscure get out the pencil-and-paper-computer and play with it a bit (har!). It is a critical concept for understanding microcontrollers.

We are going to use: `(1<<PINB4)|(1<<PINB6)|(1<<PINB7)` several places in our code, so let's look at a new item that will simplify our lives, the #define preprocessor directive. If we put:

```
#define PINB_MASK ((1<<PINB4)|(1<<PINB6)|(1<<PINB7))
```

In our code, usually after the #include directives and before the main() function, the preprocessor will substitute `((1<<PINB4)|(1<<PINB6)|(1<<PINB7))` for each occurrence of PINB_MASK in the code. So we can write:

```
PCMSK1 |= PINB_MASK;
```

in our source file but the C compiler will see:

```
PCMSK1 |= ((1<<PINB4)|(1<<PINB6)|(1<<PINB7))
```

The External Interrupt Mask Register, EIMSK, and External Interrupt Flag Register, EIFR are discussed on page 78 of the data book. We set them to enable the PCI1 interrupt as follows:

```
EIFR = (1<<PCIF0)|(1<<PCIF1);
EIMSK = (1<<PCIE0)|(1<<PCIE1);
```

The program will jump to the interrupt routine when the interrupt is triggered, but where is the interrupt routine? The location is determined by the address 'vector' listed in Table 22, page 47 of the data book. We use the following code to access the PCI1 interrupt:

```
SIGNAL(SIG_PIN_CHANGE1)
{
        // Do something
}
```

SIGNAL is defined in the WinAVR include directory in signal.h, which defines some macros to handle interrupt functions using the gcc compiler. We'll get to macros later. Interrupt handling is defined specifically for a particular microcontroller and a particular C compiler and it is not portable like most of C. The original Butterfly code was built using the IAR C compiler and uses this format for interrupts:

```
#pragma vector = PCINT0_vect
__interrupt void PCINT0_interrupt(void)
{
        // Do something
}
```

We'll get to pragmas later. IAR handles interrupts one-way and WinAVR does it another.

Let's review:
- We setup a register, PCMSK1, to indicate which port B pins can cause interrupts.
- We setup the External Interrupt Mask Register, EIMSK, and External Interrupt Flag Register, to enable the PCI1 interrupt.
- We provided the SIGNAL(SIG_PIN_CHANGE1) code to be called when the interrupt occurs.

Projects

Grab your joystick – and test your interrupts

Create a new directory Joystick and copy the PC_comm. and Demonstrator .c and .h files from the PC_comm. directory.

In Programmers Notepad change Demonstrator.h to:

```
// Demonstrator.h Joystick version

#include <avr/signal.h>
#include <inttypes.h>

#define KEY_UP        0
#define KEY_DOWN      1
#define KEY_LEFT      2
#define KEY_RIGHT     3
#define KEY_PUSH      4
#define KEY_INVALID   5

#define BUTTON_A      6    // UP
#define BUTTON_B      7    // DOWN
#define BUTTON_C      2    // LEFT
#define BUTTON_D      3    // RIGHT
#define BUTTON_O      4    // PUSH

#define PINB_MASK ((1<<PINB4)|(1<<PINB6)|(1<<PINB7))
#define PINE_MASK ((1<<PINE2)|(1<<PINE3))

#define TRUE 1
#define FALSE 0

// declare functions
void PinChangeInterrupt(void);
char getkey(void);

void initializer(void);
void parseInput(char *);
void joystick(void);
```

Open the Demonstrator.c and change it to:

```c
// Demonstrator.c Joystick version

#include "PC_Comm.h"
#include "Demonstrator.h"

// declare global variables
volatile char KEY = 0;
volatile char KEY_VALID = 0;
volatile char ENABLED = 0;

void initializer()
{

        // Calibrate the oscillator:
        OSCCAL_calibration();

        // Initialize the USART
        USARTinit();

        // Init port pins
        DDRB |= 0xD8;
        PORTB |= PINB_MASK;
        DDRE = 0x00;
        PORTE |= PINE_MASK;

        // Enable pin change interrupt on PORTB and PORTE
        PCMSK0 = PINE_MASK;
        PCMSK1 = PINB_MASK;
        EIFR = (1<<6)|(1<<7);
        EIMSK = (1<<6)|(1<<7);

        DDRD = 0xFF; // set PORTD for output
        DDRB = 0X00; // set PORTB for input

        PORTB = 0xFF; // enable pullup on for input
        PORTD = 0XFF; // set LEDs off

        // say hello
        sendString("\rPC_Comm.c ready to communicate.\r");
        // identify yourself specifically
        sendString("You are talking to the JoyStick demo.\r");

}
```

```
void parseInput(char s[])
{
  // parse first character
  switch (s[0])
  {
      case 'j':
            if( (s[1] == 'o') && (s[2] == 'y'))
            joystick();
            break;
      case 'd':

if((s[1]=='e')&&(s[2]=='m')&&(s[3]=='o')&&(s[4]=='?') )
            sendString("You are talking to the JoyStick
demo.\r");
            break;
          default:
            sendString("\rYou sent: '");
            sendChar(s[0]);
            sendString("' - I don't understand.\r");
            break;
      }
      s[0] = '\0';
}

void joystick()
{
      if(ENABLED == 0) ENABLED = 1;
      else ENABLED = 0;
}


SIGNAL(SIG_PIN_CHANGE0)
{
    PinChangeInterrupt();
}

SIGNAL(SIG_PIN_CHANGE1)
{
    PinChangeInterrupt();
}

void PinChangeInterrupt(void)
{
    char buttons;
    char key;
```

116

```
    buttons = (~PINB) & PINB_MASK;
    buttons |= (~PINE) & PINE_MASK;

    // Output virtual keys
    if (buttons & (1<<BUTTON_A))
        key = KEY_UP;
    else if (buttons & (1<<BUTTON_B))
        key = KEY_DOWN;
    else if (buttons & (1<<BUTTON_C))
        key = KEY_LEFT;
    else if (buttons & (1<<BUTTON_D))
        key = KEY_RIGHT;
    else if (buttons & (1<<BUTTON_O))
        key = KEY_PUSH;
    else
        key = KEY_INVALID;

    if(key != KEY_INVALID)
    {
        if (!KEY_VALID)
        {
            KEY = key;              // Store key in global key buffer
            KEY_VALID = TRUE;
        }
    }

    //Delete pin change interrupt flags
    EIFR = (1<<PCIF1) | (1<<PCIF0);

      if(ENABLED)
      {
            getkey();
      }
}

char getkey(void)
{
    char k;

    cli(); // disable interrrupts so 'KEY' won't change while in
use

    if (KEY_VALID) // Check for unread key in buffer
    {
        k = KEY;
        KEY_VALID = FALSE;
```

```
    }
    else
        k = KEY_INVALID; // No key stroke available

    sei(); // enable interrupts

      if(k != KEY_INVALID)
      {
            sendString("The joystick position is: ");

            switch(k)
            {
                  case KEY_UP:
                        sendString("UP");
                        break;
                  case KEY_DOWN:
                        sendString("DOWN");
                        break;
                  case KEY_LEFT:
                        sendString("LEFT");
                        break;
                  case KEY_RIGHT:
                        sendString("RIGHT");
                        break;
                  case KEY_PUSH:
                        sendString("PUSH");
                        break;
                  default:
                        sendString("?");
                        break;
            }

            sendChar('\r');
      }

    return k;
}
```

Compile it and download to the Butterfly (remembering to browse to the correct directory).

Using joystick

Using HyperTerminal, you should see:

PC_Comm.c ready to communicate.
You are talking to the Joystick demo.

Type in:
joy

Move the joystick to the left and you should receive:
The joystick position is: LEFT

Move the joystick to the right and you should receive:
The joystick position is: RIGHT

Move the joystick up and you should receive:
The joystick position is: UP

Move the joystick down and you should receive:
The joystick position is: DOWN

Push the joystick while centered t and you should receive:
The joystick position is: PUSH

I'm tired and going to bed. Tomorrow we'll look at timers. I may get so excited that I won't be able to sleeeeeppp ummm errr zzzzzz…

Timers/Counters

Good morning! In Blinky.c we set the timing of the blinks using the _delay_loop_2(delaycount). The delay function uses a 16-bit count that takes 4 cycles/loop. This loop runs in the CPU, which can do nothing else while it is running. You set the period of the delay by sending a parameter for the number of '4 cycles' you want to waste. Knowing the time per cycle allows you to set the time of the delay. Cycle wasting delays are a simple way to control some types of periodic events, but the simplicity comes at the cost of totally occupying the CPU while wasting the specified time. That's a good idea if you don't need to do anything else while the delay is running, but it makes a lousy way to mark time if you have anything else going on. Timers are peripheral devices that run independent of the CPU and only bother the CPU when set up to do so. The bothering can take the form of setting a flag that the CPU can poll, or throwing an interrupt to break into normal operations.

The reason we usually see Timer/Counter hooked together is that the Timer/Counter peripheral keeps time by counting pulses. The pulses can come from a synchronous periodic source providing an accurate time count, or the pulses can come from an asynchronous non-periodic source providing an accurate count of the input pulses. In the first case we could be counting pulses from the 32.768 kHz watch crystal and keep accurate clock time. In the second case we could be counting pulses from a light beam interrupter circuit and keep an accurate count of the number of people entering a door and breaking the light beam.

The ATmega169 has three Timer/Counters, two 8 bit and one 16 bit. A timer interrupt overflows when it counts up to its maximum value (255 for the 8 bit and 65535 for the 16 bit devices) and resets to 0. We can get the Timer to overflow at lower values by putting a value in the OCR, Output Compare Register, for the specified timer and that timer will compare the value with the count and when they match it will set a flag or throw an interrupt. It can also be set to overflow to 0 on a match.

The timers can be configured for input capture events, where a change on a pin will cause the timer to save the count when the event occurred. This input capture count can be used to measure the width of an external pulse. If the external pulses are periodic, we have a frequency counter.

The Timer/Counter is a peripheral and runs independent of program execution. There are three ways for the program to monitor and react to Timer/Counter events.

1. Poll the overflow flags.
2. Break program execution with an interrupt.
3. Let the timer automatically change the level of output pins.

The clock of the Timer/Counters uses a prescaler connected to a multiplexer The prescaler is used to divide the input clock and the multiplexer selects which of the divided signals is used as the input clock. The clock source for the prescaler can be an external clock such as the 32.768 kHz crystal or it can use the system clock.

Calibrating the Butterfly oscillator:

We first used the OSCCAL_calibration() function in the PC_Comm project, claiming that we would explain it later. Well, it's later and, wow, it's time to understand how it works.

If you try to tell time with the uncalibrated oscillator built into the ATmega169, you can expect to gain or lose a couple of hours a day. These oscillators produce very precise pulse trains, but due to manufacturing variables, the pulse timing varies from chip to chip and do not correlate to 'real' time. Real time is determined by the National Bureau of Standards and references an atomic clock. To calibrate the built-in oscillator to real time requires an external crystal that has been precisely trimmed to pulse at a rate calibrated to the NBS clock. The Butterfly uses an external 32.768 kHz watch crystal to calibrate the oscillator to run at 8 MHz. Watch crystals are accurate, cheap, and make keeping human time easy ('easy' being another relative term).

We can get an accurate count of a time period by counting pulses from the watch crystal. For instance if we count 32768 pulses we know that one second has passed. We use a shorter known good period to calibrate the internal oscillator by setting the oscillator to generate x pulses in the known good time period. Remember that the oscillator is running at about 8 MHz, so we are going to get a lot more counts from it than we will get from the watch crystal. If we count 32768 pulses from the watch crystal and 8 million pulses from the oscillator in the same period, we know the 8 MHz is accurate. That is, we get 8 million counts from the oscillator in the same period we get 32768 counts (one second) from the crystal meaning the oscillator is running at exactly 8 million pulses per second. But we will actually use a much shorter period and have smaller counts. If the oscillator count is too small for the period we change the value in a register to speed it up, and if it is too large we change the register to slow it down. We do this in a loop to keep bracketing the speed until it gets as accurate as we can make it. Sounds easy, but as you'll quickly see, it is a real pain just to get the registers all set up properly.

In this section we will learn how the Butterfly oscillator is calibrated. This is presented in two sections, the first shows the OSCCAL_calibration function, and the second gives a detailed explanation.

OSCCAL_calibration() function – the code:

```
/*********************************************************************
*
*    Function name : OSCCAL_calibration
*
*    Returns :        None
*
*    Parameters :     None
*
*  Purpose :  Calibrate the internal OSCCAL byte, using the external
*                  32,768 kHz crystal as reference
*
*********************************************************************/
void OSCCAL_calibration(void)
{
    unsigned char calibrate = FALSE;
    int temp;
    unsigned char tempL;

    CLKPR = (1<<CLKPCE);         // set Clock Prescaler Change Enable
    // set prescaler = 8, Inter RC 8MHz / 8 = 1MHz
    CLKPR = (1<<CLKPS1) | (1<<CLKPS0);

    TIMSK2 = 0;            //disable OCIE2A and TOIE2

     ASSR = (1<<AS2);        //select  asynchronous  operation  of  timer2
                            (32,768kHz)

    OCR2A = 200;             // set timer2 compare value

    TIMSK0 = 0;             // delete any interrupt sources

    TCCR1B = (1<<CS10);     // start timer1 with no prescaling
    TCCR2A = (1<<CS20);     // start timer2 with no prescaling

    //wait for TCN2UB and TCR2UB to clear
    while((ASSR & 0x01) | (ASSR & 0x04));

    Delay(1000);    // wait for external crystal to stabilise

    while(!calibrate)
    {
        cli(); // mt __disable_interrupt();  // disable global
                                                  interrupt

        TIFR1 = 0xFF;   // delete TIFR1 flags
        TIFR2 = 0xFF;   // delete TIFR2 flags
```

122

```
        TCNT1H = 0;      // clear timer1 counter
        TCNT1L = 0;
        TCNT2 = 0;       // clear timer2 counter

        // wait for timer2 compareflag
        while ( !(TIFR2 && (1<<OCF2A)) );

        TCCR1B = 0; // stop timer1

        sei(); // __enable_interrupt();  // enable global interrupt

        if ( (TIFR1 && (1<<TOV1)) )
        {
            temp = 0xFFFF; // if timer1 overflows, set the temp to 0xFFFF
        }
        else
        {   // read out the timer1 counter value
            tempL = TCNT1L;
            temp = TCNT1H;
            temp = (temp << 8);
            temp += tempL;
        }

        if (temp > 6250)
        {
            OSCCAL--;   //RC oscillator runs to fast, decrease OSCCAL
        }
        else if (temp < 6120)
        {
            OSCCAL++;//RC oscillator runs to slow, increase OSCCAL
        }
        else
            calibrate = TRUE;    // the interRC is correct

        TCCR1B = (1<<CS10); // start timer1
    }
}
```

OSCCAL_calibration() function – detailed explanation

The 'System Clock and Clock Options' section of the ATmega169 data book tells more than you'll ever want to know about the ATmega169's clock. Let's focus on only what we need for our system.

The Clock Prescale Register, CLKPR, is discussed beginning on page 30 of the data book. Bit 7 of CLKPR is the prescaler enable bit, CLKPCE (an alias for bit 7), so the statement:

```
CLKPR = (1<<CLKPCE);
```

enables the Clock Prescaler Change.

The Clock Prescaler Select Bits CLKPS0, CLKPS1, CLKPS2, and CLKPS3 are alias for the lower 4 bits of CLKPR and are used to select a clock division factor. Since registers are preset to 0, we OR CLKPS1 and CLKPS0 as 1 and get 0011 which provides a clock division factor of 8, this divides the 8 MHz oscillator by 8 giving a 1 MHz clock:

```
CLKPR = (1<<CLKPS1) | (1<<CLKPS0);
```

The Timer/Counter2 Interrupt Mask Register, TIMSK2, is set to 0 to disable the OCIE2A, output compare, and TOIE2, overflow enable, interrupts (p 141 data book if you want the gory details).

```
TIMSK2 = 0;
```

We must set the Asynchronous Timer/Counter2, AS2, bit 3 of the Asynchronous State Register, ASSR, to allow an external clock connected to the Timer Oscillator, TOSC1, pin 24 of the microcontroller to be used to for asynchronous operation of timer2 (32,768kHz):

```
ASSR = (1<<AS2);
```

The Output Compare Register A, OCR2A, contains a value, 200, that will be continuously compared with the Timer Count 2, TCNT2, register

```
OCR2A = 200;
```

The Timer/Counter0 Interrupt Mask Register, TIMSK0, is set to 0 to delete any interrupt sources (p 93 data book).

```
TIMSK0 = 0;
```

The Timer/Counter1 Control Register B, TCCR1B and the Timer/Counter2 Control Register A, TCCR2A, are set to start timer1 and timer2 with no prescaling:

```
TCCR1B = (1<<CS10);
TCCR2A = (1<<CS20);
```

After setting all these registers we wait for the TCNT2 and the TCRU2B registers to be set from temporary memory, by waiting for the Timer/Counter2 Update Busy, TCN2UB, and the Timer/Counter2 Update Register Busy,TCCR2A, bits of the ASSR register to be cleared (p 139 data book).

```
while((ASSR & 0x01) | (ASSR & 0x04));
```

Wait a while for the crystal to stabilize:

```
Delay(1000);
```

ALL THIS AND WE HAVEN'T EVEN STARTED CALIBRATING YET!

Getting registers set properly to do much of anything in a microcontroller can be a long and frustrating exercise, and another good reason to steal code where possible.

We start calibrating by running a loop in which we make adjustments to the internal oscillator and compare the results to the external clock, looping until we get it right.

Set a flag:

```
unsigned char calibrate = FALSE;
```

to terminate the loop when true:

```
while(!calibrate)
```

On each pass you do the following:

Disable global interrupts:

```
cli();
```

Clear the timer interrupt flags:

```
TIFR1 = 0xFF;
TIFR2 = 0xFF;
```

Clear the timer counts:

```
TCNT1H = 0;
TCNT1L = 0;
TCNT2 = 0;
```

Wait for the timer to reach the count

```
while ( !(TIFR2 && (1<<OCF2A)) );
```

Stop the timer:

```
TCCR1B = 0;
```

Enable global interrupts

```
sei();
```

Has Timer/Counter1 overflowed? If so set our temp variable to 0xFFFF.

```
if ( (TIFR1 && (1<<TOV1)) )
{
        //if timer1 overflows, set the temp to 0xFFFF
        temp = 0xFFFF;
}
```

Otherwise read the timer1 counter value into the temp variable

```
else
{
    tempL = TCNT1L;
    temp = TCNT1H;
```

```
    temp = (temp << 8);
    temp += tempL;
}
```

Is temp greater than 6250? If so decrement the Oscillator Calibration Register, OSCCAL

```
if (temp > 6250)
{
 OSCCAL--;//RC oscillator runs to fast, decrease OSCCAL
}
```

Otherwise, if temp is less than 6120, increment OSCCAL.

```
else if (temp < 6120)
{
   OSCCAL++;  //RC oscillator runs to slow, increase OSCCAL
}
```

If temp is between 6250 and 6120 the calibration is complete and we can go home.

```
else
     calibrate = TRUE;   // the interRC is correct
```

But before we turn out the light, we start the timer:

```
TCCR1B = (1<<CS10); // start timer1
```

Now if you are beginning to think all this is mighty confusing, you are finally beginning to understand the core truth of microcontroller programming. It **IS** mighty confusing. And frustrating and bug infested and time consuming and ego destroying and… well, you name it. But finally getting something working is the greatest pleasure known to mankind, (if you overlook sex, eating, parenting, and anything else you like to do). A word of advice: if you don't actually get some pleasure from working out these puzzles you don't need to be doing this for a career. Try professional knife fighting… you'll survive longer. This complexity is primary reason to 'reuse' code. And speaking of stealing them naked, the following project uses code lifted directly from the WinAVR port of the ATMEL Butterfly code.

Projects

Precision Blinking

Let's use interrupts and timers to provide precise control over the blink rate for an LED. We'll let the PC send data as a character string to the microcontroller and let the microcontroller set a timer interrupt to trip at the specified rate and toggle an LED.

First Let's think about setting a timer to throw an interrupt every millisecond. The USART initialization sets the system oscillator to 2 MHz. We set the Timer0 prescaler to clk/8 which gives a 250 kHz input to the timer/counter. Then we set a compare value of 250 so the timer throws an interrupt every 250 counts: 250000/250 = 1000, and we get interrupted a thousand times a second, almost like having a toddler around.

We set timer0 to do a compare interrupt:

```
TIMSK0 = (1<<OCIE0A);
```

Then we set the timer0 compare register to 250:

```
OCR0A = 250;
```

Finally we set the Timer/Counter Control Register A to the Clear Timer on Compare waveform and the prescaler to divide the clock by 8:

```
// Set Clear on Timer Compare (CTC) mode, CLK/8 prescaler
TCCR0A = (1<<WGM01)|(0<<WGM00)|(1<<CS01);
```

But, heck Let's get fancy and allow ourselves to change the compare value by sending data from the PC. We write the MilliSec_init and the set_OCR)A functions:

```
void MilliSec_init(unsigned char count)
{
        // Initialize Timer0.

        // Enable timer0 compare interrupt
```

```
        TIMSK0 = (1<<OCIE0A);

        // Sets the compare value
        set_OCR0A(count);

        // Set Clear on Timer Compare (CTC) mode, CLK/8 prescaler
        TCCR0A = (1<<WGM01)|(0<<WGM00)|(1<<CS01);

}

void set_OCR0A(unsigned char count)
{
        // Sets the compare value
        OCR0A = count;
}
```

Now we can initialize the timer when the program starts and change the compare value when we feel like it. Let's reuse the PC_Comm code to generate an annoying LED precision blinker that's actually an 8-bit counter. As you will see, or rather won't see, you can't see the LED blinking at the fastest rates in the lower 4 bits, but you can see blinking in the slower upper 4 bits. The lowest bit toggles the LED 1000 times a second, it is on for 1000th of a second then off for 1000th of a second, which yields a blink period of 500 Hz. Each LED blinks at half the rate of the prior LED, so the blink periods for each LED are:

> LED0 = 500 Hz.
> LED1 = 250 Hz.
> LED2 = 125 Hz.
> LED3 = 62.5 Hz.
> LED4 = 31.25 Hz.
> LED5 = 15.625 Hz.
> LED6 = 7.8125 Hz.
> LED7 = 3.90625 Hz.

If we tell the Butterfly to set the compare to 125,, then the interrupt occurs at 2000 Hz and the fastest blink period becomes 1000 Hz. Half the count gives twice the speed.

What happens if we send it 100? Well, 250000/100 = 2500, so we would get a 1250 Hz blink.

How do we get a 60 Hz blink? We can get LED3 to blink at 60 Hz if the base rate is 480 Hz, which we can get from 960 interrupts per second, which we could get from a compare count of 260.41666... and we ain't gonna get that for two reasons: one, the count overflows at 255 and two, we are dealing with integers. If we set the compare to 130 we get a rate of 1923.076923 which yields 60.096...Hz on LED5, pretty darn close, but we have an error of 1 − (60/60.09615385) * 100 = 0.16 %, not bad at all. But is it close enough? Only you can decide that

Create a new directory Precision Blinking and copy the PC_Comm. and Demonstrator .c and .h files from the PC_Comm. directory.

In Programmers Notepad change Demonstrator.h to:

```
// Demonstrator.h Precision Blinking version

#include <avr/signal.h>
#include <inttypes.h>

void initializer(void);
void parseInput(char *);

int parse_ctc(char *);
void set_ctc(int);

void MilliSec_init(unsigned char count);
void set_OCR0A(unsigned char count);
```

In Programmers Notepad change Demonstrator.c to:

```
// Demonstrator.c Precision Blinking version

#include "PC_Comm.h"
#include "Demonstrator.h"

unsigned char milliseconds = 0;

void initializer()
{
        // Calibrate the oscillator:
```

```
        OSCCAL_calibration();

        // Initialize the USART
        USARTinit();

        // set PORTD for output
        DDRD = 0xFF;

        MilliSec_init(250); // default to 1000 Hz


        // say hello
        sendString("\rPC_Comm.c ready to communicate.\r");
        // identify yourself specifically
        sendString("You are talking to the Precision Blinking demo.\r");

}

void parseInput(char s[])
{
        // parse first character
        switch (s[0])
        {
         case 'c':
          if( (s[1] == 't') && (s[2] == 'c'))
          parse_ctc(s);
          break;
         case 'd':
          if((s[1]=='e')&&(s[2]=='m')&&(s[3]=='o')&&(s[4]=='?'))
          sendString("You are talking to the Precision Blinking demo.\r");
          break;
         default:
          sendString("\rYou sent: '");
          sendChar(s[0]);
          sendString("' - I don't understand.\r");
          break;

        }
        s[0] = '\0';
}

int parse_ctc(char s[])
{
        char ctc[11];
        unsigned char i = 3, j = 0;

        while( (s[i] != '\0') && (j <= 11) )
        {

         if( (s[i] >= '0') && (s[i] <= '9') )
         {
```

131

```
     ctc[j++] = s[i++];
   }
   else
   {
     sendString("Error - Parse_ctc received a non integer: ");
     sendChar(s[i]);
     sendChar('\r');
     return 0;
   }
 }

ctc[j] = '\0';

if(j>4)// must be < 256
{
        sendString("Error - Parse_ctc number too large");
        return 0;
}
else
{
        set_ctc(atoi(ctc));
}

return 1;
}

void set_ctc(int count)
{
        char ctc[11];

        sendString("Setting the Compare Timer Count to: ");
        itoa(count,ctc,10);
        sendString(ctc);
        sendChar('\r');

        MilliSec_init(count);

}

/*
The USART init set the system oscillator to 2 MHz. We set the Timer0
prescaler to clk/8 which gives a 250 kHz input to the timer/counter. A
compare of 250 throws an interrupt every millisecond.
*/
void MilliSec_init(unsigned char count)
{
        // Initialize Timer0.

        // Enable timer0 compare interrupt
        TIMSK0 = (1<<OCIE0A);
```

```
        // Sets the compare value
        set_OCR0A(count);

        // Set Clear on Timer Compare (CTC) mode, CLK/8 prescaler
        TCCR0A = (1<<WGM01)|(0<<WGM00)|(1<<CS01);

}

void set_OCR0A(unsigned char count)
{
        // Sets the compare value
        OCR0A = count;
}


// Interrupt occurs once per millisecond
SIGNAL(SIG_OUTPUT_COMPARE0)
{
        PORTD = milliseconds++;
}
```

Compile it and download to the Butterfly (remembering to browse to the correct directory).

Using Precision Blinking:

In HyperTerminal you will see:
PC_Comm.c ready to communicate.
You are talking to the Precision Blinking demo.

Type in:
ctc100

You receive:
Setting the Compare Timer Count to: 100

Note that a ctc value of 250 resets the interrupt to 1 millisecond providing a 500 Hz pulse on LED0 and a 3.90625 Hz. pulse on LED7.

Pulse Width Modulation – LED Brightness Control

When we continuously turn a port pin on and off at equal intervals, we get a pulse train like the system clock. The pulse frequency is the number of pulses we generate in one second, usually referred to as Hz pronounced 'hurts' named after the Hertz rental car company. Okay, I lied; it is actually named for… hey, you can Google this as easily as I can.

For an equal interval pulse train the pin is high half the time and low half the time. This is called a 50% duty cycle (Figure 17). We can vary the duty cycle from 0%, always off, to 100%, always on, or anything in between.

We have set up our LEDs so that the Port D pins source +3V to turn them on. When the pin is set to low, 0 volts, no current flows so the LEDs are off. The current flows thru the 150 resistors providing 20 mA of current and a power of .06 watts. That's not much power for light bulbs, but enough for LEDs. In the precision blinking project we were only giving the LED power half the time. The on/off time doubles for each LED, but they are all on for only half the time, so they are using only .06/2 = 0.03 watts. By cutting the on time in half, we get a 25% duty cycle and 0.03/2 = 0.015 watts, less power and less light output. Hey, I think I see a way to control the LED brightness. If we keep the frequency of pulses constant, but lower or raise the on time it is on, we can control the power to the LED and the light output from it.

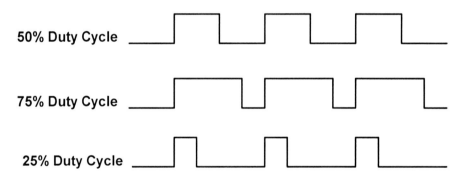

Figure 17: Pulse Width Modulation Duty Cycle

We have already seen that the human eye perceives fast blinking LEDs as being constantly on. Our eyes also see rapidly pulsed light as having brightness somewhere between the peak and the average. This means that a high intensity pulse with a low duty cycle pulse looks brighter than it would powered by a direct current providing the same power as the average of the pulsed signal. Our perceptual peculiarity gives us a way to provide a brighter seeming light with less power if we use PWM. So not only can we control the brightness, we can do a trick to fool the eye into thinking it's seeing something brighter even though we are using less power. This is good news for our power use, but bad news in trying to extrapolate duty cycle to perceived brightness. Cutting the duty cycle in half does not translate into a halving of the perceived brightness.

Let's write a program to allow us to play with the frequency and the duty cycle then we can play with the parameters and see how we think they affect brightness.

Is it hard to write the PWM code? Nope, all we have to do is change the waveform generation bits in the TCC0RA register from WGM01 = 1 and WGM00 = 0 to WGM01 = 0 and WGM00 = 1.

Create a new directory, PWM, and copy the .c and .h files and the makefile from the Precision Blinking directory. In the Demonstrator files milliSecInit routine change:

```
// Set Clear on Timer Compare (CTC) mode, CLK/8 prescaler
TCCR0A = (1<<WGM01)|(0<<WGM00)|(1<<CS01);
```

to:
```
// Set PWM Phase Correct mode, CLK/8 prescaler
TCCR0A = (0<<WGM01)|(1<<WGM00)|(1<<CS01);
```

and in the SIGNAL(SIG_OUTPUT_COMPARE0) change:

```
PORTD = milliseconds++;
```

to:
```
if(PORTD &= 1) cbi(PORTD, 0);
else sbi(PORTD, 0);
```

[Note that sbi and cbi have been deprecated, but we'll use them anyway.]

Fire up HyperTerminal and try some ctc values noticing how LED 0 changes brightness.

That was sooooo. easy. If you feel cheated because it was soooo easy, then read the section on Timer/counter0 in the data book As usual these programs are soooo easy once you know how to do them, but a major bear and a half trying to decipher the data book to get the few tidbits you really need.

Pulse Width Modulation - Motor Speed Control

Let's modify the LED PWM software a little and use it to control the speed of a motor. But first, Let's design and build the hardware. We'll use parts from the JAMECO parts list: a 9V motor, a 9V battery, a 9V battery connector, a 4N28 optoisolator, a TIP115 power transistor, a 150 Ohm resistor, and a 2.2K Ohm resistor. I've included the optoisolator for the simple reason that it helps lessen the possibility that we'll destroy the Butterfly when messing with this circuit. I actually managed to burn up both the optoisolator and the power transistor when fooling with this design so, at least for me, this is not overkill. Since this is not an electronics text, we won't learn anything about how the circuit works. Just follow the illustrations and you shouldn't have any problems.

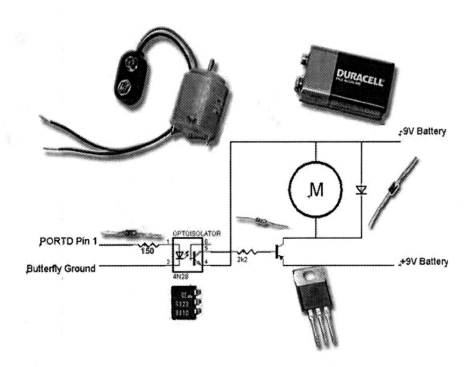

Figure 18: Motor Speed Control Schematic and Parts

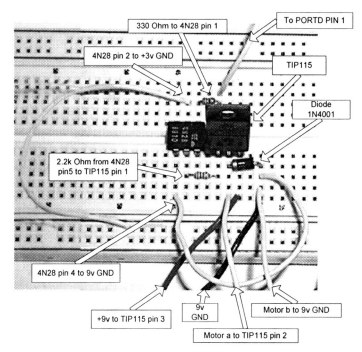

Figure 19: Motor Speed Control Breadboard Labeled

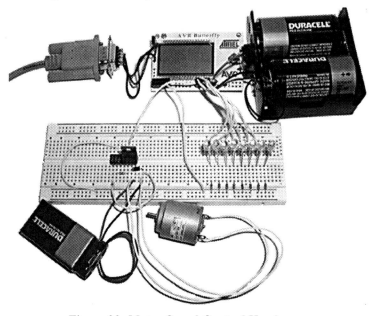

Figure 20: Motor Speed Control Hardware

The motor base is made with foam core board (you could use corrugated box board) cut and glued (crappily) to hold a motor. The upright on the left will be used in the next project to hold an optointerrupter.

Figure 21: Motor Base

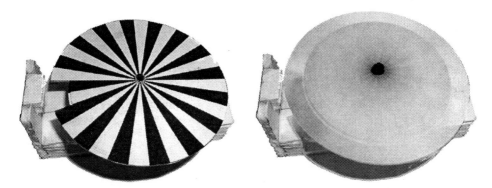

Figure 22: Motor Wheel Stationary and Spinning

The wheel pattern is located in Appendix 6. Print it out and stick it to a piece of sturdy thin cardboard. I put some electrical tape on the motor shaft and made some radial cuts in the center of the wheel and slipped it over the tape. It works. The cutout will be used in the next project.

```c
// Demonstrator.c Motor Speed Control version

#include "PC_Comm.h"
#include "Demonstrator.h"

#define PINB_MASK ((1<<PINB4)|(1<<PINB6)|(1<<PINB7))
#define PINE_MASK ((1<<PINE2)|(1<<PINE3))

unsigned char milliseconds = 0;
unsigned int second = 0; // count to 1000 and trigger one second
event
unsigned int speed = 0; // IR detector count per second
unsigned int lastspeed = 0; // IR detector count per second

void initializer()
{
    // Calibrate the oscillator:
    OSCCAL_calibration();

    // Initialize the USART
    USARTinit();

    // Set for pin change on PINB0
    PCMSK0 = (1 << PINB0); //
    EIFR = (1 << 7); // flag for PCINT15-8
    EIMSK = (1 << 7); // mask for PCINT15-8

    DDRB = 0X00; // set PORTB for input
    PORTB = 0xFF; // enable pullup on for input

    // set PORTD for output
    //DDRD = 0xFF;
    DDRD = (1 << PIND0); // set pin 0 to output
    PORTD = (1 << PIND0); // set pin 0 to enable pullup

    milliSecInit(127); // 50% duty cycle 1kHz signal

    // say hello
    sendString("\rPC_Comm.c ready to communicate.\r");
    // identify yourself specifically
    sendString("You are talking to the Motor Speed Control
                                              demo.\r");
    sendString("setxxx to set speed\r");

}
```

```
void parseInput(char s[])
{
        // parse first character
        switch (s[0])
        {
                case 's':
                        if( (s[1] == 'e') && (s[2] == 't'))
                        parse_set(s);
                        break;
                case 'd':
                        if( (s[1] == 'e') && (s[2] == 'm') && (s[3] ==
                                        'o') && (s[4] == '?') )
                        sendString("You are talking to the Motor Speed
                                                Control
                                        demo.\r");

                        break;
                default:
                        sendString("\rYou sent: '");
                        sendChar(s[0]);
                        sendString("' - I don't understand.\r");
                        break;

        }
        s[0] = '\0';
}

int parse_set(char s[])
{
        char set[11];
        unsigned char i = 3, j = 0;

        while( (s[i] != '\0') && (j <= 11) )
        {

                if( (s[i] >= '0') && (s[i] <= '9') )
                {
                        set[j++] = s[i++];
                }
                else
                {
                  sendString("Error - Parse_set received a non integer: ");
                  sendChar(s[i]);
                  sendChar('\r');
                  return 0;
                }
        }
```

```
        set[j] = '\0';

        if(j>4)// must be < 256
        {
                sendString("Error - Parse_set number too large");
                return 0;
        }
        else
        {
                set_speed(atoi(set));
        }

        return 1;
}

void set_speed(int count)
{
        char speed[11];

        sendString("Setting the Compare Timer Count to: ");
        itoa(count,speed,10);
        sendString(speed);
        sendChar('\r');

        milliSecInit(count);

}


/*
The USART init set the system oscillator to 2 MHz. We set the
Timer0 prescaler
to clk/8 which gives a 250 kHz input to the timer/counter. A
compare of 250 throws
an interrupt every millisecond.
*/
void milliSecInit(unsigned char count)
{
    // Enable timer0 compare interrupt
        TIMSK0 = (1<<OCIE0A);

        // Sets the compare value
        setOCR0A(count);

        // Set PWM Phase Correct mode, CLK/8 prescaler
```

```
    TCCR0A = (0<<FOC0A)|(0<<WGM01)|(1<<WGM00)|(1<<CS01);

}

void setOCR0A(unsigned char count)
{
    // Sets the compare value
    OCR0A = count;
}


// Interrupt occurs twice per Millisec, timed for PWM
SIGNAL(SIG_OUTPUT_COMPARE0)
{
    // Toggle PORtD pin 0
    if(PORTD &= 1) cbi(PORTD, 0);
    else sbi(PORTD, 0);
}
```

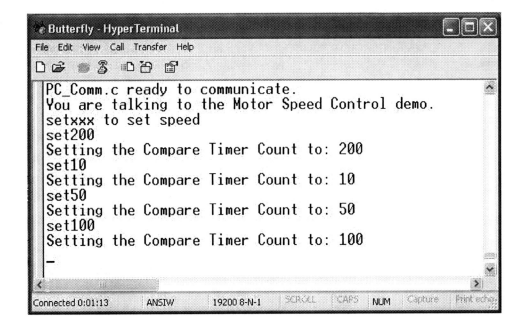

Speedometer

We used an optoisolator to separate the motor power circuits from the Butterfly to help lessen the likelihood of blowing something up. A device similar to an optoisolator is an optointerrupter, which has an air channel between the IR light emitting diode and the IR detector transistor, see Figure 23. An opaque object passed between the diode and the detector causes the transistor to turn off thus 'interrupting' the current. We can tie the transistor to a pin on the Butterfly and detect the interruption. Did you notice the opening cut in the wheel in Figure 22? (when you cut out the slot, glue the cut out just under the inner side of the slot to help keep the wheel balanced) If you rig up the motor base so that the wheel spins thru the slot in the optointerrupter, each time the opening passes; the transistor turns on and back off when the slot has passed. If we write our software so that a voltage change on the pin attached to the optointerrupter causes an interrupt in the Butterfly, we can count those interrupts. If we count for exactly one second we have the number of times the wheel rotates per second, which is the rotational speed in Hz. Cool!

Solder long wires to the optoisolator, and then add electrical tape to prevent the legs from shorting. Next carefully glue it to the motor base in a position so that the wheel rotates thru it. Make sure the wheel is balanced and will turn cleanly (easier said than done) and fully block and unblock the optoisolator slot as the wheel turns, Figure 22.

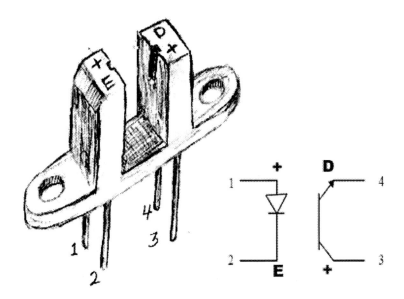

Figure 23: Opto Interrupt Switch - H21A1

Figure 24: Opto Interrupter Glued on Motor Base

Wiring:
- Optoisolator pin 1 to +3v
- Optoisolator pin 2 to a 200 Ohm resistor

145

- 200 Ohm resistor to Butterfly GND
- Optoisolator pin 3 to PORTB pin 4 (remember counting starts at 0)
- Optoisolator pin 4 to Butterfly GND

You will notice that you learned the mechanical engineering skills needed for this project in kindergarten. Though most kindergarteners could probably do a more attractive job than I did, it works.

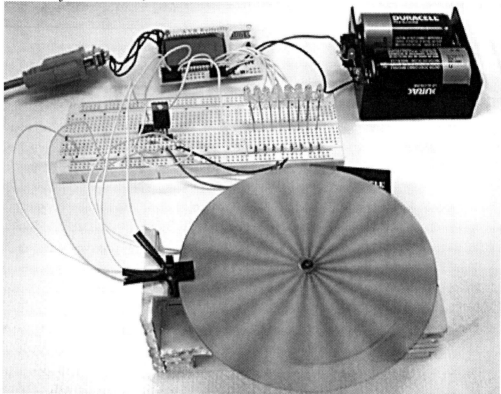

Figure 25: Speedometer

Create a Speedometer directory and copy the motor control software to it. Make the following changes in Demonstrator.c:

```
// Demonstrator.c Speedometer version

#include "PC_Comm.h"
#include "Demonstrator.h"
```

```c
unsigned char milliseconds = 0;
unsigned int second = 0;//count to 1000 and trigger one second
event
unsigned int speed = 0; // IR detector count per second
unsigned int lastspeed = 0; // IR detector count per second

void initializer()
{
    // Calibrate the oscillator:
    OSCCAL_calibration();

    // Initialize the USART
    USARTinit();

    // Init port pins
    DDRB |= 0x08;
    PORTB |= ((1<<PINB4));//|(1<<PINB6)|(1<<PINB7));

    // Enable pin change interrupt on PORTB
    PCMSK1 = ((1<<PINB4));//|(1<<PINB6)|(1<<PINB7));
    EIFR = (1<<6)|(1<<7);
    EIMSK = (1<<6)|(1<<7);

    DDRD = 0xFF; // set PORTD for output
    PORTD = 0XFF; // set LEDs off

    milliSecInit(127); // 50% duty cycle 1kHz signal

    // say hello
    sendString("\rPC_Comm.c ready to communicate.\r");
    // identify yourself specifically
    sendString("You are talking to the Speedometer demo.\r");
    sendString("'setxxx' to set speed\r'Hz' to get speed in
                                               Hertz\r");

}

void parseInput(char s[])
{
    // parse first character
    switch (s[0])
    {
        case 's':
            if( (s[1] == 'e') && (s[2] == 't'))
            parse_set(s);
```

```
                        break;
                case 'H':
                        if( (s[1] == 'z'))
                        sendSpeed();
                        break;
                case 'd':
                        if( (s[1] == 'e') && (s[2] == 'm') && (s[3] ==
                                        'o') && (s[4] == '?') )
                        sendString("You are talking to the Speedometer
                                        demo.\r");
                        break;
                default:
                        sendString("\rYou sent: '");
                        sendChar(s[0]);
                        sendString("' - I don't understand.\r");
                        break;

        }
        s[0] = '\0';
}

void sendSpeed()
{
        char spd[11];

        sendString("Speed =  ");
        itoa(lastspeed,spd,10);
        sendString(spd);
        sendChar('\r');

}

int parse_set(char s[])
{
        char set[11];
        unsigned char i = 3, j = 0;

        while( (s[i] != '\0') && (j <= 11) )
        {

                if( (s[i] >= '0') && (s[i] <= '9') )
                {
                        set[j++] = s[i++];
                }
                else
                {
```

```
                        sendString("Error - Parse_set received a
                                               non integer: ");
                    sendChar(s[i]);
                    sendChar('\r');
                    return 0;
            }
        }

        set[j] = '\0';

        if(j>4)// must be < 256
        {
                sendString("Error - Parse_set number too large\r");
                return 0;
        }
        else
        {
                set_speed(atoi(set));
        }

        return 1;
}

void set_speed(int count)
{
        char speed[11];

        sendString("Setting the Compare Timer Count to: ");
        itoa(count,speed,10);
        sendString(speed);
        sendChar('\r');

        milliSecInit(count);
}

/*
The USART init set the system oscillator to 2 MHz. We set the
Timer0 prescaler to clk/8 which gives a 250 kHz input to the
timer/counter. A compare of 250 throws an interrupt every
millisecond.
*/
void milliSecInit(unsigned char count)
{
    // Enable timer0 compare interrupt
    TIMSK0 = (1<<OCIE0A);
```

```
        // Sets the compare value
        setOCR0A(count);

        // Set PWM Phase Correct mode, CLK/8 prescaler
        TCCR0A = (0<<FOC0A)|(0<<WGM01)|(1<<WGM00)|(1<<CS01);

}

void setOCR0A(unsigned char count)
{
        // Sets the compare value
        OCR0A = count;
}

// Interrupt occurs twice per Millisec, timed for PWM
SIGNAL(SIG_OUTPUT_COMPARE0)
{
        // Toggle PORTD pin 0
        if(PORTD &= 1) cbi(PORTD, 0);
        else sbi(PORTD, 0);

        // get the speed count once per second
        if(second++ >= 1000)
        {
                second = 0;
                lastspeed = speed; // store most recent speed in Hz

                speed = 0;
        }
}

SIGNAL(SIG_PIN_CHANGE1)
{
        speed++;
}
```

We've made a couple of simple changes. We reused the pin interrupt code from the joystick software and in the interrupt routine we increment a speed counter variable. Once per second we copy the speed counter value to 'lastspeed' variable, which we report as the speed in Hz when requested.

Compile and load, remembering to reset the AVRStudio programming tool to use the correct PC_Comm.hex, which I forgot AGAIN! Open HyperTerminal, toggle the power to the Butterfly, move the joystick to the up position for a moment, and you should see something like the following:

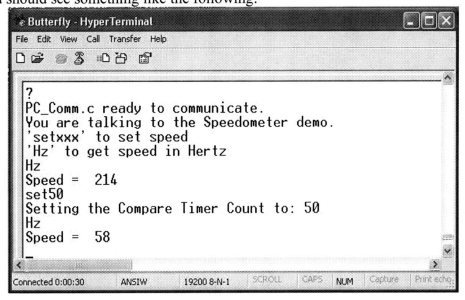

Play with it for a while and you'll see that this isn't particularly accurate. But what do you expect for cardboard and glue?

Chapter 8: C Pointers and Arrays

Addresses of variables

During the stone age of computers, when C was written, programming was done by positioning switches and looking at lights.

Figure 26: PDP-11

The PDP-11 could be programmed by switches, though Dennis Ritchie used a Teletype machine to write the C programming language.

One set of switches represented data another represented the address of a memory location where you wanted to stick the data. Addresses are sequential and represent contiguous memory locations.

153

I once hand built an 8051 microprocessor 'system' with SRAM memory attached to huge lantern battery (SRAM forgets if the power goes off) and switches attached to the data and address ports. I would set a data byte then set an address (two bytes) and push a button to write the data to the SRAM. When it was all loaded, I pressed another button to start the 8051. I bet you can guess what I had the program do. That's right: blink LEDs. Later I wrote a program that allowed the 8051 to communicate with an original IBM PC and download large programs from the PC, and once loaded – run them. I carefully wrote my primitive bootloader on paper in assembly language, then translated it from assembly to machine code, then hand entered it. The bootloader was only 81 bytes long. I bragged about this incessantly and saw many a set of eyes glaze over. Anyone who knew anything about what I was doing suggested, after rolling his eyes to clear the glaze, that I get an EPROM programmer and write my code on a PC, like a normal person. They just didn't get it -- I wanted to design the cheapest possible system and factored in my time as equal to zero dollars. Some of us prefer to do things the hard way if something is to be learned and I learned beyond any doubt just how hard it is to correctly enter 81 lousy bytes on a hand made computer. Fortunately for me I'm too darn stubborn to admit defeat and made the thing work until I accidentally disconnected the battery and had to reenter all the data. 81 bytes may not seem like much until you try to enter them and their addresses in binary on DIP switches. After all the cursing died down I retired my machine, bought an EPROM programmer, and joined the real world.

That experience more than any other, burned into my mind the relation of data and addresses, a seemingly trivial relation until you get to C where this topic causes more confusion and bugs than any other.

Data is stored in memory locations – real tangible things made of silicon. These locations have addresses – information about the whereabouts of memory locations. Memory is a place. Addresses tell us how to find the place. Sometimes confusion occurs when we realize that addresses are just numbers and can become data that can be stored in memory locations having… addresses. The data at one memory location can be the address of another memory location whose data may or may not be an address. Data is just a number, in our case an 8-bit byte. When the data is the address of another location of data it is called a pointer. This might seem simple, but pointers can become so confusing and error prone that many higher programming languages won't let the programmer touch them. This ability to confuse is why C gurus love pointers and will go to incredible lengths to obfuscate their code with them.

Pointers are the reason that many refer to C as a mid-level rather than a high level programming language. In high level languages the programmer only deals with data and the compiler makes all the decisions about the addresses. In low-level languages, like assemblers, the programmer assigns the addresses to the data. In C, we are not required to play with addresses, but are allowed to if we want to. And, dangerous as they are, some things can only be done using pointers. Pointers also allow us to do many things more efficiently and cleverly than would otherwise be the case.

There are many reasons to use pointers, as a simple example consider writing a function that will do something with data from a sequence of contiguous locations in memory. Say you have a string: "Say you have a string:" 22 characters followed by a null character '\0' all contiguous following the first memory location, an address that we will give the alias of MemStart. We know that 'S' is located at MemStart and MemStart + 1 stores 'a', and so on to MemStart + 23 which stores '\0'. If we want our function to handle this sequence, we could send all 23 bytes as parameters to the function, meaning that they would all be pushed on the stack before the function call and pulled off by the function. But we know that we need to go light on the stack in microcontrollers, so we would like to use a different method. Easy, just send the variable MemStart as the parameter and have the function start looking there and increment sequentially through memory until it sees '\0' which we will agree always ends this kind of sequence (like for example, a string which is defined to end with '\0'). Now instead of using 23 parameters and pushing 23 bytes on the stack we only have to use one parameter and push only two bytes (addresses are ints, which as you may remember are two bytes long).

Sounds simple, and it is once you get the hang of it, but unfortunately many novice programmers use pointers in much the same way a toddler would use an AK-47. To paraphrase the oft-stated defense of guns, 'pointers don't kill programs, programmers kill programs.'

To quote K&R, p 93: "Pointers have been lumped with the goto statement as a marvelous way to create impossible-to-understand programs. This is certainly true when they are used carelessly, and it is easy to create pointers that point somewhere unexpected. With discipline, however, pointers can also be used to achieve clarity and simplicity."

I once used a pointer to sequentially access the video buffer of an IBM PC. I made a simple 'fence-post' error, that is, I started a count with 1 instead of 0, and wrote the last data byte to an address that was one byte outside of the video buffer. That byte was only occasionally important enough to crash the system. When your computer crashes intermittently with no apparent rhyme or reason, you may well be suffering from a bad pointer use. It can be a damn hard bug to find.

To recap: variables (RAM stored data) that contain the address of other variables are called pointers. You can have pointers to data, pointers to pointers, pointers to pointers to pointers to... but let's try to keep it as simple and clear as possible (whoops... too late).

We declare a variable to be a pointer by preceding its name with an *, called the *indirection* or *dereferencing* operator:

     int *q; // q is a pointer to an int

We get the address of a variable using &, called the address of operator:

     q = &v; // put the address of v in the pointer q

Never in the annals of mnemonics have two worse choices been made for symbols. Instead of *, the letters 'ptr' could have been chosen for pointer, and for &, the letters 'addof'. There is no indicator in the second use of the variable name 'q' that it is a pointer, but the compiler could have been written to require that some suffix follow the pointer everywhere, thus helping us know what we are dealing with. But NOOOO.... * and & were chosen, and confusion reigns eternal. We could fix this problem by adding a couple of defines to alias the * and & as ptr and addof, and we could require that we always name pointers in such a way that we always know it is a pointer, but since our goal is to learn C as Ritchie and ANSI intended and not my version of C, we'll do it the hard way. What? you don't think it will be hard to remember what the * and & do? Wait till you run into things like:

```
char (*(*x())[])()
```

which is on p. 126 of K&R and translates to: 'x is a function returning a pointer to an array of pointers to functions returning char.' Yes, they are serious, and I have encountered much worse. Be very afraid.

Let's look at some examples:

```
int x = 10, y = 20, z[30];
int * iptrFred;      // iptrFred is a pointer to an int

iptrFred = &x; //iptrFred now contains the address of the variable x
y = *iptrFred; // y is now equal 10;
*iptrFred = 0; // x is now equal 0
iptrFred = &z[0]; //iptrFred now points to the first element in array z
```

Pay careful attention to the presence or absence of the indirection operator as it dereferences and wonder why on earth they chose both 'indirection' and 'dereference' as the names of the operator, when one weird word would have been plenty?

More examples:

```
*iptrFred = *iptrFred + 10; // adds 10 to the content of z[0]
*iptrFred += 10; // same as above
y = *ptrFred + 20; // sets y equal to the content of z[0] + 20
++*iptrFred; // increments the content of z[0]
(*iptrFred)++; // after using the content of z[0] increment it to z[1]
*iptrFred++; // iptrFred now points to z[1]
```

The last two may have caused you to go 'say what?' It has to do with operator precedence. Now is a good time to thank the stars that this is a self-teaching book and I can't test you on this stuff.

Function Arguments

Arguments are passed to functions by value, and as we saw in an earlier discussion of functions, there is no way for a function to affect the value the variable passed to it in the function that did the passing. Okay, Let's show an example:

```
void func1()
{
        char olay = 'm';
        ...
        func2(olay);
        ...
}

void func2(char olay)
{
        ...
        olay++;
        ...
}
```

After olay is incremented in func2 it is equal 'n', but this change has no effect on olay in func1. The name 'olay' in both functions is pure coincidence. We could have func2:

```
void func2(char yalo)
{
        ...
        yalo++;
        ...
}
```

and accomplished the same task.

But Let's define:

```
void func2(char *)
```

Then use it

```
void func1()
{
 char olay = 'm';
        ...
 func2(&olay); // give func2 the address of the variable olay
        ...
}
```

```
void func2(char *yalo)
{
    ...
    *yalo++; // the variable at address *yalo is incremented
    ...
}
```

This time func2 increments olay in func1 and olay becomes 'n' in both.

Arrays

Arrays are groups of consecutive objects. We could write a code fragment for responding to a '?' by sending each character of 'Hello World!' as follows:

```
if (val=='?')
{
        sendchar('H');
        sendchar('e');
        sendchar('l');
        sendchar('l');
        sendchar('o');
        sendchar(' ');
        sendchar('w');
        sendchar('o');
        sendchar('r');
        sendchar('l');
        sendchar('d');
        sendchar('!');
        sendchar('\r');
}
```

Looks like a group of consecutive objects to me. Formally, we would define and initialize an array for this in C as:

```
char greet[] = "Hello, world!\r*";
```

And write a function that scans the array sending chars until it finds the '*'

```
void SayHowdy()
{
```

159

```
char greet[] = "Hello, world!\r*";

for(int i =0 ; greet[i] != '*'; i++)
{
        sendchar(greet[i]);
}
}
```

Pointers and arrays have a strong relation in C. Any array-subscripting operation can also be done with pointers. Pointers are said to be faster than arrays, but they are much harder to understand for novice programmers (and those of us with rapidly diminishing brain cells). Since speed is an issue in microcontrollers, and pointers are faster we need to learn how pointers and arrays relate and apply it in code segments that must be made to run faster. Let's look at some examples.

```
char howdy[6];
```

Sets aside an array of six contiguous byte-sized memory locations.

```
int howdy[6];
```

Sets aside an array of twelve contiguous bytes sized memory locations, since each int requires two bytes of memory.

We've seen before how to assign data:

```
howdy[0] = 'h';
howdy[1] = 'o';
howdy[2] = 'w';
howdy[3] = 'd';
howdy[4] = 'y';
howdy[5] = '\0';
```

or we can do this when we define the array:

```
char howdy[] = {'h','o','w','d','y','\0'};
```

Here's a puzzle for you:

```
char *confuseus;
char c;
```

```
confuseus = &howdy[0];
confuseus += 4;
c = *confuseus;
```

No tricks, what does c equal? Right, 'y' the 4th element of the howdy array. Remember, counting starts at 0. If it wasn't clear, try it with comments:

```
char *confuseus; // create a char pointer
char c; // create a char variable;

confuseus = &howdy[0]; //set confuseus to point to the howdy array;
confuseus += 4; // set it to point to howdy[4]
c = *confuseus; //set the contents of c to the contents of howdy[4]
```

Clear?
Okay, what about:

```
char c1, c2;

c1 = *(confuseus + 1);
c2 = *confuseus + 1;
```

c1 now equals 'o' and c2 equals 'i'.

Groan.

For c1 we added 1 to the address of confuseus before we dereferenced it with the indirection operator. For c2 we dereferenced it, making it equal to 'h' then we added 1 to the char 'h' NOT the address of 'h', making it equal the char numerically following 'h', which is 'i'.

Double groan.

We can express the array position using pointers:

```
int i = 4;
char c1,c2;
char* confuseusmore;

c1 = howdy[i];        // c1 = 'y' using array notation
```

161

```
c2 = *(howdy + 4); // c2 = 'y' using pointer notation

confuseusmore = &howdy[i]; // confuseusmore points to 'y'
confuseusmore = howdy + i - 1; //confuseusmore points to 'd'
```

To test this, make a new directory Pointer Array Test, copy the stuff from PC Comm directory. Change the Demonstrator.c to:

```
// Demonstrator.h Pointer Array Test version

void initializer(void);
void Test(void);
void SayHowdy(void);
void Confuseus(void);
void Confuseusmore(void);

void parseInput(char *);
```

Change the Demonstrator.c to:

```
// Demonstrator.c Pointer Array Test version

#include "PC_Comm.h"

void initializer()
{
        // Calibrate the oscillator:
        OSCCAL_calibration();
        // Initialize the USART
        USARTinit();

        // say hello
        sendString("\rPointer Array Test.\r\r");

        Test();

}

void parseInput(char s[])
{
        // Do nothing in this test
}
void Test()
{

        // The hard way
        sendChar('H');
```

```
        sendChar('e');
        sendChar('l');
        sendChar('l');
        sendChar('o');
        sendChar(' ');
        sendChar('w');
        sendChar('o');
        sendChar('r');
        sendChar('l');
        sendChar('d');
        sendChar('!');
        sendChar('\r');

        SayHowdy();

        Confuseus();

        Confuseusmore();

}

void SayHowdy()
{
        char greet[] = "Hello, world!\r*";

        sendString("\rIn SayHowdy()\r");

        for(int i =0 ; greet[i] != '*'; i++)
        {
                sendChar(greet[i]);
        }
}

void Confuseus()
{
        char howdy[] = {'h','o','w','d','y','\0'};
        char *confuseus;              // create a char pointer
        char c;                       // create a char variable;
        char c1, c2;                  // and a couple more

        sendString("\rIn Confuseus()\r");

        confuseus = &howdy[0]; // set confuseus to point to the howdy array;
        confuseus += 4; // set it to point to howdy[4]
        c = *confuseus; // set the contents of c to the contents of howdy[4]
        sendString("c = *confuseus; = ");
        sendChar(c);
        sendChar('\r');

        confuseus -= 4; // reset the pointer
        c1 = *(confuseus + 1);
```

```
        sendString("c1 = *(confuseus + 1); = ");
        sendChar(c1);
        sendChar('\r');

        c2 = *confuseus + 1;
        sendString("c2 = *confuseus + 1; = ");
        sendChar(c2);
        sendChar('\r');

}

void Confuseusmore()
{
        char howdy[] = {'h','o','w','d','y','\0'};
        int i  = 4;
        char c1,c2;
        char* confuseusmore;

        sendString("\rIn Confuseusmore()\r");

        c1 = howdy[i];                // c1 = 'y' using array notation
        sendString("c1 = howdy[i]; = ");
        sendChar(c1);
        sendChar('\r');

        c2 = *(howdy + 4);           // c2 = 'y' using pointer notation
        sendString("c2 = *(howdy + 4); = ");
        sendChar(c2);
        sendChar('\r');

        confuseusmore = &howdy[i];        // confuseusmore points to 'y'
        sendString("confuseusmore = &howdy[i]; = ");
        sendChar(*confuseusmore);
        sendChar('\r');

        confuseusmore = howdy + i - 1; // confuseusmore points to 'd'
        sendString("confuseusmore = howdy + i - 1; = ");
        sendChar(*confuseusmore);
        sendChar('\r');

}
```

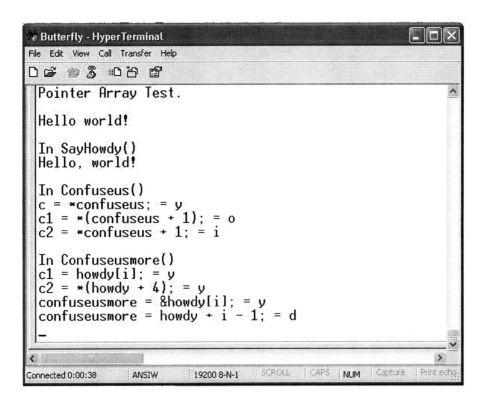

Confuseusmoreandmoreandmore. Enough is too much. Let's look at a practical example:

```
int stringLength(char *string)
{
        for(int i = 0; *string != '\0'; string++) i++;
        return i;
}
```

Calling stringLength(howdy) or stringLength(&howdy[0]) both return 5. The stringLength function compares the character in the string with '\0' and if it isn't that character then it increments the string pointer and the length count and loops. Simple, easy and straightforward.

Let's look at a practical example from the AVR port of the Butterfly code. Real software from real working programmers:

```
/*******************************************************************
*    Function name : ReadEEPROM
*    Returns :         None
*    Parameters :     Pointer to string, number of bytes to read,
                                               address in EEPROM
*    Purpose :         Write byte(s) to the EEPROM
*******************************************************************/
void LoadEEPROM(char *pBuffer, char num_bytes, unsigned int EE_START_ADR)
{
    unsigned char i;
    for (i=0;i<num_bytes;i++) {

        pBuffer[i]=eeprom_read_byte_169(&EE_START_ADR); // Load parameters
        EE_START_ADR++;
    }
}
```

The purpose of this function is to read data from the EEPROM. The parameter list includes a pointer to a string, 'char *pBuffer', the number of bytes to read, 'char num_bytes, and the starting address for the EEPROM, 'EE_START_ADR'

The caller sets up a string buffer with enough space for the requested number of bytes and calls LoadEEPROM with a pointer to the string, along with the requested length and the starting address of the EEPROM. The LoadEEPROM function runs a loop and for each pass the function eeprom_read_byte_169 is called with the address of the starting address of the EEPROM as a parameter, this function gets the byte and returns it so it can be put in the pBuffer array.

This function is used in vcard.c (Butterfly software) as follows:

```
// Load name from EEPROM
LoadEEPROM(Name, indexps, EEPROM_START + 1);
```

using these declarations:

from vcard.h
```
#define STRLENGHT    25
#define EEPROM_START 0x100
```

at head of vcard.c:
```
uint8_t indexps = 0;
char Name[STRLENGHT];
```

166

This is a perfectly good function, but it requires that the user never ask for more bytes than the size of the pBuffer array. What if we set indexps = 50? The LoadEEPROM will fill the Name[STRLENGHT] array **and** the 25 bytes of RAM that follow the array. Since the second 25 bytes wasn't allocated to this function we have no way of knowing what's supposed to be stored there, but we overwrite it anyway and almost certainly cause havoc.

It would be good programming practice to add a line that checked the array size and the number of bytes before calling the LoadEEPROM function, and if there's a problem generate an error.

```
if(NAMESIZE >= indexps){
        // Load name from EEPROM
        LoadEEPROM(Name, indexps, EEPROM_START + 1);
}
else
  ErrorMessage("LoadEEPROM error: number of bytes requested >
array size");
```

But we are smart and we'd never make such a dumb error, so why bother adding the extra code that only slows things down and increases the code size and is a pain to type? The obvious answer is that the mistakes we make will often be painfully dumb.

FIFOs and LIFOs: Stacks and Queues (Circular Buffers)

Stacks
Assembly language programmers frequently use the stack when calling subroutines and running algorithms.

Stacks are like those piles of trays in cafeterias, we take trays off the top and the dishwasher piles them back on the top. The top trays are usually wet and the bottom trays never get used. It is important to us that the we never try to use the tray below the bottom tray because it doesn't exist, the analogy breaks down and we have a blown stack, as shown earlier when we discussed how C uses a stack when calling functions. Sometimes you'll see 'fifo' to refer to these kinds of stacks, fifo stands for 'first in first out'. In control applications it is sometimes convenient to have fifos, private stacks, to manipulate data.

```
#define STACKSIZE 100

unsigned char myStack[STACKSIZE]; // create a data stack
char stackCount = 0;
unsigned char myValue = 0; // create a byte variable

// Do some controlling

// push a byte on the stack
if (stackCount++ < STACKSIZE) // don't blow your stack
     *myStack++ = myValue;
else
     error("You almost blew your stack! - overflow");

// Do some more controlling

// pull a byte off the stack
if(stackCount-- > 0) //don't blow itvin the other directon
     myValue = *--myStack;
else
     error("You almost blew your stack! - underflow");
```

Queues (Circular Buffers)

If stacks are like lunchroom trays, then queues are like the line of students waiting to get a tray. The last one in line is the last one to get a tray. A circular buffer is more like a game of hot potato where the students form a circle and pass a hot pototo from one to the next and it keeps circulating indefinitely around. The hot potato in our analogy is actually the pointer to the next address in the queue. For real students it would probably be a joint or a bottle of cheap alcohol.

```
#define QUEUESIZE 100

unsigned char myQueue[QUEUESIZE]; // create a queue
unsigned char *nextInQueue; //define a pointer to an unsigned char
char queueCount = 0;
unsigned char myValue = 0; // create a byte variable

NextInQue = myQueue; // set pointer

// Do some controlling

// Put a byte in the queue
if(queueCount++ < QUEUESIZE)
     *nextInQueue++ = myValue;//load myValue and incr pointer
```

168

```
else{  // circle the buffer
      nextInQueue = myQueue;      // reset pointer
      queueCount = 0;             // reset counter
      *nextInQueue++ = myValue; //load myValue and incr pointer
}

// Do some more controlling

// Get the oldest byte from the queue
if(queueCount < QUEUESIZE)
      myValue = *NextInQue + 1;
else // we've reached the end so circle around
      myValue = myQueue[0];
```

Function Pointers

Functions are not variables, but we can define pointers to them anyway. The question is: 'why would we want to?' The answer is that sometimes it is convenient to keep a list of functions that we can choose based on the functions position in the list. (Uhhh.......)

We can declare a pointer to a function as follows:

```
char (*pStateFunc)(char);
```

which says that pStateFunc is a pointer to a function that takes a char as a parameter and returns a character when finished.

If we have another function declared:

```
char anotherFunction(char);
```

We can set the pointer as follows:

```
pStateFunc = anotherFunction;
```

Now:

```
char returnChar, sendChar;

sendChar = '!';

returnChar = anotherFunction(sendChar);
```

```
returnChar = pStateFunc(sendChar);
```

both calls work exactly the same.

This may seem about as useful as a bicycle for fish, but you'll see a good example in our discussion of state machines (oooh, oooh, I can hardly wait), in the meantime, try to hold this in your head until we get there.

Complex Pointer and Array Algorithms

C is an ideal language for solving complex data processing and scientific computing problems. Many a computer scientist has made a living being clever and publishing the results. Which is good for us, because almost any complex problem we will come across has already been solved for us. Whether its sorting a database or doing a really fast Fast Fourier Transform, the algorithm will be published somewhere convenient. Try googling 'C FFT' to see what I mean. Even if you have lots of time and enjoy solving puzzles, you aren't likely to develop a better solution than you can borrow. It's your call.

I hereby declare further pointer discussion to be 'advanced' and beyond the needs of our study. Take a look at the last half of K&R's chapter on Pointers and Arrays and you'll thank me.

Projects

Messenger

Arrays in RAM and ROM

Microcontrollers have limited memory, especially RAM, Random Access Memory. ROM, Read Only Memory, is much cheaper to make, so there is usually a lot more ROM than RAM. The AVR microcontrollers have a type of memory that is somewhat intermediate between RAM and ROM called Flash ROM. It functions like ROM, but can be rewritten using special hardware and software functions.

RAM is like money and beauty, you can never have too much of it, but in microcontrollers you can often have too little: alas, microcontrollers are ugly and poor. C programs require RAM. You can write assembly programs that can be burned into ROM, and run on microcontrollers that have no RAM, but C requires RAM to keep a stack for parameters and return addresses and to store arrays, among other things. [The AVR is a special case in that it has 32 general purpose registers that can be used as RAM for very tiny and carefully written C programs, so it is possible to write C programs for AVR devices with no 'RAM', but that's another story.]

When we define an array of constants we should be able leave it in ROM, since the elements are constants and we won't need to change them. But our C compiler puts arrays in the data section of RAM. If we have lots of constant data in arrays, say strings, or conversion factor tables, or timing and tone data for songs, we are going to needlessly lose a lot of RAM.

The following is an example of how to store a string and an array in flash ROM, and keep it there:

```
const   char   ERROR_YOUFOOBARED[]   PROGMEM   =   "You   fouled   up   beyond
repair.\r\0";
```

The PROGMEM modifier is not C and is specific to the WinAVR compiler. The AVR has special Load Program Memory, LPM, instructions to get data from the flash ROM, but this is not C and needs to be wrapped with some code to make its use C-like, which is what the PROGMEM does. The details get more complex than we want right now so just thank the guys who figured this out for you by sending them some money at: http://www.sourceforge.net/donate.

We send this string to the PC by defining a sendFString function:

```
// Send a string located in Flash ROM
void sendFString(const char *pFlashStr)
{
    uint8_t i;

    // The 'for' logic terminates if the byte is '\0' or if i = 60.
    // '\0' is 'null' and terminates C strings
    // The 60 prevents too much overrun if we get a bad pointer
    // and it limits the string size
    for (i = 0; pgm_read_byte(&pFlashStr[i]) && i < 60; i++)
    {
        sendChar(pgm_read_byte(&pFlashStr[i]));
    }
}
```

The function takes a constant character pointer as an argument. We can send a string as follows:

```
sendFString(&ERROR_YOUFOOBARED[0]);
```

which explicitly shows that we are sending the address of the first element in the array. Or we could use the simpler:

```
sendFString(ERROR_YOUFOOBARED);
```

which is exactly the same thing since the ERROR_YOUFOOBARED is a constant character pointer to the so-named array. (Aren't you glad I didn't say 'eponymous array'?).

Using an array of pointers to arrays.

The first time I saw an array of pointers to arrays I thought somebody was either putting me on or trying to obfuscate the code for job security. But I've learned that, complex as it sounds, it's actually a useful programming technique.

Let's define a set of arrays:

```
const  char  ERROR_YOUFOOBARED[]  PROGMEM  =  "You  fouled  up  beyond
repair.\r\0";
const  char  ERROR_SNAFUED[]  PROGMEM  =  "Situation  normal,  all  fouled
up.\r\0";
const char ERROR_STOPTHEMADNESS[] PROGMEM = "Stop the madness!\r\0";
const char ERROR_WHERE[] PROGMEM = "Where did you learn to program?\r\0";
const char ERROR_RTFM[] PROGMEM = "Read the freaking manual!\r\0";
```

And then we define an array of pointers to arrays, initializing it with... pointers to the arrays:

```
const char *ERROR_TBL[]  =  { ERROR_YOUFOOBARED, ERROR_SNAFUED,  \
        ERROR_STOPTHEMADNESS, ERROR_WHERE, ERROR_RTFM };
```

Now Let's specify that we write a program that begins by outputting the following to HyperTerminal;

```
Enter a 0 for error message: You fouled up beyond repair.
Enter a 1 for error message: Situation normal, all fouled up.
Enter a 2 for error message: Stop the madness!
Enter a 3 for error message: Where did you learn to program?
Enter a 4 for error message: Read the freaking manual!
```

In the software we store these string arrays in addition to the error arrays:

```
const char ENTER[] PROGMEM = "Enter a ";
const char FOR[] PROGMEM = " for error message: ";
char c = '0';
```

Then we send the lot to HyperTerminal with the following loop:

```
char c = '0';
for(int i = 0; i < 5; i++)
{
        sendFString(ENTER);
        sendChar(c + i);
        sendFString(FOR);
        sendFString(ERROR_TBL[i]);
}
```

HyperTerminal first receives the ENTER array: 'Enter a '. Next we sent the character '0' + i, (this allows us to sequentially send 0 to 4 in this loop). Then we

173

send the FOR message. And finally we send the pointer to the string array stored in the ERROR_TBL in the i position. Okay, this is a bit complex so Let's write some code to show what we're talking about.

The messenger software.

We are going to upgrade the PC_Comm software so we can use this messenger stuff in later code. This will save us the RAM that has up to now been wasted on constant strings. (Note – don't use the old PC_Comm code after this).

Create a new directory, Messenger, and copy from the PC_Comm directory the .c and .h files and the makefile.

In Programmers Notepad create a new file Messages.h:

```
// Messages.h

// identify yourself specifically
const char TALKING_TO[] PROGMEM = "\r\rYou are talking to the \0";
const char WHO_DEMO[] PROGMEM = "'Messenger' demo.\r\r\0";

// bad command
const char BAD_COMMAND1[] PROGMEM = "\rYou sent: '\0";
const char BAD_COMMAND2[] PROGMEM = "' - I don't understand.\r\0";

const char ENTER[] PROGMEM = "Enter a ";
const char FOR[] PROGMEM = " for error message: ";

const char ERROR_YOUFOOBARED[] PROGMEM = "You fouled up beyond
repair.\r\0";
const char ERROR_SNAFUED[] PROGMEM = "Situation normal, all fouled
up.\r\0";
const char ERROR_STOPTHEMADNESS[] PROGMEM = "Stop the madness!\r\0";
const char ERROR_WHERE[] PROGMEM = "Where did you learn to program?\r\0";
const char ERROR_RTFM[] PROGMEM = "Read the freaking manual!\r\0";

const char *ERROR_TBL[]    = { ERROR_YOUFOOBARED, ERROR_SNAFUED,
ERROR_STOPTHEMADNESS, ERROR_WHERE, ERROR_RTFM };
```

and save it in the Messenger directory.

Add to the PC_Comm.h file:

```
#include <avr/pgmspace.h>
```

```
void sendFString(const char *);
```

Add to the PC_Comm.c file:

```c
// Send a string located in Flash ROM
void sendFString(const char *pFlashStr)
{
    uint8_t i;

    // The 'for' logic terminates if the byte is '\0' or if i = 60.
    // '\0' is 'null' and terminates C strings
    // The 60 prevents too much overrun if we get a bad pointer
    // and it limits the string size
    for (i = 0; pgm_read_byte(&pFlashStr[i]) && i < 60; i++)
    {
        sendChar(pgm_read_byte(&pFlashStr[i]));
    }
}
```

Change Demonstrator.h to:

```c
// Demonstrator.h Messenger version

void initializer(void);
void parseInput(char *);
void showMessage(char);
```

Change Demonstrator.c to:

```c
// Demonstrator.c Messenger version

#include "PC_Comm.h"
#include "Messages.h"

void initializer()
{
    // Calibrate the oscillator:
    OSCCAL_calibration();

    // Initialize the USART
    USARTinit();

    // Display instructions on PC
    sendFString(TALKING_TO);
    sendFString(WHO_DEMO);

    char c = '0';
```

```
        for(int i = 0; i < 5; i++)
        {
                sendFString(ENTER);
                sendChar(c + i);
                sendFString(FOR);
                sendFString(ERROR_TBL[i]);
        }
}

void parseInput(char s[])
{
        if( (s[0] <= '4') && ( s[0] >= '0') ) // 5 error messages
        {
                showMessage(s[0]);
        }
        else
        {
                // parse first character
                switch (s[0])
                {
                 case 'd':
                   if((s[1]=='e')&&(s[2]=='m')&&(s[3]=='o')&&(s[4]=='?') )
                        sendFString(TALKING_TO);
                        sendFString(WHO_DEMO);
                        break;
                 default:
                        sendFString(BAD_COMMAND1);
                        sendChar(s[0]);
                        sendFString(BAD_COMMAND2);

                        break;
                }
        s[0] = '\0';
        }
}

void showMessage(char mess)
{

        int num = atoi(&mess);

        sendFString(ERROR_TBL[num]);      // Send the song title to the PC

}
```

Compile, load to the Butterfly, and in HyperTerminal you will see:

```
You are talking to the 'Messenger' demo.
```

```
Enter a 0 for error message: You fouled up beyond repair.
Enter a 1 for error message: Situation normal, all fouled up.
Enter a 2 for error message: Stop the madness!
Enter a 3 for error message: Where did you learn to program?
Enter a 4 for error message: Read the freaking manual!
```

Test it as follows:

```
2
Stop the madness!
0
You fouled up beyond repair.
1
Situation normal, all fouled up.
3
Where did you learn to program?
4
Read the freaking manual!
5

You sent: '5' - I don't understand.
```

Let me add a postscript to this by saying again that this memory use is not about C, it is about the AVR microcontroller and how to conserve limited RAM by using Flash ROM. It is important to keep C and the microcontroller specific 'fixes' separate in your head, because what we just learned works great on the AVR using the WinAVR compiler, but won't work using other compilers for the AVR, and is completely useless for other microcontrollers.

Does anybody know what time it is? A Real Time Clock.

Let's combine our knowledge of interrupts with what we learned in the messenger project to make a simple real time clock. This was derived from the more capable clock in the Butterfly software.

A one second interrupt

We saw how to use the 32.768kHz watch crystal to calibrate the cpu clock oscillator in the chapter on timers and interrupts. While that calibration makes the oscillator accurate enough for communicating with the PC via the USART, it isn't accurate enough to keep real time like a watch. We will use Timer/counter2 with the watch crystal as an input so that when the count reaches 32768, we will know that one-second has passed and can throw an interrupt allowing us to do something at exact one second intervals. Notice that 32768 is 0x8000 in hexadecimal and 1000000000000000 in binary, this is no accident since the crystals were designed to allow digital systems to keep real time (well, 'real' to humans anyway). The low speed (kilohertz verus mega or giga hertz) and precision timing allowed watches more accurate than expensive mechanical chronometers to be manufactured so cheaply that its not unusual to find one as a prize in a box of cereal, though they aren't milk proof and are a bit too crunchy.

We start the software by using a delay loop to wait for the external crystal to stabilize.

```
for(int i = 0; i < 10; i++)
        _delay_loop_2(30000);
```

Disable global interrupts.

```
cli();
```

Clear the Timer/Counter 2 Output Interrupt Enable, TOIE2, bit in the Timer/Counter 2 Interrupt Mask Register, TIMSK2, to disable the timer output interrupt enable.

```
cbi(TIMSK2, TOIE2);
```

Select Timer2 asynchronous operation AS2: Asynchronous Timer/Counter2, AS2 bit in the Asynchronous Status Register, ASSR.

```
ASSR = (1<<AS2);
```

Clear the Timer/Counter 2, TCNT2, count register.

```
TCNT2 = 0;
```

Select the divide by 128 prescale factor in the Timer Counter Control Register, TCCR2A. The watch crystal pulses 32768 times in one second and 128*256 = 32768, so with a 128 prescaler, the timer counts to 256 and overflows once per second.

```
TCCR2A |= (1<<CS22) | (1<<CS20);
```

Wait for the TCN2UB: Timer/Counter2 Update Busy and the TCR2UB: Timer/Counter Control Register2 Update Busy bits of the, ASSR, to be cleared.

```
while((ASSR & 0x01) | (ASSR & 0x04));
```

Clear the Timer/Counter2 Interrupt Flags Register, TIFR2.

```
TIFR2 = 0xFF;
```

Set the Timer/Counter 2 Output Interrupt Enable, TOIE2, bit in the Timer/Counter 2 Interrupt Mask Register, TIMSK2, to enable the timer output interrupt enable.

```
sbi(TIMSK2, TOIE2);
```

And finally, enable the global interrupts.

```
sei();
```

Now the SIGNAL(SIG_OVERFLOW2) function will be called once per second (as shown in the code section) so we can use it to keep track of seconds.

Converting Computer Time to Human Readable Time

We can keep a count of seconds, but what good does it do us if our watch reads 40241? If the count started at midnight then this number of seconds would indicate that the time is ten minutes and 41 seconds after eleven in the morning. And that conversion is easy compared to the numbers you get if you set your watch at thirty-three seconds after three twenty in the afternoon on May 11th of 2005 and you are reading the number two years seventy-eight days six hours fourteen minutes and seven seconds later. So we are going to need to do some computing to convert the count to something we can read.

We'll briefly explore one way to convert time from byte sized data to ASCII text strings that we can understand.

BCD - Binary Coded Decimal

Binay Coded Decimal is a coding trick that eases the storage and conversion of binary numbers, say a count of the crystal beats, to decimal numbers, like you'd want to display on a watch LCD. We can divide an 8-bit byte into two 4-bit nibbles each of which can represent a number with a range of 0 to 16. That's one of the reasons for the use of hexadecimal notation discussed earlier. And it allows us to store as single decimal integers, 0 to 9, in a nibble and two in a byte, one integer in each nibble.

If a the decimal number in a byte is less than 99, we can convert it to a BCD byte using the following algorithm:

Set the initial byte (in C we use char) to some two digit value.

```
char initialbyte = 54;
```

Declare a variable for the upper nibble value.

```
char high = 0;
```

Count the tens in initialbyte.

```
while (initialbyte >= 10)
{
        high++;
        initialbyte -= 10;
}
```

After this runs the initialbyte now contains only the ones integer from the original byte and high char contains the tens, that is: high = 5 and intialbyte = 4. We combine the high and low nibbles to get the converted byte.

```
convertedbyte  =  (high << 4) | initialbyte;
```

This algorithm is used in the CHAR2BCD2 function in the software.

Converting a byte to the ASCII equivalent decimal character using BCD.

We define two bytes Tens and Ones and a third byte, Number, which we set to a value in the range of 0 to 99.

```
char Tens = 0;
char Ones = 0;
char Number = 54;
```

We use the character to BCD algorithm written as the function CHAR2BCD2(char) in the software section below to convert the Number to the BCD equivalent in Tens.

```
Tens = CHAR2BCD2(Number);
```

Now Tens has the BCD of the tens in the upper nibble and of the ones in the lower nibble. We can convert this to an ASCII character for the integer by remembering that the numerical value of ASCII '0' is 48 and each following char integer is a simple increment of the previous one. Meaning that adding the number 4 to the value of the ASCII character '0', which is 48, yields the ASCII character '4', (48+4 = 52 which is the ASCII decimal value of the character '4'). So the conversion of a decimal integer to its ASCII equivalent character is the simple addition of 48 to the decimal integer.

Since the CHAR2BCD2 function loaded both the tens and ones parts of Number into Tens, we need to extract the Ones and the Tens so that we can add 48 to get the ASCII characters for Number.

```
Ones = Tens;
Ones = (Ones & 0x0F) + '0';
```

Finally we get the Tens by right shifing the byte 4-bits, which we use as the ASCII character offset.

```
Tens = (Tens >> 4) + '0';
```

We'll use these ideas in the showClock function in the software.

The Real Timer Clock Software

In the software you will encounter: uint8_t, which is WinAVR specific and denotes what would normally we called 'unsigned char' and is the same as a byte.

Create a new directory, Real Time Clock, and copy the .c and .h files and the makefile from the Messenger directory.

Open Messenger.h in Programmers Notepad and write:

```
// identify yourself specifically
const char TALKING_TO[] PROGMEM = "\rYou are talking to the ";
const char WHO_DEMO[] PROGMEM = "'Real Time Clock' demo.\r";

// bad command
const char BAD_COMMAND1[] PROGMEM = "\rYou sent: '";
const char BAD_COMMAND2[] PROGMEM = "' - I don't understand.\r";

const char ENTER[] PROGMEM = "Enter ";
const char TEXT_GET[] PROGMEM = "'get' to get the time and
date.\r";
const char TEXT_SEC[] PROGMEM = "'secXX' to set the second";
const char TEXT_MIN[] PROGMEM = "'minXX' to set the minute";
const char TEXT_HOUR[] PROGMEM = "'hourXX' to set the hour";
const char TEXT_TOXX[] PROGMEM = " to XX.\r";

const char ERROR_NUMBER[] PROGMEM = "\rERROR - number must be
less than ";
const char ERROR_60[] PROGMEM = " 60.\r";
const char ERROR_12[] PROGMEM = " 12.\r";

const char THE_TIME_IS[] PROGMEM = "The time is: ";

Open Demonstrator.h and write:
```

```c
// Demonstrator.h Real Timer Clock version

void initializer(void);
void parseInput(char *);

void setSecond(char *);
void setMinute(char *);
void setHour(char *);

char CHAR2BCD2(char input);
void RTC_init(void);

void showClock(void);
void setClock(void);
```

Open Demonstrator.c and write:

```c
// Demonstrator.c Real Time Clock version

#include "PC_Comm.h"
#include "Messages.h"

unsigned char gSECOND;
unsigned char gMINUTE;
unsigned char gHOUR;

void initializer()
{
        // Calibrate the oscillator:
    OSCCAL_calibration();

        // Initialize the USART
        USARTinit();

        // Initialize the RTC
        RTC_init();

        // Display instructions on PC
        sendFString(TALKING_TO);
        sendFString(WHO_DEMO);
        sendFString(ENTER);
        sendFString(TEXT_GET);
        sendFString(ENTER);
        sendFString(TEXT_SEC);
        sendFString(TEXT_TOXX);
        sendFString(ENTER);
        sendFString(TEXT_MIN);
        sendFString(TEXT_TOXX);
        sendFString(ENTER);
```

```c
        sendFString(TEXT_HOUR);
        sendFString(TEXT_TOXX);

}

void parseInput(char s[])
{

        // parse first character
        switch (s[0])
        {

                case 'g':
                        if( (s[1] == 'e') && (s[2] == 't') )
                        showClock();
                        break;
                case 's':
                        if( (s[1] == 'e') && (s[2] == 'c') )
                        setSecond(s);
                        break;
                case 'm':
                        if( (s[1] == 'i') && (s[2] == 'n') )
                        setMinute(s);
                        break;
                case 'h':
                        if( (s[1] == 'o') && (s[2] == 'u') && (s[3] == 'r'))
                        setHour(s);
                        break;
                case 'd':

        if((s[1]=='e')&&(s[2]=='m')&&(s[3]=='o')&&(s[4]=='?'))
                        sendFString(TALKING_TO);
                        sendFString(WHO_DEMO);
                        break;
                default:
                        sendFString(BAD_COMMAND1);
                        sendChar(s[0]);
                        sendFString(BAD_COMMAND2);

                        break;

        }
        s[0] = '\0';

}

void setSecond(char s[])
{
        char str[] = {0,0,'\0'};
        int sec;
```

184

```
        str[0] = s[3];
        str[1] = s[4];

        sec = atoi(str);
        if( sec <= 60)
        {
                gSECOND = (uint8_t)sec;
        }
        else
        {
                sendFString(ERROR_NUMBER);
                sendFString(ERROR_60);
        }
}

void setMinute(char s[])
{
        char str[] = {0,0,'\0'};
        int min;

        str[0] = s[3];
        str[1] = s[4];

        min = atoi(str);
        if( min <= 60)
        {
                gMINUTE = (uint8_t)min;
        }
        else
        {
                sendFString(ERROR_NUMBER);
                sendFString(ERROR_60);
        }
}

void setHour(char s[])
{
        char str[] = {0,0,'\0'};
        int hour;

        str[0] = s[4];
        str[1] = s[5];

        hour = atoi(str);
        if( hour <= 12)
        {
                gHOUR = (uint8_t)hour;
        }
        else
        {
                sendFString(ERROR_NUMBER);
```

185

```
                    sendFString(ERROR_12);
        }
}

void showClock(void)
{
        uint8_t HH, HL, MH, ML, SH, SL;

        HH = CHAR2BCD2(gHOUR);

        HL = (HH & 0x0F) + '0';
        HH = (HH >> 4) + '0';

        MH = CHAR2BCD2(gMINUTE);
        ML = (MH & 0x0F) + '0';
        MH = (MH >> 4) + '0';

        SH = CHAR2BCD2(gSECOND);
        SL = (SH & 0x0F) + '0';
        SH = (SH >> 4) + '0';

        sendFString(THE_TIME_IS);
        sendChar(HH);
        sendChar(HL);
        sendChar(':');
        sendChar(MH);
        sendChar(ML);
        sendChar(':');
        sendChar(SH);
        sendChar(SL);
        sendChar('\r');


}

// convert a character into a binary coded decimal chracter in the range
// 0 to 99 resulting byte has tens in high nibble and ones in low nibble
char CHAR2BCD2(char input)
{
    char high = 0;

    while (input >= 10)                 // Count tens
    {
        high++;
        input -= 10;
    }

    return  (high << 4) | input;        // Add ones and return answer
}
```

186

```
// initialize Timer/counter2 as asynchronous using the 32.768kHz watch
// crystal.
void RTC_init(void)
{
    // wait for external crystal to stabilise
    for(int i = 0; i < 10; i++)
        _delay_loop_2(30000);

    cli();                  // disable global interrupt

    cbi(TIMSK2, TOIE2);     // disable OCIE2A and TOIE2

    ASSR = (1<<AS2);        // select asynchronous operation of Timer2

    TCNT2 = 0;                          // clear TCNT2A

    // select precaler: 32.768 kHz / 128 = 1 sec between each overflow
    TCCR2A |= (1<<CS22) | (1<<CS20);

    // wait for TCN2UB and TCR2UB to be cleared
    while((ASSR & 0x01) | (ASSR & 0x04));

    TIFR2 = 0xFF;               // clear interrupt-flags
    sbi(TIMSK2, TOIE2);         // enable Timer2 overflow interrupt

    sei();                      // enable global interrupt

    // initial time and date setting
    gSECOND  = 0;
    gMINUTE  = 0;
    gHOUR    = 0;
}

// one second interrupt from 32kHz watch crystal
SIGNAL(SIG_OVERFLOW2)
{
    gSECOND++;              // increment second

    if (gSECOND == 60)
    {
        gSECOND = 0;
        gMINUTE++;          // increment minute

        if (gMINUTE > 59)
        {
            gMINUTE = 0;
            gHOUR++;        // increment hour

            if (gHOUR > 12)
```

187

```
            {
                gHOUR = 0;
            }
        }
    }
}
```

Using Real Time Clock:

After compiling and loading the code, in HyperTerminal you should see:

```
You are talking to the 'Real Time Clock' demo.
Enter 'get' to get the time and date.
Enter 'secXX' to set the second to XX.
Enter 'minXX' to set the minute to XX.
Enter 'hourXX' to set the hour to XX.
```

Get the current time:

```
get
The time is: 12:00:03
```

Which initially should be a few seconds past 12. Set the current time as follows:

```
sec45
min4
hour11
```

Then you can get the correct time:

```
get
The time is: 11:05:01
get
The time is: 11:05:12
get
The time is: 11:05:17
```

Music to my ears. "Play it again Sam."

We are going to pillage the Butterfly code again and play some tunes to further illustrate the use of pointers and arrays.

More on pointers to arrays

In the original Butterfly code written with the IAR compiler, in sound.c, songs are selected using these definitions:

```
__flash int __flash *Songs[]    = { FurElise, Mozart, /*Minuet,
AuldLangSyne,*/ Sirene1,  Sirene2, Whistle, 0};

int __flash *pSong;    // pointer to the different songs in flash
```

The __flash is not C, it is a special IAR modifier that allows access to Flash ROM as if it was regular C style RAM. In use:

```
    pSong = Songs[song];             // point to this song
```

Loads pSong with the pointer to the tune indicated by the song variable. All nice and C like. Unfortunately, the WinAVR compiler isn't quite as C-like in the way it allows access to Flash ROM. Not that I'm criticizing, I think the WinAVR port of the gcc tools to the AVR platform is a miracle of dedication and technical prowess, not to mention: free. But I won't mention free. Especially not repeatedly: free, free, free. So this is a miraculous little **free** compiler (send them some money at: http://www.sourceforge.net/donate.)

The port of the Butterfly code from not-free IAR compiler to the free WinAVR was done by:
Martin Thomas, Kaiserslautern, Germany
mthomas@rhrk.uni-kl.de
http://www.siwawi.arubi.uni-kl.de/avr_projects/

who did an outstanding job. When you finally learn enough to really evaluate the Butterfly code, you will come to appreciate the intelligence and hard work that this gentleman (my assumption) did for you. Yes, you. And for free. So when you see the way he translated the relatively simple appearing song selection statement, you can agree with his comment below: '// looks too complicated', without getting fussy about it.

First look at his version of the definitions:

```
// pointer-array with pointers to the song arrays
const  int  *Songs[] PROGMEM     = {  FurElise,  Mozart,  Minuet,
AuldLangSyne, Sirene1, Sirene2, Whistle, 0};

const int *pSong; // mt point to a ram location (pointer array
Songs)
```

The __flash of the IAR compiler is replaced by the PROGMEM. And the actual use is as follows:

```
// mt pSong = Songs[song];    // point to this song
pSong=(int*)pgm_read_word(&Songs[song]); // looks too
complicated...
```

Yep, I agree: '// looks too complicated', but I have no intention to try to fix it and make it look more C-like. I doubt seriously that I have the time or the skill. In programming microcontrollers in C we sometimes have to dance lightly around ANSI C and use what works.

What the statement says is: we equate a constant integer pointer pointer to a cast of an integer pointer of the function pgm_read_word, which takes as a parameter the address of the song element of the Songs[] array. What we are doing is sending this address to a function that knows how to extract a pointer to Flash RAM. Looks too complicated… but so what, it works.

Setting the frequency

Tones are setup by putting an integer from the song table in the Timer1 Input Capture Register 1, ICR1, which in this case is used to set the counter top value. The values are taken from the Butterfly code and are based on a cpu clock running at 1 MHz. Since we are using a cpu clock of 2 MHz for the USART, adjustments are made that help but do not truly compensate for the difference.

We select a base frequency of 220Hz (the A note) and calculate the frequency for subsequent notes using the notes position on the musical scale following a. For instance, C0 is 3 after A:

```
Tone = 220*2^(NOTE/12)
```

When NOTE = C0 we get:

```
Tone = 220*2^(3/12) = 261.6256.
```

We get the frequency to generate for the tone with:

```
Timer value = 1MHz / Tone / 2
```

For the C0 we would have:

```
Timer value = 1000000 / 261,6256... / 2 = 1911
```

So when we want to generate a C0 we set Timer1 to generate a phase/frequency correct PWM with a top value calculated as above. We then compensate for our using a 2MHz cpu clock by doubling the value using a left bit shift of one position. (In case you didn't get this earlier, left shifting a byte or integer doubles it if there is headroom. Headroom means the value is less than half the possible value, 256/2 for a byte.)

A few tones from the sound.h table:

```
#define a    2273     // tone 0
#define xa   2145     // tone 1
#define ax   2145     // tone 1
#define b    2024     // tone 2
#define c0   1911     // tone 3
```

Setting the tempo

The tempo, in this case, is the length of time we play the tone. The Timer0 calls the Play_Tune function at 10ms intervals. It begins by getting the tempo from the first position of the array and putting it into a Tempo variable. The next time Play_Tune is called, if Tempo is not 0, it decrements the tempo and exits. It continues to do this until the Tempo is 0, when it rereads the tempo and starts over.

Setting the duration

The duration and the frequency are paired values in the table. The duration is the length of time that the following tone should be played. Play_Tune gets the duration
and tone from the table and loads them into the Duration variable and the Timer1 top count. It starts the tone and then exits. When called again by Timer0, if the Duration is not 0, Duration is decremented and the function exits leaving the tone playing. When Duration is decremented to 0, Play_Tune gets the next set of values for the Duration and the timer and starts the next tone. If the Duration value read from the table is 0, this indicates that the tune has been played through, so it checks the next byte and if that byte is 1, it starts the tune over, if 0 it ends the tune. Clever, eh?

An example song array – Fur Elise

```
const int FurElise[] PROGMEM=
{
3,
8,e2, 8,xd2, 8,e2, 8,xd2, 8,e2, 8,b1, 8,d2, 8,c2, 4,a1,
8,p, 8,c1, 8,e1, 8,a1, 4,b1, 8,p, 8,e1, 8,xg1, 8,b1, 4,c2,
8,p, 8,e1, 8,e2, 8,xd2, 8,e2, 8,xd2, 8,e2, 8,b1, 8,d2,
8,c2, 4,a1, 8,p, 8,c1, 8,e1, 8,a1, 4,b1, 8,p, 8,e1, 8,c2,
8,b1, 4,a1,
0, 1
};
```

Using the Piezo-element to make sound

The piezo-element is the large black square on the back of the Butterfly. It contains a sheet of material that deforms when electricity is applied to it (the piezo electric effect). This deformation can be made at audio frequencies allowing the element to produce sound waves in the air. Our piezo-element is connected to PortB pin 5, which is also the OC1A pin that can be configured as an output for the Timer1 waveform generator. We will configure the Timer1 waveform generator so that it will use PWM to generate tones.

Initializing the Timer1 for PWM to the piezo-element.

We initialize Timer1 to generate a PWM waveform as follows:

We set Timer/Counter Control Register A, TCCR1A, so that the OC1A pin (PortB pin 5) will be set when up counting and cleared when down counting.

```
TCCR1A = (1<<COM1A1);
```

We set the TCCR1B for phase and frequency correct PWM with a top value in ICR1.

```
TCCR1B = (1<<WGM13);
```

We set the TCCR1B to start Timer 1 with no prescaling

```
sbi(TCCR1B, CS10);
```

We set the Output Compare Register 1 High to 0 and Low to the value in the Volume variable. A lower value of Volume will produce a higher volume.

```
OCRA1H = 0;
OCRA1L = Volume;
```

Generating the tone using PWM from Timer1

When Play_Tune is called periodically by Timer0, we set the Timer1 TCCR1B, the Timer/Counter1 High and Low registers, TCNT1H TCNT1L , and the Input Capture Register 1, ICR1H, which in this case is used to set the counter top value.

In Play_Tune:

If the song calls for a pause we stop Timer1, otherwise we start it

```
if((pgm_read_word(pSong + Tone) == p) | (pgm_read_word(pSong + Tone) == P))
        cbi(TCCR1B, CS10); // stop Timer1, prescaler(1)
else
        sbi(TCCR1B, CS10); // start Timer1, prescaler(1)
```

We then load the tone value from the song array.

```
temp_hi = pgm_read_word(pSong + Tone); // read out the PWM-value
```

The Tone is an integer, so we get it into a temporary variable and shift it right by 8 bits and load that value into the high byte of the counter top. Except that we actually only shift it right by 7 bits to adjust it (cut it in half) to compensate for the use of a 2MHz system clock in this applications (for the USART) when a 1 MHz clock was used in the original Butterfly code.

```
temp_hi >>= 7;
```

We clear the Timer1 count.

```
TCNT1H = 0;
TCNT1L = 0;
```

We load the counter top value high byte.

```
ICR1H = temp_hi;
```

Finally we load the counter top value low byte and adjust it for the 2 MHz clock.

```
ICR1L = pgm_read_word(pSong + Tone);
ICR1L <<= 1;
```

Using the Timer0 interrupt to play a tune

As mentioned above the Timer0 interrupt calls the Play_Tune function every 10 ms. We set up the Timer0 much as we've seen before:

```
  // Enable timer0 compare interrupt
TIMSK0 = (1<<OCIE0A);

// Sets the compare value
OCR0A = 38;

// Set Clear on Timer Compare (CTC) mode, CLK/256 prescaler
TCCR0A = (1<<WGM01)|(0<<WGM00)|(4<<CS00);
```

The Play it again Sam Software.

For some reason, the Butterfly code commented out the songs Minuet and AuldLangSyne, but the WinAVR version uses them, so we get to hear two songs absent on the store-bought Butterfly.

Create a new directory: Play it again Sam, and copy the .c and .h files and the makefile from the Messenger directory. From the WinAVR Butterfly port, bf_gcc directory copy sound.c and sound.h. In Programmers Notepad, create a new C/C++ file, tunes.h and add:

```
// tunes.h

#include "sound.h"
```

Then copy the following from sound.c to tunes.h

```
/************************************************************
 * A song is defined by a table of notes. The first byte sets
 * the tempo. A high byte will give a low tempo, and opposite.
 * Each tone consists of two bytes. The first gives the length of
 * the tone, the other gives the frequency. The frequencies for
 * each tone are defined in the "sound.h". Timer0 controls the
 * tempo and the length of each tone, while Timer1 with PWM gives
 * the frequency. The second last byte is a "0" which indicates
 * the end, and the very last byte makes the song loop if it's
 * "1", and not loop if it's "0".
 ************************************************************?

// mt __flash char TEXT_SONG1[]      = "Fur Elise";
const char TEXT_SONG1[] PROGMEM     = "Fur Elise";

// __flash int FurElise[] =
const int FurElise[] PROGMEM=
{
    3,
    8,e2, 8,xd2, 8,e2, 8,xd2, 8,e2, 8,b1, 8,d2, 8,c2, 4,a1,
    8,p, 8,c1, 8,e1, 8,a1, 4,b1, 8,p, 8,e1, 8,xg1, 8,b1, 4,c2,
    8,p, 8,e1, 8,e2, 8,xd2, 8,e2, 8,xd2, 8,e2, 8,b1, 8,d2,
    8,c2, 4,a1, 8,p, 8,c1, 8,e1, 8,a1, 4,b1, 8,p, 8,e1, 8,c2,
    8,b1, 4,a1, 0, 1
};
```

```
//__flash char TEXT_SONG2[]        = "Turkey march";
const char TEXT_SONG2[] PROGMEM  = "Turkey march";

//__flash int Mozart[] =
const int Mozart[] PROGMEM =
{
      3,
      16,xf1, 16,e1, 16,xd1, 16,e1, 4,g1, 16,a1, 16,g1, 16,xf1,
      16,g1,4,b1, 16,c2, 16,b1, 16,xa1, 16,b1, 16,xf2, 16,e2,
      16,xd2, 16,e2, 16,xf2, 16,e2, 16,xd2, 16,e2, 4,g2, 8,e2,
      8,g2, 32,d2, 32,e2, 16,xf2, 8,e2, 8,d2, 8,e2, 32,d2, 32,e2,
      16,xf2, 8,e2, 8,d2, 8,e2, 32,d2, 32,e2, 16,xf2, 8,e2, 8,d2,
      8,xc2, 4,b1, 0, 1
};

// mt song 3 & 4 where commented out by ATMEL - see their readme
// well, the gcc-geek wants all the songs ;-)
const char TEXT_SONG3[] PROGMEM        = "Minuet";

const int Minuet[] PROGMEM =
{
      2,
      4,d2, 8,g1, 8,a1, 8,b1, 8,c2, 4,d2, 4,g1, 4,g1, 4,e2, 8,c2,
      8,d2, 8,e2, 8,xf2, 4,g2, 4,g1, 4,g1, 4,c2, 8,d2, 8,c2,
      8,b1, 8,a1, 4,b1, 8,c2, 8,b1, 8,a1, 8,g1, 4,xf1, 8,g1,
      8,a1, 8,b1, 8,g1, 4,b1, 2,a1,
      0, 1
};



char TEXT_SONG4[] PROGMEM    = "Auld Lang Syne";

const int AuldLangSyne[] PROGMEM =
{
      3,
      4,g2, 2,c3, 8,c3, 4,c3, 4,e3, 2,d3, 8,c3, 4,d3, 8,e3, 8,d3,
      2,c3, 8,c3, 4,e3, 4,g3, 2,a3, 8,p, 4,a3, 2,g3, 8,e3, 4,e3,
      4,c3, 2,d3, 8,c3, 4,d3, 8,e3, 8,d3, 2,c3, 8,a2, 4,a2, 4,g2,
      2,c3, 4,p,
      0, 1
};


//__flash char TEXT_SONG5[]        =   "Sirene1";
const char TEXT_SONG5[] PROGMEM =   "Sirene1";
```

```
//__flash int Sirene1[] =
const int Sirene1[] PROGMEM =
{
     0,
     32,400, 32,397, 32,394, 32,391, 32,388, 32,385, 32,382,
     32,379, 32,376, 32,373, 32,370, 32,367, 32,364, 32,361,
     32,358, 32,355, 32,352, 32,349, 32,346, 32,343, 32,340,
     32,337, 32,334, 32,331, 32,328, 32,325, 32,322, 32,319,
     32,316, 32,313, 32,310, 32,307, 32,304, 32,301, 32,298,
     32,298, 32,301, 32,304, 32,307, 32,310, 32,313, 32,316,
     32,319, 32,322, 32,325, 32,328, 32,331, 32,334, 32,337,
     32,340, 32,343, 32,346, 32,349, 32,352, 32,355, 32,358,
     32,361, 32,364, 32,367, 32,370, 32,373, 32,376, 32,379,
     32,382, 32,385, 32,388, 32,391, 32,394, 32,397, 32,400,
     0, 1
};

//__flash char TEXT_SONG6[]      =    "Sirene2";
const char TEXT_SONG6[] PROGMEM =    "Sirene2";

//__flash int Sirene2[] =
const int Sirene2[] PROGMEM =
{
     3,
     4,c2,  4,g2,
     0, 1
};


//__flash char TEXT_SONG7[]      =    "Whistle";
const char TEXT_SONG7[] PROGMEM      =    "Whistle";

//__flash int Whistle[] =
const int Whistle[] PROGMEM =
{
     0,
     32,200, 32,195, 32,190, 32,185, 32,180, 32,175, 32,170,
     32,165, 32,160, 32,155, 32,150, 32,145, 32,140, 32,135,
     32,130, 32,125, 32,120, 32,115, 32,110, 32,105, 32,100,
     8,p, 32,200, 32,195, 32,190, 32,185, 32,180, 32,175,
     32,170, 32,165, 32,160, 32,155, 32,150, 32,145, 32,140,
     32,135, 32,130, 32,125, 32,125, 32,130, 32,135, 32,140,
     32,145, 32,150, 32,155, 32,160, 32,165, 32,170, 32,175,
     32,180, 32,185, 32,190, 32,195, 32,200,
     0, 0
};
```

197

```
// pointer-array with pointers to the song arrays
// mt: __flash int __flash *Songs[]     = { FurElise, Mozart,
// /*Minuet, AuldLangSyne,*/ Sirene1, Sirene2, Whistle, 0};
const int *Songs[] PROGMEM   = { FurElise, Mozart, Minuet,
AuldLangSyne, Sirene1, Sirene2, Whistle, 0};

//mt: __flash char __flash *TEXT_SONG_TBL[]    = { TEXT_SONG1,
// TEXT_SONG2, /*TEXT_SONG3, TEXT_SONG4,*/TEXT_SONG5, TEXT_SONG6,
// TEXT_SONG7, 0};
//// mt: 16 ram-bytes (8 words) "wasted" - TODO
//// PGM_P TEXT_SONG_TBL[] PROGMEM   = { TEXT_SONG1, TEXT_SONG2,
// /*TEXT_SONG3, TEXT_SONG4,*/TEXT_SONG5, TEXT_SONG6, TEXT_SONG7,
// 0};
const char *TEXT_SONG_TBL[]    = { TEXT_SONG1, TEXT_SONG2,
TEXT_SONG3, TEXT_SONG4, TEXT_SONG5, TEXT_SONG6, TEXT_SONG7, 0};

//__flash char PLAYING[]          = "PLAYING";
const char PLAYING[] PROGMEM   = "PLAYING";

//mt: int __flash *pSong; //pointer to the different songs in flash
const int *pSong; // mt point to a ram location (pointer array Songs)

static char Volume = 80;
static char Duration = 0;
static char Tone = 0;
static char Tempo;
```

Save tunes.h to the Play it again Sam directory.

Copy the sounds.h file from the WinAVR port of the Butterfly code, bf_gcc directory to the Play it again Sam directory. No changes, we'll just steal the whole thing.

Change the contents of the messages.h file to:

```
// identify yourself specifically
const char TALKING_TO[] PROGMEM = "\rYou are talking to the ";
const char WHO_DEMO[] PROGMEM = "'Play it again Sam' demo.\r";

// bad command
const char BAD_COMMAND1[] PROGMEM = "\rYou sent: '";
```

```
const char BAD_COMMAND2[] PROGMEM = "' - I don't understand.\r";

const char ENTER[] PROGMEM = "Enter ";
const char TEXT_FUR_ELISE[] PROGMEM = "1 for Fur Elise.\r";
const char TEXT_TURKEY_MARCH[] PROGMEM = "2 for Turkey march.\r";
const char TEXT_MINUET[] PROGMEM = "3 for Minuet.\r";
const char TEXT_AULD_LANG_SYNE[] PROGMEM = "4 for Auld Lang
Syne.\r";
const char TEXT_SIRENE1[] PROGMEM = "5 for Sirene1.\r";
const char TEXT_SIRENE2[] PROGMEM = "6 for Sirene2.\r";
const char TEXT_WHISTLE[] PROGMEM = "7 for Whistle.\r";
const char VOLUME_UP[] PROGMEM = "+ to increase";
const char VOLUME_DOWN[] PROGMEM = "- to decrease";
const char THE_VOLUME[] PROGMEM = " the volume.\r";
const char STOP[] PROGMEM ="stop to stop the music.\r" ;
```

Change the Demonstrator.c to:

```
// Demonstrator.c PWM version

#include "PC_Comm.h"
#include "Messages.h"

#include "tunes.h"

void initializer()
{
        // Calibrate the oscillator:
         OSCCAL_calibration();

        // Initialize the USART
        USARTinit();

        // Initialize timer0 to play a tune
        Timer0_Init();

        // initialize piezo-element
        sbi(DDRB, 5);                   // set OC1A as output
        sbi(PORTB, 5);                  // set OC1A high

        // Display instructions on PC
        sendFString(TALKING_TO);
        sendFString(WHO_DEMO);
        sendFString(ENTER);
        sendFString(TEXT_FUR_ELISE);
```

```
        sendFString(ENTER);
        sendFString(TEXT_TURKEY_MARCH);
        sendFString(ENTER);
        sendFString(TEXT_AULD_LANG_SYNE);
        sendFString(ENTER);
        sendFString(TEXT_SIRENE1);
        sendFString(ENTER);
        sendFString(TEXT_SIRENE2);
        sendFString(ENTER);
        sendFString(TEXT_WHISTLE);
        sendFString(ENTER);
        sendFString(VOLUME_UP);
        sendFString(THE_VOLUME);
        sendFString(ENTER);
        sendFString(VOLUME_DOWN);
        sendFString(THE_VOLUME);
        sendFString(ENTER);
        sendFString(STOP);


}

void parseInput(char s[])
{
  if( (s[0] <= '7') && ( s[0] >= '1') ) // 7 tunes
  {
      startTune(s[0]);
  }
  else
  {
   // parse first character
   switch (s[0])
   {
     case '+':
       volumeUp();
       break;
     case '-':
       volumeDown();
       break;
     case 's':
       if( (s[1] == 't') && (s[2] == 'o') && (s[3] == 'p'))
         stopTune();
      break;
    case 'd':
      if((s[1]=='e')&&(s[2]=='m')&&(s[3]=='o')&& (s[4 =='?'))
        sendFString(TALKING_TO);
```

```c
            sendFString(WHO_DEMO);
            break;
      default:
        sendFString(BAD_COMMAND1);
        sendChar(s[0]);
        sendFString(BAD_COMMAND2);
        break;

    }
    s[0] = '\0';
  }
}

void volumeUp()
{
    if(Volume >= 250)
        Volume = 250;
    else
        Volume += 50;

    OCRA1H = 0;
    OCRA1L = Volume;

}

void volumeDown()
{
    if(Volume < 11)
        Volume = 6;
    else
        Volume -= 50;

      OCRA1H = 0;
    OCRA1L = Volume;
}

void stopTune()
{
    cbi(TCCR1B, 0);     // stop Playing
    TCCR1A = 0;
    TCCR1B = 0;
    sbi(PORTB, 5);      // set OC1A high
}


void startTune(char tune)
```

```
{
        int song = atoi(&tune) - 1;

        stopTune();
        Tone = 0;
        Tempo = 0;
        Duration = 0;

        // Send the song title to the PC
        sendFString(TEXT_SONG_TBL[song]);
        sendChar('\r');

        // looks too complicated..
        pSong=(int*)pgm_read_word(&Songs[song]);

        Sound_Init();
}


void Sound_Init(void)
{
        // Set OC1A when upcounting, clear when downcounting
        TCCR1A = (1<<COM1A1);
        // Phase/Freq-correct PWM, top value = ICR1
        TCCR1B = (1<<WGM13);

        sbi(TCCR1B, CS10); // start Timer1, prescaler(1)
        // Set a initial value in the OCR1A-register
        OCRA1H = 0;

        // This will adjust the volume on the buzzer, lower value
        // =>higher volume
        OCRA1L = Volume;
}

void Play_Tune(void)
{
    int temp_hi;

    char loop;

    if(!Tone)
    {
        Duration = 0;
```

```c
        Tempo = (uint8_t)pgm_read_word(pSong + 0);
        Tempo <<= 1; // compensate for using 2 MHz clock
        Tone = 1;    //Start the song from the beginning
    }

    if(!Tempo)
    {
        if(Duration) // Check if the length of the tone has "expired"
        {
            Duration--;
        }
        else if(pgm_read_word(pSong + Tone))// If not the song end
        {
          // store the duration
          Duration = (DURATION_SEED/pgm_read_word(pSong+Tone));
          Duration <<= 1;// compensate for using 2 MHz clock
          Tone++; // point to the next tone in the Song-table

          // if pause
          if((pgm_read_word(pSong+Tone) == p)|
             (pgm_read_word(pSong+Tone) == P))

              cbi(TCCR1B, CS10); // stop Timer1, prescaler(1)
          else
              sbi(TCCR1B, CS10); // start Timer1, prescaler(1)

          cli();

          // read out the PWM-value
          temp_hi = pgm_read_word(pSong + Tone);
          temp_hi >>= 7; // move integer 8 bits to the right

          TCNT1H = 0; // reset TCNT1H/L
          TCNT1L = 0;

          ICR1H = temp_hi; // load ICR1H/L
          ICR1L = pgm_read_word(pSong + Tone);
          ICR1L <<= 1; // compensate for using 2 MHz clock

          sei();

          Tone++;  // point to the next tone in the Song-table
        }
      else    // the end of song
      {
        Tone++; // point to the next tone in the Song-table
```

203

```
        // get the byte that tells if the song should loop or not
        loop = (uint8_t)pgm_read_word(pSong + Tone);

        if( loop )
        {
            Tone = 1;
        }
        else          // if not looping the song
        {
            Tone = 0;
            cbi(TCCR1B, 0); // stop Playing
            TCCR1A = 0;
            TCCR1B = 0;
            sbi(PORTB, 5); // set OC1A high
        }
        }

        Tempo = (uint8_t)pgm_read_word(pSong + 0);
    }
    else
        Tempo--;

}


void Timer0_Init(void)
{
        // Initialize Timer0.
        // Used to give the correct time-delays in the song

        // Enable timer0 compare interrupt
        TIMSK0 = (1<<OCIE0A);

        // Sets the compare value
        OCR0A = 38;

        // Set Clear on Timer Compare (CTC) mode, CLK/256 prescaler
        TCCR0A = (1<<WGM01)|(0<<WGM00)|(4<<CS00);
}


SIGNAL(SIG_OUTPUT_COMPARE0)
{
        Play_Tune();
}
```

Finally change Demonstrator.h to:

```
// Demonstrator.h PWM version

void initializer(void);
void parseInput(char *);

int parseTune(char *);
void startTune(char);

void volumeUp(void);
void volumeDown(void);
void stopTune(void);

void Sound_Init(void);
void Timer0_Init(void);
```

Using Play it again Sam:

This is what you should see in HyperTerminal, and an example of use:

```
You are talking to the 'Play it again Sam' demo.
Enter 1 for Fur Elise.
Enter 2 for Turkey march.
Enter 3 for Minuet.
Enter 4 for Auld Lang Syne.
Enter 5 for Sirene1.
Enter 6 for Sirene2.
Enter 7 for Whistle.
Enter + to increase the volume.
Enter - to decrease the volume.
Enter stop to stop the music.
4
Auld Lang Syne
1
Fur Elise
```

Chapter 9 – Digital Meets Analog – ADC and DAC

But First - A Debugging Tale

In the ADC project that follows, I liberally 'borrowed' code from the Butterfly, adding my own inimitable style to allow a user from the PC to ask for a measure of light, temperature, and voltage. All was well except for a tiny problem with the voltage measurement. Tiny as in the first time I tried to measure voltage on the Butterfly I destroyed it. Well destroyed is a bit harsh. It looks just like it always did, but it doesn't work. Fortunately I know myself so I had ordered six Butterflys because, as I said elsewhere, my nickname is Smoky Joe since my favorite learning method is producing copious quantities of smoke in my hardware projects. The Butterfly didn't smoke though. It just died. Belly up, legs in the air, ready for a pin thru the thorax to be box mounted in the Dead Butterfly Museum. But Lepidopteron death is not what this is about. I eventually found that I had done something unbelievably stupid and since you wouldn't believe it, I won't relate that tale. Lets just say this event led me to becoming a bit paranoid about the voltage measurement part of the Butterfly hardware and I went forward on tiptoes and slightly hyperventilating as I proceeded with the ADC code.

My next version was able to read the light just fine, and the temperature just fine, and the voltage just one time.

When I requested: volt the hardware responded to HyperTerminal with:

The reading is 1.1 volts.

And promptly died. No further responses to the PC. My response involved lots of obscenities and complaints about flushing another $19.99, but the Butterfly wasn't destroyed this time, it rebooted just fine and only crashed when I asked for 'volt'. My first assumption, reasonable I thought, was that it's the light level in the room. Sound crazy? Well, it seems that the light sensor affects the Butterfly voltage reference and we have to measure the ambient room light to calibrate the voltage reference before we measure volts. So I covered the light sensor and the Butterfly still crashed. Then I went the other direction and put a bright light on it to no avail. So I thought that if it is all that sensitive to light derived voltages maybe the USART traffic voltage is propagating about unpredictably and screwing things up. The USART uses a higher voltage than the Butterfly and they have included a voltage inverter circuit that looked like a prime candidate to radiate messy voltages that might combine with a voltage on the Voltage In pin and might, theoretically, cause a problem. So I changed PC_Comm so that it sent the PC a '!' every time it received a character. In HyperTerminal I got:

So after requesting 'volt' the Butterfly was no longer exclaiming with a '!' but decided it wanted to play cards with a black club, or perhaps more reasonably, I thought, the '!' was being scrambled on reception by the PC because the Baud rate had changed (I've seen that happen before). So I reread the data sheet on the USART and diddled with the Butterfly schematics and tried a few coding changes. Hours passed and still no fix. I messed with the USART initialization function, the ADC initialization function, the ADC read function, the oscillator calibration function and generally had myself a merry old goose chase for about half a day. Nothing fixed the problem, but at least the Butterfly didn't explode nor make the least bit of smoke, the code was consistently responding with a black club rather than the '!' but at least it was running.

Finally, in total desperation, I tried what I should have tried in the first place. I bracketed code by commenting out sections (putting // in front of a line) to see where exactly the problem occurred. Eventually I got to the getVolt function and started commenting out sections. This is a time consuming process, each time you comment something out, you have to recompile, load, and test the code. It takes a while. So here is the getVolt code:

```
void getVolt()
{
      char voltintpart[]= {''0','\0'};
      char voltfractpart[]= {'0','\0'};
      int intpart = 0;
      int fractpart = 0;
      int ADCresult = 0;

      ADCresult = ADC_read();
```

```
intpart = ADCresult/50;
fractpart = ADCresult%50;

itoa(intpart, voltintpart, 10);
itoa(fractpart, voltfractpart, 10);

// Send the voltage to the PC
sendString("The reading is ");
sendChar(voltintpart [0]);
sendChar('.');
sendChar(voltfractpart [0]);
sendString(" volts.\r");
}
```

I commented out each logical part and still nothing worked. Finally, because there was nothing logical to try, I commented out the itoa functions. And the Butterfly no longer messed up. Also, it started returning '!' rather than the black club for each character I sent it. Of course, it didn't return the correct voltage, because I wasn't converting it to ASCII, but it was running fine otherwise and correctly returned the light and temperature. The itoa function is in the standard library, so I assumed that it must have a problem. I changed it to the itoa function (and the other support functions) that we wrote at the end of Chapter 6. Guess what? They also fail! I went for a long walk.

Later, after more staring at the function I noticed:

```
char voltintpart[]= {''0','\0'};
char voltfractpart[]= {'0','\0'};
```

These can't be the problem, can they? They work just fine in the original Butterfly code. But many years ago I learned the hard way that if you assign memory to an array and then foolishly write beyond that memory, say to voltintpart[2], the third element of the array which only has two elements you will in fact write to the byte in memory that follows the array bytes which may not cause a problem if nothing else is using that byte, or it might just change it from the ASCII code for an explanation point to the Microsoft extended ASCII code for a black club. So I enlarged them to:

```
char voltintpart[]= {'0','0',0,'\0'};
char voltfractpart[]= {''0',0,'0','\0'};
```

And the code works just fine. Why, you may ask, didn't the designers of the standard library require the itoa function to check the size of the array before using it? Good question. My guess is that the standard library functions were written to be as fast and small as possible. They also likely assumed nobody would be stupid enough to send it an array that was too small, and if they are that dumb, they deserve what they get. C is fast, small, and mean. C++ was designed to take out some of the meanness by forcing features that protect the programmer from himself, but this was done at the expense of size, speed, and simplicity. Other higher-level languages provide even more protection and are even larger, slower, and more complex. You almost certainly won't be using C to write programs for Windows© based programs on a PC where you've got plenty of hardware speed and memory and high level development tools, but for microcontrollers with their limited speed and memory, C probably has the best set of tradeoffs. I acknowledge that the arguments for the choice of a programming language borders on the religious, so I say that if you choose not to use C, you will be eternally damned.

Debugging can be a maddeningly frustrating process, especially if you are on a deadline. I spent half a day finding this problem. I didn't make my array large enough. HALF A DAY! Am I stupid? No, I'm not. This kind of debugging is part and parcel of working with microcontrollers. If you have the wrong attitude, you will drive yourself nuts trying to find these bugs. What is the right attitude? It is to understand that you have to be really smart, work very hard, and know a lot about C programming and microcontrollers to make a mistake this dumb. You have to keep telling yourself over and over: "This is better than putting shingles on roofs in the summer." I understand that alcohol also helps as does having an obsessive-compulsive disorder. Speaking of which, Let's move on to the next project.

Analog to Digital Conversion

What is Analog to Digital Conversion?

During a discussion with one of my EE professors about Analog to Digital Conversion, I made the mistake of bringing up Heraclitus and Democritus and the ancient debate about the fundamental nature of reality: is reality made of a continuum of a single thing (analog) or of bits of multiple things (digital). He shook his head, as my profs often did, and said, "Son, I don't give a damn what some sheep header said 3,000 years ago, this **IS** an analog world!" Humpf! I say it depends on your perspective. To electronics, Heraclitus was right and the world is analog and you can't step in the same river twice since the only constant is change. To computers, Democritus was right, the world is digital (well, he said atomic, but it's the same thing philosophically speaking) and you can theoretically step in the same river twice if you arrange the atoms (bits) of the river the same way.

Another professor of mine, also shaking his head, said, "Son, a difference that makes no difference is no difference!" So Let's drop this right here and say that the world we want to control is analog and the world we will use to control it is digital, and somewhere up there in philosopher heaven Heraclitus and Democritus can give each other a big hug.

Analog to Digital Conversion by Successive Approximation

We want to measure voltage, and in the real world, voltages can be any value whatever, they represent a continuum of electromotive force. There are many ways to convert an analog signal to a digital value each having strengths and weaknesses, we will examine successive approximation since that is what the AVR uses.

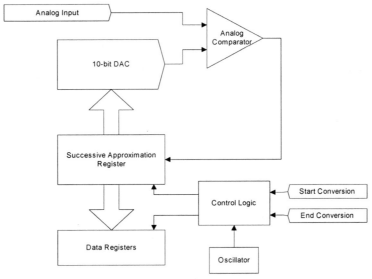

Figure 27: 10-bit successive approximation ADC Figure

Figure 27 shows a simplified diagram of a successive approximation ADC. This method uses an analog comparator and a digital to analog converter. An analog comparator, in this case, is a device that has two analog inputs one for the external voltage and the other for the voltage from the DAC (Digital to Analog Converter that can accept a digital number and output a voltage proportional to that number – we'll examine these later). If the voltage on the DAC is lower than the external voltage, the analog comparator outputs a 0, if it is higher, it outputs a 1. The ATmega169 DAC is 10-bits, meaning that it can output 1024 steps from 0 and its maximum voltage.

Let's look at the case where the maximum voltage that the DAC can produce is 3.0 volts. We have 10-bits to play with so we can keep approximating in 0.00293 (3.0/1024) volt steps. Let's set the input voltage to 1.234 volts. We use a binary search technique that starts in the middle and bisects each successive voltage. We start by bisecting the 3 volts by sending the number 512 to the DAC, which then outputs 1.5 volts; the comparator will output a 1, meaning that the DAC voltage is too high. So we bisect the 1.5 volts by sending the DAC 256 to reset it to 0.75 volt and get a 0 meaning that the DAC voltage is now lower than the input voltage. Next we bisect the 1.5-0.75 volts by sending 384 to the DAC output 1.215 volts and get a 0, too low. We keep successively approximating until we find that the voltage is between1.233 and 1.236 volts. This is the best we can do with 0.003 volt steps.

Analog to Digital Conversion with the ATMEGA169

The ATmega169 has its 10-bit successive approximation Analog to Digital Converter connected to an 8-channel analog multiplexer allowing connection to one of eight voltage inputs on PortF. During conversion the voltage is held constant by a sample and hold circuit. Look in the data book on page 195, figure 82 for a block diagram of the ADC circuit.

The minimum value is GND and the maximum is determined by the voltage on the AREF pin (minus 1-bit in the least significant bit). We can use an external voltage reference attached to this pin, or we can tell the AVR to connect it to either AVCC or to an internal 1.1 volt reference. This setup allows us to improve noise immunity by connecting a decoupling capacitor to the AREF to help stabilize the internal voltage reference. The Butterfly uses a 100 nF capacitor for this purpose.

There are 8 analog input channels ADC0 – ADC7 on the Port F pins PF0 – PF7. These pins are connected to an analog multiplexer that can connect any of the pins to the analog comparator. The channel is selected by setting the MUX0 – MUX4 bits in the ADMUX register.

The ADC is enabled/disabled by setting/clearing the ADEN bit in the ADCSRA (ADC Control and Status Register A). Since the ADC consumes power it is recommended that you turn it off when not in use.

The ADC readings are put in the ADC Data Registers ADCH and ADCL. In normal operation you read the ADCL first, then the ADCH to ensure that both registers contain the value of a single conversion.

An ADC interrupt can be set to trigger when a conversion is complete.

Starting a Conversion

There are several ways to start a conversion. You can write a 1 to the ADC Start Conversion bit ADSC to start a conversion. This bit stays high while the conversion is in progress and is cleared by the hardware when the conversion completes.

You can enable auto triggering by setting the ADC Auto Trigger bit, ADATE. The trigger source is determined by setting the ADTS2:0 ADC Auto Trigger Source bits in the ADCSRB register. The triggers can be:

- Free Running mode
- Analog Comparator
- External Interrupt Request 0
- Timer/Counter0 Compare Match
- Timer/Counter0 Overflow
- Timer Counter Compare Match B
- Timer/Counter1 Overflow
- Timer/Counter 1 Capture Event

Conversion Timing

The successive approximations are clocked between 50kHz and 200kHz to get the maximum resolution. You can use higher sampling rate frequencies, but you get lower resolution. The sampling rate is determined by the input clock and by a prescaler value set in the ADPS bits of the ADCSRA register. The first conversion takes 25 clock cycles to initialize the hardware. Normal conversions take 13 clock cycles and auto triggered conversions take 13.5.

Changing Channels

There are some complexities involved in changing channels and voltage references that lead to the recommendation that you always wait till a conversion is complete before making a change.

Digital Noise Reduction

The CPU and I/O peripherals can generate a lot of electrical noise that affect the accuracy of the ADC. We can put the system to sleep to shut it up and then take our ADC readings in the quietened environment. Details in the data book.

Conditioning the Analog Input Signal

The accuracy of the conversion will depend on the quality of the input signal. A few recommendations:

- Filter out signal components higher than the Nyquist sampling frequency (double the frequency of interest) with a low pass filter.
- Sampling time depends on the time needed to charge the sample and hold circuit so always use a source with an output impedance of 10 kOhm or less.
- Use only slowly varying signals.
- Keep analog signal paths as short as possible.
- Use the ADC noise canceller function.
- If any of the ADC port pins are used for digital output, don't switch them while a conversion is going on.

Accuracy

The data book has some cursory discussion of the extremely dense topic of ADC accuracy. Just be aware that in the accompanying project we don't use any of these recommendations, so take the accuracy of our measurements with a grain of salt.

Projects

We will write code to allow us to use HyperTerminal to request a reading from the light, temperature and voltage sensors of the Butterfly. You've already seen the debugging tale above so you know how much fun I had writing this stuff, so enjoy it or else.

Initializing the ADC

The Butterfly has the ATmega169 pin 62, (AREF) connected to a bypass capacitor to help lessen noise on the ADC, so we set the ADMUX bits 6 and 7 to 0 to select the 'use external reference' option. We use the 'input' variable to set the multiplexer. to connect the ADC to pin 61 (ADC0) using the ADMUX register (data book p 207).

```
ADMUX = input;    // external AREF and ADCx
```

Next we set the ADC Control and Status Register A. The ADEN bit enables the ADC. The ADPSx bits select the prescaler.

```
// set ADC prescaler to , 1MHz / 8 = 125kHz
ADCSRA = (1<<ADEN) | (1<<ADPS1) | (1<<ADPS0);
```

Finally we take a dummy reading, which basically allows the ADC to hack up any hairballs before we take any real readings

```
input = ADC_read();

void ADC_init(char input)
{
    ADMUX = input;    // external AREF and ADCx

    // set ADC prescaler to , 1MHz / 8 = 125kHz
    ADCSRA = (1<<ADEN) | (1<<ADPS1) | (1<<ADPS0);

    input = ADC_read();  // clear hairballs
}
```

Reading the ADC

We save power by turning off the voltage on the light and temperature sensors when they are not used, so now we turn them on, in case they are being used.

```
sbi(PORTF, PF3); // deprecated, but so what?
sbi(DDRF, DDF3); // deprecated, but so what?
```

Next we enable the ADC.

```
sbi(ADCSRA, ADEN);      // Enable the ADC
```

Then we do another hairball clearing dummy read.

```
ADCSRA |= (1<<ADSC);         // do single conversion
```

And we wait till the conversion is complete.

```
while(!(ADCSRA & 0x10));//wait for conversion done, ADIF flag
active
```

Now we repeat this 8 times for better accuracy.

```
    // do the ADC conversion 8 times for better accuracy
    for(i=0;i<8;i++)
    {
        ADCSRA |= (1<<ADSC); // do single conversion

        // wait for conversion done, ADIF flag active
        while(!(ADCSRA & 0x10));

        ADC_temp = ADCL; // read out ADCL register
        ADC_temp += (ADCH << 8); // read out ADCH register

        // accumulate result (8 samples) for later averaging
        ADCr += ADC_temp;
    }
```

We divide by 8, which conveniently is done by right shifting 3 bits. Weren't we lucky that we chose to do 8 samples and save processing time by avoiding a division?

```
    ADCr = ADCr >> 3;      // average the 8 samples
```

We turn the sensors off to save power.

```
cbi(PORTF,PF3); // mt cbi(PORTF, PORTF3);  // disable the VCP
cbi(DDRF,DDF3); // mt cbi(DDRF, PORTF3);
```

And we disable the ADC and return the calculated value.

```
cbi(ADCSRA, ADEN);        // disable the ADC

return ADCr;
```

Giving us the ADC_read function:

```
int ADC_read(void)
{
    char i;
    int ADC_temp;
    // mt int ADC = 0 ;
    int ADCr = 0;

    // To save power, the voltage over the LDR and the NTC is
    // turned off when not used. This is done by controlling the
    // voltage from an I/O-pin (PORTF3)
    sbi(PORTF, PF3); // Enable the VCP (VC-peripheral)
    sbi(DDRF, DDF3); // sbi(DDRF, PORTF3);

    sbi(ADCSRA, ADEN);        // Enable the ADC

    //do a dummy readout first
    ADCSRA |= (1<<ADSC);           // do single conversion

    // wait for conversion done, ADIF flag active
    while(!(ADCSRA & 0x10));

    // do the ADC conversion 8 times for better accuracy
    for(i=0;i<8;i++)
    {
        ADCSRA |= (1<<ADSC);           // do single conversion

        // wait for conversion done, ADIF flag active
        while(!(ADCSRA & 0x10));

        ADC_temp = ADCL;               // read out ADCL register
```

```
        ADC_temp += (ADCH << 8);      // read out ADCH register

        // accumulate result (8 samples) for later averaging
        ADCr += ADC_temp;
    }

    ADCr = ADCr >> 3;      // average the 8 samples

    cbi(PORTF,PF3); // disable the VCP
    cbi(DDRF,DDF3); // mt cbi(DDRF, PORTF3);

    cbi(ADCSRA, ADEN);       // disable the ADC

    return ADCr;
}
```

Light Meter

The Butterfly has a Light Dependent Resistor, LDR, connected to ADC channel 2. The resistance of the LDR decreases as the light increases, so the voltage measured will decrease as light decreases.
We write the getLight function:

```
void getLight()
{
    char light[]= {'0','0','0','\0'};
    int ADCresult = 0;

    // Initialize the ADC to the light sensor channel
    ADC_init(2);

    ADCresult = ADC_read();

    itoa(ADCresult, light, 10);

    // Send the temperature to the PC
    sendString("The light reading is ");
    sendString(light);
    sendString(" somethings.\r");

}
```

This is straightforward and returns a value for the light. The light units 'somethings' is a precise scientific measure that means: 'I don't have a clue as to how the ADC value translates to light intensity'. I have no idea what the data means other than the amount of light is inversely proportional to the magnitude of the data sent back, just like it is supposed to be. I guess we could try to calibrate it in Lumens, or furlongs or something… nah, Let's move on.

Temperature Meter

We will measure the temperature in Fahrenheit and use an array of constants to convert the value from a voltage to a temperature. The table is from the Butterfly code.

```
// Positive Fahrenheit temperatures (ADC-value)
const int TEMP_Fahrenheit_pos[] PROGMEM =
{    // from 0 to 140 degrees
      938, 935, 932, 929, 926, 923, 920, 916, 913, 909, 906, 902,
      898, 894, 891, 887, 882, 878, 874, 870, 865, 861, 856, 851,
      847, 842, 837, 832, 827, 822, 816, 811, 806, 800, 795, 789,
      783, 778, 772, 766, 760, 754, 748, 742, 735, 729, 723, 716,
      710, 703, 697, 690, 684, 677, 670, 663, 657, 650, 643, 636,
      629, 622, 616, 609, 602, 595, 588, 581, 574, 567, 560, 553,
      546, 539, 533, 526, 519, 512, 505, 498, 492, 485, 478, 472,
      465, 459, 452, 446, 439, 433, 426, 420, 414, 408, 402, 396,
      390, 384, 378, 372, 366, 360, 355, 349, 344, 338, 333, 327,
      322, 317, 312, 307, 302, 297, 292, 287, 282, 277, 273, 268,
      264, 259, 255, 251, 246, 242, 238, 234, 230, 226, 222, 219,
      215, 211, 207, 204, 200, 197, 194, 190, 187,
};

void getTemperature()
{
      char fahr[]= {'0','0','0','\0'};

      int ADCresult = 0;
      int i = 0;

      // Initialize the ADC to the temperature sensor channel
      //ADC_init(0);
      ADMUX = 0;//input;

      ADCresult = ADC_read();

      /* The pgm_read_word() function is part of WinAVR and reads
      a word from the program space with a 16-bit (near) address,
```

as in the table. When a table entry is found that is less than the ADC result we break and i equals the temperature in Fahrenheit. Pretty clever, huh? Wish I thought of it, but I borrowed it from the WinAVR version of the Butterfly code. I'll quit owning up to all this theft and from now on if you see something clever (the good kind of clever) just assume that I stole it. */

```
for (i=0; i<=141; i++)
{
 if (ADCresult > pgm_read_word(&TEMP_Fahrenheit_pos[i]))
 {
     break;
 }
}
```

/* Next we convert the integer ADCresult to a string that we can transmit to the PC. Let's use a function from the standard library. We add #include <stdlib.h> to our file. Then we can use the itoa() function, which converts and integer to an ASCII character array terminated with '\0'. */

```
itoa(i, fahr, 10);

// Send the temperature to the PC
sendString("The temperature is ");
sendString(fahr);
sendString(" degrees Fahrenheit.\r");

}
```

The @#%#&*#!!!! Volt Meter

If you read the debugging tale, you know where the "@#%#&*#!!!!" comes from.

```
void getVolt()
{
        char voltintpart[]= {'0','0','0','\0'};
        char voltfractpart[]= {'0','0','0','\0'};
        int intpart = 0;
        int fractpart = 0;
        int ADCresult = 0;
```

```
    ADCresult = ADC_read();
    intpart = ADCresult/50;
    fractpart = ADCresult%50;

    itoa(intpart, voltintpart, 10);
    itoa(fractpart, voltfractpart, 10);

    // Send the voltage to the PC
    sendString("The reading is ");
    sendChar(voltintpart [0]);
    sendChar('.');
    sendChar(voltfractpart [0]);
    sendString(" volts.\r");
}
```

The initializer and the parseInput functions:

Open a new directory, ADC, and copy the Demonstrator and PC_Comm .c and .h files from the last project. Change the Demonsrator.c by adding the following functions and the above functions. Compile, load, and test.

```
#include "PC_Comm.h"
#include "Demonstrator.h"

void initializer()
{
    // Calibrate the oscillator:
    OSCCAL_calibration();

    // Initialize the USART
    USARTinit();

    ADC_init(1);

    // say hello
    sendString("\rPC_Comm.c ready to communicate.\r");
    // identify yourself specifically
    sendString("You are talking to the ADC demo.\r");
    // show commands
    sendString("Commands:\r");
    sendString("light - returns a light value\r");
    sendString("temp - returns the temperature in fahrenheit\r");
    sendString("volt - returns a voltage value\r");

}
```

```
void parseInput(char s[])
{
 // parse first character
 switch (s[0])
 {
  case 'l':
   if((s[1]=='i') && (s[2]=='g')&& (s[3]=='h') && (s[4 =='t'))
      getLight();
      break;
  case 't':
   if((s[1] == 'e') && (s[2] == 'm')&& (s[3] == 'p'))
      getTemperature();
      break;
  case 'v':
   if((s[1] == 'o') && (s[2] == 'l')&& (s[3] == 't'))
      getVolt();
      break;
  case 'd':
   if((s[1]=='e') && (s[2]=='m') && (s[3]=='o') && (s[4]=='?'))
      sendString("You are talking to the ADC demo.\r");
      break;
  default:
      sendString("\rYou sent: '");
      sendChar(s[0]);
      sendString("' - I don't understand.\r");
      break;

 }
  s[0] = '\0';
}
```

Using ADC

When you turn on the Butterfly you should see the following on HyperTerminal:

```
PC_Comm.c ready to communicate.
You are talking to the ADC demo.
Commands:
light - returns a light value
temp - returns the temperature in fahrenheit
volt - returns a voltage value
```

Type in:

```
temp
```

The response looks like:

```
The temperature is 78 degrees Fahrenheit.
```

Turn on a fan! 78 degrees Fahrenheit is too darn hot to work.

Put a flashlight on the light sensor and type in:

```
light
```

The response is a low number for a high light level:

```
The light reading is 236 somethings.
```

Using the room light and type in:

```
light
```

The response is a medium number for a medium light level:

```
The light reading is 645 somethings.
```

Put your finger over the sensor to block the room light and type:

```
light
```

The response is a high number for a low light level:

```
The light reading is 1004 somethings.
```

Type in:

volt

The response looks like:

```
The reading is 0.0 volts.
```

Urrrrmmmm… Oh yes, if we are going to measure voltage, we need to put a voltage on pin 2 of J407 on the Butterfly. But first we need solder some wires on a potentiometer so we can vary a voltage. The JAMECO parts list has a 10 k Ohm potentiometer listed. As in Figure 28, we connect one side to +3V and the other to GND, then we connect the middle to pin 1 of J407, the ADC connector, as shown in Figure 26. By turning the potentiometer shaft we move a wiper connected to the center wire up or down. The full +3V is dropped across the potentiometer and the center leg 'sees' a voltage proportional to the resistance above and below it.

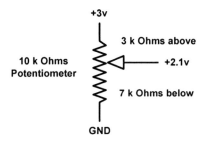

Figure 28: Potentiometer Schematic

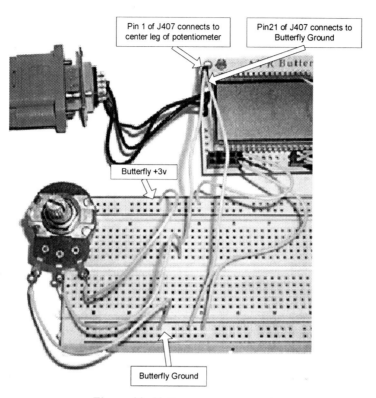

Figure 29: Voltage measurement

Now we can get some responses. Try turning the potentiometer to various settings and in response to a volt command you should see something like:

```
volt
The reading is 2.1 volts.
volt
The reading is 3.0 volts.
volt
The reading is 1.4 volts.
volt
The reading is 0.4 volts.
```

DAC and ADC - Function Generator / Digital Oscilloscope

In this project we will use a Digital to Analog Converter, DAC, made with a R-2R resistor ladder circuit that will output voltages from 0 to +3V in 255 steps. We will use voltage values stored in look-up tables to generate 'functions' which in this case are repeating wave forms: sine, square, triangle, and sawtooth. Since this is an educational enterprise we will reuse the software with the millisecond interrupt making our 'wave' frequencies pretty slow.

We will also develop a Digital Oscilloscope, using the Butterfly's ADC and reusing the ADC project software to read the data from our Function Generator. Since Digital Oscilloscopes normally cost tens of thousands of dollars, you can expect some compromises. This thing is very very very ... very slow. (And the 'screen' is rotated 90 degrees.) If you set the 'ctc' to 250 you can see the wave output on HyperTerminal. If you set 'ctc' to 1, you can see the signal on a real oscilloscope.

We will output the look-up table data on port D and attach the pins as shown in Figure 30. An R-2R resistor ladder looks a little magical, and the circuit analysis, though simple in concept, turns out to be fairly complex, but it makes a reasonably accurate DAC for very little cost. Usually you'll see two resistor values in this type circuit, in our case we would use a single 4.4k Ohm resistor in place of the two 2.2k resistors, but since we got 100 2.2k resistors from our JAMECO list, Let's just use two of each for the 4.4k resistors. The 2.2k and 4.4k are not magical numbers; you can use any value for R as long as the other is 2R and not be so low as to drain the battery or so high as to block the current.

Using the 2.2k resistors from the JAMECO list construct your DAC using the schematic in Figure 30, which is illustrated by the close-up photo in Figure 31, a medium distant photo in Figure 32, and the full setup in Figure 33 complete with a sine wave on an oscilloscope.

If you don't have an oscilloscope, just connect the output of the DAC to the Butterfly ADC on J407, just like with the potentiometer as shown in Figure 29. Now you can read the output using HyperTerminal and have a really slow crappy sideways oscilloscope as shown in Figure 34.

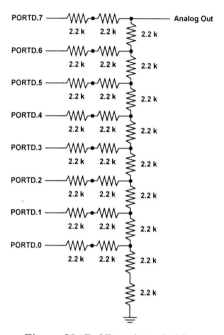

Figure 30: R-2R resistor ladder

Figure 31: Breadboard of R-2R DAC

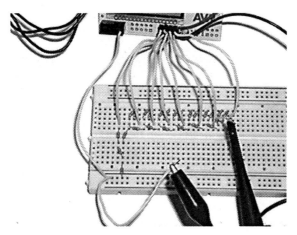

Figure 32: Breadboard R-2R DAC wiring

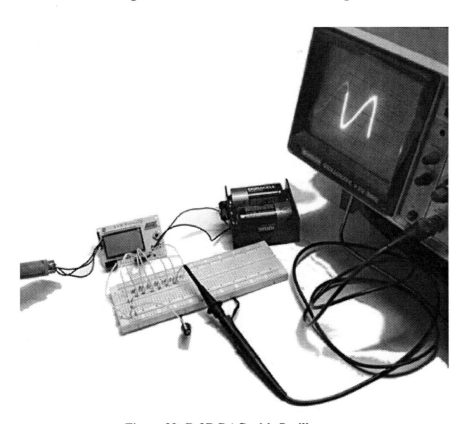

Figure 33: R-2R DAC with Oscilloscope

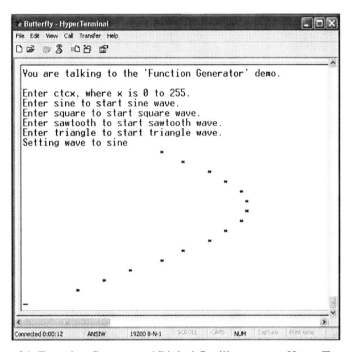

Figure 34: Function Generator / Digital Oscilloscope on HyperTerminal

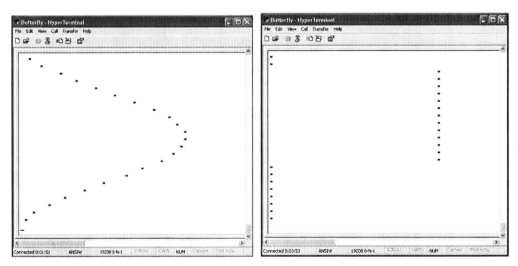

Figure 35: Sine Wave

Figure 36: Square Wave

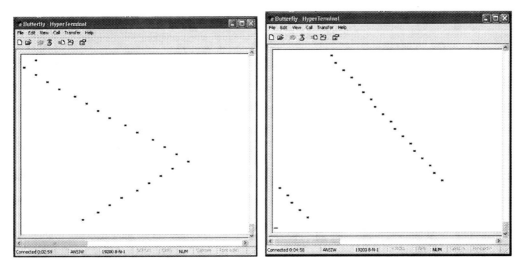

Figure 37: Triangle Wave   **Figure 38: Sawtooth Wave**

Your skills as a C programmer should be to the point where you can read and understand all the software for this project without further comment. So I'll just give you the listing and let you have at it.

```
// Demonstrator.h Function Generator / Digital Oscilloscope version

void initializer(void);
void parseInput(char *);
void showMessage(char);


int parse_ctc(char *);
void set_ctc(int);

void startWave(int);
void startSine(void);
void startSquare(void);
void startSawtooth(void);
void startTriangle(void);

void DigitalOscilloscopeTimerInit(void);

void MilliSec_init(unsigned char count);
void set_OCR0A(unsigned char count);

void ADC_init(void);
int ADC_read(void);


// Demonstrator.c Function Generator / Digital Oscilloscope version
```

231

```
#include "PC_Comm.h"
#include "Messages.h"
#include "WaveTables.h"

unsigned char count = 0;
unsigned char tenth = 0;
//unsigned long signal = 0; // used for test

void initializer()
{
        // Calibrate the oscillator:
        OSCCAL_calibration();

        // Initialize the USART
        USARTinit();

        // set PORTD for output
        DDRD = 0xFF;

        // Display instructions on PC
        sendFString(TALKING_TO);
        sendFString(WHO_DEMO);

        sendFString(ENTER);
        sendFString(TEXT_CTC);

        sendFString(ENTER);
        sendFString(TEXT_SINE);
        sendFString(TO_START);
        sendFString(TEXT_SINE);
        sendFString(WAVE);

        sendFString(ENTER);
        sendFString(TEXT_SQUARE);
        sendFString(TO_START);
        sendFString(TEXT_SQUARE);
        sendFString(WAVE);

        sendFString(ENTER);
        sendFString(TEXT_SAWTOOTH);
        sendFString(TO_START);
        sendFString(TEXT_SAWTOOTH);
        sendFString(WAVE);

        sendFString(ENTER);
        sendFString(TEXT_TRIANGLE);
        sendFString(TO_START);
        sendFString(TEXT_TRIANGLE);
        sendFString(WAVE);


        MilliSec_init(250); // default to 1000 Hz

        DigitalOscilloscopeTimerInit();

        ADC_init();
```

```
            startSine();
}

void parseInput(char s[])
{

  // parse first character
  switch (s[0])
  {
    case 's':
        if( (s[1] == 'i') && (s[2] == 'n')&& (s[3] == 'e'))
            startSine();
        else if((s[1]=='q')&&(s[2]=='u')&&(s[3]=='a')&&(s[4]=='r')&&(s[5]=='e'))
            startSquare();
        else if((s[1]=='a')&&(s[2]=='w'&&(s[3]=='t')&&(s[4]=='o')&&(s[5]=='o')
        &&(s[6]=='t')&&(s[7]=='h'))
            startSawtooth();
            break;
     case't':
        if((s[1]=='r')&&(s[2]=='i')&&(s[3]=='a')&&(s[4]=='n')&&(s[5]=='g')&&(s[6]=
            ='l')&&(s[7]=='e'))
            startTriangle();
            break;
    case 'c':
        if( (s[1] == 't') && (s[2] == 'c'))
            parse_ctc(s);
            break;
    case 'd':
        if( (s[1] == 'e') && (s[2] == 'm') && (s[3] == 'o') && (s[4] == '?') )
            sendFString(TALKING_TO);
            sendFString(WHO_DEMO);
            break;
    default:
            sendFString(BAD_COMMAND1);
            sendChar(s[0]);
            sendFString(BAD_COMMAND2);

            break;
    }
    s[0] = '\0';
}

int parse_ctc(char s[])
{
        char ctc[11];
        unsigned char i = 3, j = 0;

        while( (s[i] != '\0') && (j <= 11) )
        {

                if( (s[i] >= '0') && (s[i] <= '9') )
                {
                        ctc[j++] = s[i++];
                }
                else
                {
                        sendFString(ERROR_NONINT);
```

```
                        sendChar(s[i]);
                        sendChar('\r');
                        return 0;
                }
        }

        ctc[j] = '\0';

        if(j>4)// must be < 256
        {
                sendFString(ERROR_NUMTOLARGE);
                return 0;
        }
        else
        {
                set_ctc(atoi(ctc));
        }

        return 1;
}

void set_ctc(int count)
{
        char ctc[11];

        sendString("Setting the Compare Timer Count to: ");
        itoa(count,ctc,10);
        sendString(ctc);
        sendChar('\r');

        MilliSec_init(count);

}

void startWave(int wave)
{
        sendFString(TEXT_SETTING);
        sendFString(TEXT_WAVE_TBL[wave]);      // Send the song title to the PC
        sendChar('\r');

        pWave=(int*)pgm_read_word(&Waves[wave]); // looks too complicated..
}

void startSine()
{
        startWave(0);
}
void startSquare()
{
        startWave(1);
}
void startSawtooth()
{
        startWave(2);
}
void startTriangle()
{
```

```
        startWave(3);
}


/*
The USART init set the system oscillator to 2 MHz. We set the Timer0 prescaler
to clk/8 which gives a 250 kHz input to the timer/counter. A compare of 250 throws
an interrupt every millisecond.
*/
void MilliSec_init(unsigned char count)
{
        // Initialize Timer0.

        // Enable timer0 compare interrupt
        TIMSK0 = (1<<OCIE0A);

        // Sets the compare value
        set_OCR0A(count);

        // Set Clear on Timer Compare (CTC) mode,
        TCCR0A = (1<<WGM01)|(0<<WGM00)|(1<<CS02)|(0<<CS01)|(0<<CS00);

}

// Initialize for 1 millisecond interrupt
void DigitalOscilloscopeTimerInit()
{
        // Initialize Timer2.

    // Enable timer2 compare interrupt
        TIMSK2 = (1<<OCIE2A);

        // Sets the compare value
        OCR2A = 1;

        // Set Clear on Timer Compare (CTC) mode,
        TCCR2A = (1<<WGM21)|(0<<WGM20)|(1<<CS22)|(0<<CS21)|(0<<CS20);

}


void set_OCR0A(unsigned char count)
{
        // Sets the compare value
        OCR0A = count;
}


// Interrupt occurs once per millisecond
SIGNAL(SIG_OUTPUT_COMPARE0)
{
//      signal += pgm_read_word(pWave + count);  // used for test
        PORTD = pgm_read_word(pWave + count++);     // read table
        tenth++;
}
```

```
// Interrupt occurs once per millisecond
SIGNAL(SIG_OUTPUT_COMPARE2)
{
        int sig = 0;

        sig = ADC_read();

        if (tenth >= 10)
        {
                tenth = 0;

                for(int i = 0; i < (sig/4); i++)
                {
                        sendChar(' ');
                }
                sendChar('*');
                sendChar('\r');
        }

/*      // Test code to output wave from table to HyperTerminal
        if (tenth >= 10)
        {
                tenth = 0;
                signal /= 50;

                for(int i = 0; i < signal; i++)
                {
                        sendChar(' ');
                }
                sendChar('*');
                sendChar('\r');
                signal = 0;
        }
*/

}

/*******************************************************************************
*
        ADC common functions
********************************************************************************
*/

void ADC_init()
{
        int dummy = 0;

    ADMUX = 1;

    // set ADC prescaler to , 1MHz / 8 = 125kHz
    ADCSRA = (1<<ADEN) | (1<<ADPS1) | (1<<ADPS0);

    //  Take a dummy reading , which basically allows the ADC
    // to hack up any hairballs before we take any real readings
    dummy = ADC_read();
}
```

```
int ADC_read(void)
{
    char i;
    int ADC_temp;
        // mt int ADC = 0 ;
        int ADCr = 0;

    // To save power, the voltage over the LDR and the NTC is turned off when not
used
    // This is done by controlling the voltage from a I/O-pin (PORTF3)
    sbi(PORTF, PF3); // mt sbi(PORTF, PORTF3);          // Enable the VCP (VC-
peripheral)
    sbi(DDRF, DDF3); // sbi(DDRF, PORTF3);

    sbi(ADCSRA, ADEN);      // Enable the ADC

    //do a dummy readout first
    ADCSRA |= (1<<ADSC);        // do single conversion
    while(!(ADCSRA & 0x10));    // wait for conversion done, ADIF flag active

    for(i=0;i<8;i++)                // do the ADC conversion 8 times for better
accuracy
    {
        ADCSRA |= (1<<ADSC);        // do single conversion
        while(!(ADCSRA & 0x10));    // wait for conversion done, ADIF flag active

        ADC_temp = ADCL;            // read out ADCL register
        ADC_temp += (ADCH << 8);    // read out ADCH register

        ADCr += ADC_temp;           // accumulate result (8 samples) for later
averaging
    }

    ADCr = ADCr >> 3;       // average the 8 samples

    cbi(PORTF,PF3); // mt cbi(PORTF, PORTF3);       // disable the VCP
    cbi(DDRF,DDF3); // mt cbi(DDRF, PORTF3);

    cbi(ADCSRA, ADEN);      // disable the ADC

    return ADCr;
}


// WaveTables.h

const int Sine[] PROGMEM =
{
0x80,0x83,0x86,0x89,0x8c,0x8f,0x92,0x95,0x98,0x9c,0x9f,0xa2,0xa5,0xa8,0xab,0xae,
0xb0,0xb3,0xb6,0xb9,0xbc,0xbf,0xc1,0xc4,0xc7,0xc9,0xcc,0xce,0xd1,0xd3,0xd5,0xd8,
0xda,0xdc,0xde,0xe0,0xe2,0xe4,0xe6,0xe8,0xea,0xec,0xed,0xef,0xf0,0xf2,0xf3,0xf5,
0xf6,0xf7,0xf8,0xf9,0xfa,0xfb,0xfc,0xfc,0xfd,0xfe,0xfe,0xff,0xff,0xff,0xff,0xff,
0xff,0xff,0xff,0xff,0xff,0xff,0xfe,0xfe,0xfd,0xfc,0xfc,0xfb,0xfa,0xf9,0xf8,0xf7,
0xf6,0xf5,0xf3,0xf2,0xf0,0xef,0xed,0xec,0xea,0xe8,0xe6,0xe4,0xe2,0xe0,0xde,0xdc,
0xda,0xd8,0xd5,0xd3,0xd1,0xce,0xcc,0xc9,0xc7,0xc4,0xc1,0xbf,0xbc,0xb9,0xb6,0xb3,
0xb0,0xae,0xab,0xa8,0xa5,0xa2,0x9f,0x9c,0x98,0x95,0x92,0x8f,0x8c,0x89,0x86,0x83,
0x80,0x7c,0x79,0x76,0x73,0x70,0x6d,0x6a,0x67,0x63,0x60,0x5d,0x5a,0x57,0x54,0x51,
0x4f,0x4c,0x49,0x46,0x43,0x40,0x3e,0x3b,0x38,0x36,0x33,0x31,0x2e,0x2c,0x2a,0x27,
```

```
0x25,0x23,0x21,0x1f,0x1d,0x1b,0x19,0x17,0x15,0x13,0x12,0x10,0x0f,0x0d,0x0c,0x0a,
0x09,0x08,0x07,0x06,0x05,0x04,0x03,0x03,0x02,0x01,0x01,0x00,0x00,0x00,0x00,0x00,
0x00,0x00,0x00,0x00,0x00,0x00,0x01,0x01,0x02,0x03,0x03,0x04,0x05,0x06,0x07,0x08,
0x09,0x0a,0x0c,0x0d,0x0f,0x10,0x12,0x13,0x15,0x17,0x19,0x1b,0x1d,0x1f,0x21,0x23,
0x25,0x27,0x2a,0x2c,0x2e,0x31,0x33,0x36,0x38,0x3b,0x3e,0x40,0x43,0x46,0x49,0x4c,
0x4f,0x51,0x54,0x57,0x5a,0x5d,0x60,0x63,0x67,0x6a,0x6d,0x70,0x73,0x76,0x79,0x7c
};

const int Square[] PROGMEM =
{
0x00,0x00,0x00,0x00,0x00,0x00,0x00,0x00,0x00,0x00,0x00,0x00,0x00,0x00,0x00,0x00,
0x00,0x00,0x00,0x00,0x00,0x00,0x00,0x00,0x00,0x00,0x00,0x00,0x00,0x00,0x00,0x00,
0x00,0x00,0x00,0x00,0x00,0x00,0x00,0x00,0x00,0x00,0x00,0x00,0x00,0x00,0x00,0x00,
0x00,0x00,0x00,0x00,0x00,0x00,0x00,0x00,0x00,0x00,0x00,0x00,0x00,0x00,0x00,0x00,
0x00,0x00,0x00,0x00,0x00,0x00,0x00,0x00,0x00,0x00,0x00,0x00,0x00,0x00,0x00,0x00,
0x00,0x00,0x00,0x00,0x00,0x00,0x00,0x00,0x00,0x00,0x00,0x00,0x00,0x00,0x00,0x00,
0x00,0x00,0x00,0x00,0x00,0x00,0x00,0x00,0x00,0x00,0x00,0x00,0x00,0x00,0x00,0x00,
0x00,0x00,0x00,0x00,0x00,0x00,0x00,0x00,0x00,0x00,0x00,0x00,0x00,0x00,0x00,0x00,
0xff,0xff,0xff,0xff,0xff,0xff,0xff,0xff,0xff,0xff,0xff,0xff,0xff,0xff,0xff,0xff,
0xff,0xff,0xff,0xff,0xff,0xff,0xff,0xff,0xff,0xff,0xff,0xff,0xff,0xff,0xff,0xff,
0xff,0xff,0xff,0xff,0xff,0xff,0xff,0xff,0xff,0xff,0xff,0xff,0xff,0xff,0xff,0xff,
0xff,0xff,0xff,0xff,0xff,0xff,0xff,0xff,0xff,0xff,0xff,0xff,0xff,0xff,0xff,0xff,
0xff,0xff,0xff,0xff,0xff,0xff,0xff,0xff,0xff,0xff,0xff,0xff,0xff,0xff,0xff,0xff,
0xff,0xff,0xff,0xff,0xff,0xff,0xff,0xff,0xff,0xff,0xff,0xff,0xff,0xff,0xff,0xff,
0xff,0xff,0xff,0xff,0xff,0xff,0xff,0xff,0xff,0xff,0xff,0xff,0xff,0xff,0xff,0xff,
0xff,0xff,0xff,0xff,0xff,0xff,0xff,0xff,0xff,0xff,0xff,0xff,0xff,0xff,0xff,0xff
};

const int Sawtooth[] PROGMEM =
{
0x00,0x01,0x02,0x03,0x04,0x05,0x06,0x07,0x08,0x09,0x0a,0x0b,0x0c,0x0d,0x0e,0x0f,
0x10,0x11,0x12,0x13,0x14,0x15,0x16,0x17,0x18,0x19,0x1a,0x1b,0x1c,0x1d,0x1e,0x1f,
0x20,0x21,0x22,0x23,0x24,0x25,0x26,0x27,0x28,0x29,0x2a,0x2b,0x2c,0x2d,0x2e,0x2f,
0x30,0x31,0x32,0x33,0x34,0x35,0x36,0x37,0x38,0x39,0x3a,0x3b,0x3c,0x3d,0x3e,0x3f,
0x40,0x41,0x42,0x43,0x44,0x45,0x46,0x47,0x48,0x49,0x4a,0x4b,0x4c,0x4d,0x4e,0x4f,
0x50,0x51,0x52,0x53,0x54,0x55,0x56,0x57,0x58,0x59,0x5a,0x5b,0x5c,0x5d,0x5e,0x5f,
0x60,0x61,0x62,0x63,0x64,0x65,0x66,0x67,0x68,0x69,0x6a,0x6b,0x6c,0x6d,0x6e,0x6f,
0x70,0x71,0x72,0x73,0x74,0x75,0x76,0x77,0x78,0x79,0x7a,0x7b,0x7c,0x7d,0x7e,0x7f,
0x80,0x81,0x82,0x83,0x84,0x85,0x86,0x87,0x88,0x89,0x8a,0x8b,0x8c,0x8d,0x8e,0x8f,
0x90,0x91,0x92,0x93,0x94,0x95,0x96,0x97,0x98,0x99,0x9a,0x9b,0x9c,0x9d,0x9e,0x9f,
0xa0,0xa1,0xa2,0xa3,0xa4,0xa5,0xa6,0xa7,0xa8,0xa9,0xaa,0xab,0xac,0xad,0xae,0xaf,
0xb0,0xb1,0xb2,0xb3,0xb4,0xb5,0xb6,0xb7,0xb8,0xb9,0xba,0xbb,0xbc,0xbd,0xbe,0xbf,
0xc0,0xc1,0xc2,0xc3,0xc4,0xc5,0xc6,0xc7,0xc8,0xc9,0xca,0xcb,0xcc,0xcd,0xce,0xcf,
0xd0,0xd1,0xd2,0xd3,0xd4,0xd5,0xd6,0xd7,0xd8,0xd9,0xda,0xdb,0xdc,0xdd,0xde,0xdf,
0xe0,0xe1,0xe2,0xe3,0xe4,0xe5,0xe6,0xe7,0xe8,0xe9,0xea,0xeb,0xec,0xed,0xee,0xef,
0xf0,0xf1,0xf2,0xf3,0xf4,0xf5,0xf6,0xf7,0xf8,0xf9,0xfa,0xfb,0xfc,0xfd,0xfe,0xff
};

const int Triangle[] PROGMEM =
{
0x00,0x02,0x04,0x06,0x08,0x0a,0x0c,0x0e,0x10,0x12,0x14,0x16,0x18,0x1a,0x1c,0x1e,
0x20,0x22,0x24,0x26,0x28,0x2a,0x2c,0x2e,0x30,0x32,0x34,0x36,0x38,0x3a,0x3c,0x3e,
0x40,0x42,0x44,0x46,0x48,0x4a,0x4c,0x4e,0x50,0x52,0x54,0x56,0x58,0x5a,0x5c,0x5e,
0x60,0x62,0x64,0x66,0x68,0x6a,0x6c,0x6e,0x70,0x72,0x74,0x76,0x78,0x7a,0x7c,0x7e,
0x80,0x82,0x84,0x86,0x88,0x8a,0x8c,0x8e,0x90,0x92,0x94,0x96,0x98,0x9a,0x9c,0x9e,
0xa0,0xa2,0xa4,0xa6,0xa8,0xaa,0xac,0xae,0xb0,0xb2,0xb4,0xb6,0xb8,0xba,0xbc,0xbe,
0xc0,0xc2,0xc4,0xc6,0xc8,0xca,0xcc,0xce,0xd0,0xd2,0xd4,0xd6,0xd8,0xda,0xdc,0xde,
```

```
0xe0,0xe2,0xe4,0xe6,0xe8,0xea,0xec,0xee,0xf0,0xf2,0xf4,0xf6,0xf8,0xfa,0xfc,0xfe,
0xff,0xfd,0xfb,0xf9,0xf7,0xf5,0xf3,0xf1,0xef,0xef,0xeb,0xe9,0xe7,0xe5,0xe3,0xe1,
0xdf,0xdd,0xdb,0xd9,0xd7,0xd5,0xd3,0xd1,0xcf,0xcf,0xcb,0xc9,0xc7,0xc5,0xc3,0xc1,
0xbf,0xbd,0xbb,0xb9,0xb7,0xb5,0xb3,0xb1,0xaf,0xaf,0xab,0xa9,0xa7,0xa5,0xa3,0xa1,
0x9f,0x9d,0x9b,0x99,0x97,0x95,0x93,0x91,0x8f,0x8f,0x8b,0x89,0x87,0x85,0x83,0x81,
0x7f,0x7d,0x7b,0x79,0x77,0x75,0x73,0x71,0x6f,0x6f,0x6b,0x69,0x67,0x65,0x63,0x61,
0x5f,0x5d,0x5b,0x59,0x57,0x55,0x53,0x51,0x4f,0x4f,0x4b,0x49,0x47,0x45,0x43,0x41,
0x3f,0x3d,0x3b,0x39,0x37,0x35,0x33,0x31,0x2f,0x2f,0x2b,0x29,0x27,0x25,0x23,0x21,
0x1f,0x1d,0x1b,0x19,0x17,0x15,0x13,0x11,0x0f,0x0f,0x0b,0x09,0x07,0x05,0x03,0x01
};

const char TEXT_WAVE1[] PROGMEM = "sine";
const char TEXT_WAVE2[] PROGMEM = "square";
const char TEXT_WAVE3[] PROGMEM = "sawtooth";
const char TEXT_WAVE4[] PROGMEM = "triangle";

// pointer-array with pointers to the wave arrays
const int *Waves[] PROGMEM = { Sine, Square, Sawtooth, Triangle, 0};

const char *TEXT_WAVE_TBL[] = { TEXT_WAVE1, TEXT_WAVE2, TEXT_WAVE3, TEXT_WAVE4,
0};

const int *pWave;       // point to a ram location (pointer array Waves)
```

Chapter 10: C Structures

Structure Basics

A structure is a collection of variables that may be of different types all grouped together under a single name. They are like records in other programming languages and form a data unit that is convenient to handle. This convenience is very useful in large programs because it allows us to group related variables and handle them as a 'family' rather than as individuals. For example:

```
struct Pardue {
        string Joe = "Joe";
        string Clay = "Clay";
        string Beth = "Beth";
}
```

groups Joe, Clay, and Beth all in the Pardue family structure. In software we can refer to me as: Joe.Pardue or Joe->Pardue depending on the use.

Structures can come in all sizes. A small one would be useful in the PWM project to link the pulse frequency to the pulse width. A larger one could be used in the RTC project to link together all the time and date variables into a unit.

Let's look at a simple structure for pulse width modulation data. As we've seen we do PWM by varying the pulse frequency and the pulse width. We can declare a structure:

```
struct pwm {
        int pulseFreq;
        unsigned char pulseWidth;
};
```

We use the keyword struct to start the declaration, then provide the structure a name, and enclose the variable members in a block. The structure tag 'pwm' is optional and we can name the structure later when it is defined. The variable names are tied to the structure and we can legally define a variable 'int pulseFreq' later and use it separate from the structure, the compiler would differentiate between pulseFreq and pwm.pulseFreq. As we'll see in a minute, this reuse of names, normally a no-no, can help clarify code.

The structure declaration creates a data type, and like other data types variables can be declared to be of that type:

```
int x, y, z; // declare x,y,z as ints
struct pwm { … } a,b,c;  //declare a,b,c as pwm structs
```

Usually you see this done as:

```
struct pwm {
       int pulseFreq;
       unsigned char pulseWidth;
}pulser1,pulser2,pulser3;
```

which creates three instances, pulser1,pulser2,pulser3, of the struct pwm.

This 'declaration versus instantiation' of a structure is an important concept that you'll see a lot if you move on up to C++. The first declaration of pwm did not have a variable list following it, so it exists as a prototype and no memory is allocated. In the second version, where we added the variables, pulser1,pulser2, and pulser3, we actually create three copies (instances) of the structure in memory. Not only is instantiation an important word in the object oriented programming world, it's very geeky to find uses for it in ordinary conversation. "Hey babe, wanna instantiate our procreative potential?"

We can instantiate our struct and assign data to it:

```
struct pwm pulser1 = { 1000, 127};
```

which defines a pulse with a frequency of 1 kHz and a 50% duty cycle (remember that 127 is half of 255 which is 100%).

We access members of structs using the structure member operator '.':

```
int x,y;

x = pulser1.pulseFreq; // x now equals 1000
```

```
y = pulser1.pulseWidth // y now equals 127;
```

Structures can be nested:

```
struct pwms {
        struct pwm pulser1;
        struct pwm pulser2;
        struct pwm pulser2;
        int numPulsers = 3;
}myPWMS;
```

and to access pulser1 pulseFreq we use:

x = myPWMS.pulser1.pulseFreq;

While it may not seem like it at this time, this kind of syntax can make programs easier to write and understand, with the usually warning that C gurus will use them to impress and thereby confuse you.

Structures and Functions

You can do four things to a structure:

1. Copy it
2. Assign to it as a unit
3. Take its address with &
4. Access its members

Let's write some functions to modulate some pulses and see how to use structures with them. We could approach this three ways:

1. Pass components to the functions separately.
2. Pass an entire structure to the function.
3. Pass a pointer to a structure to the function.

In a moment we'll see why #3 is best.

We will write a function makePWM to initialize a PWM structure by accepting an int and an unsigned char as arguments and returning a pointer to a pwm structure. First Let's redo the struct:

```
struct {
        int pulseFreq;
        unsigned pulseWidth;
}pwm;
```

then we write our function:

```
struct pwm makePWM(int pulseFreq, unsigned char pulseWidth)
{
        struct pwm temp;

        temp.pulseFreq = pulseFreq;
        temp.pulseWidth = pulseWidth;
        return temp;
}
```

In this function we reuse the names pulseFreq and pulseWidth and cause no conflict because one set is bound to the struct and the other is bound to the function.

We can use makePWM to dynamically initialize structures:

```
struct pwm pulser1k50;
struct pwm pulser1k25;
struct pwm pulser4k10;

pulser1k50 = makePWM(1000,128);//make a 50% duty 1000 kHz pulse
pulser1k25 = makePWM(1000,64);//make a 25% duty 1000 kHz pulse
pulser4k10 = makePWM(4000,25);//make a 10% duty 4000 kHz pulse
```

When we use a structure as an argument in a function we send a copy of the structure to the function. For tiny structures, this won't matter much, but for large structures we can eat a lot of RAM, since the entire structure will be pushed onto the stack. Let's write a function to find the pulse with the greatest width in a list of 3 pwm structs:

```
struct pwm widestPWM(struct pwm pulser1, struct pwm pulser2,
        struct pwm pulser3,)
{
     if(pulser1.width > pulser2.width)
     {
          if (pulser1.width > pulser3.width) return pulser1;
     }
     else if (pulser2.width > pulser3.width) return pulser2
     return pulser3;
}
```

But that's one big memory hog. We can save stack memory by defining a function to use struct pointers as paramerters:

```
// Declare a function with struct pointers as parameters
struct pwm widestPWM(struct pwm  *, struct pwm  *, struct pwm  *);

// Define it
struct pwm widestPWM(struct pwm *p1, struct pwm *p2, struct pwm *p3)
{
     if(p1->width > p2->width)
     {
          if (p1->width > p3->width) return p1;
     }
     else if (p2->width > p->width) return p2
     return p3;
}
```

Here we use the structure pointer operator '->' to access members of the struct passed by a pointer. Novices stumble all over using the structure member operator '.' and the structure pointer operator '->' operator, so be forewarned.

We use this function as follows:

```
   struct pwm pulser1k50;
   struct pwm pulser1k25;
   struct pwm pulser4k10;

   struct pwm myWidestPWM;

 myWidestPWM = widestPWM(&pulser1k50, &pulser1k25, &pulser4k10);
```

Structure Arrays

In the last section we used:

```
struct pwm pulser1k50;
struct pwm pulser1k25;
struct pwm pulser4k10;

pulser1k50 = makePWM(1000,128);//make a 50% duty 1000 kHz pulse
pulser1k25 = makePWM(1000,64);//make a 25% duty 1000 kHz pulse
pulser4k10 = makePWM(4000,25);//make a 10% duty 4000 kHz pulse
```

We could have defined an array of these structures and made them as follows

```
struct pwm pulser[] = {
        { 1000, 128 };
        { 1000, 64 };
        { 4000, 25);
}
```

Actually the prior, non-array version probably makes more sense because the instance names carry more user information. pulser1k25 versus pulser[1]. But there are cases where arrays of structures come in real handy.

Typedef

C allows us to create new data type names with the typedef facility.

```
typedef unsigned char Byte;
```

would cause the compiler to handle anything declared as Byte as if it was an unsigned char. Only actual C types can be aliased in this manner. Typedef works somewhat like define, in that it provides an alias, but defines are handled by the preprocessor and more limited in what they can do.

Typedefs are useful in making software more readable: Byte makes more sense in our use than unsigned char. Another use is to facilitate portability of software by putting machine specific types in typedefs so you can change them as you change machines.

Unions

A union provides a way to have a type that may be of different sizes depending on the circumstances of its use.

We use a union in prgmspacehlp.h to store a float or an int in the same program memory:

```
union
{
        int i[2];
        float f;
} u;
```

Bit-fields

ANSI C defines bit-fields as a member of a structure or union that is defined to be a cluster of bits. This cluster can be a single bit, as would be used for a flag, or a 4-bit nibble, or any number of bits you might want to define. These fields can be very useful, but unfortunately, in many microcontrollers, these bit-fields slow things down (the compiler promotes bit to larger data types) so for efficiency sake, bits are best dealt with using bit masking, which compiles to faster and smaller assembly code. Bit masking simply uses a constant to define the position of a bit in a byte and allows you to read or write only that bit using the bitwise operators. We will look at the C-way, since we are learning C, then the mask-way since we want to be as efficient as possible.

Bit-Fields the C-way

In some of our examples we have often declared an object as an unsigned char when that object could only have two values: TRUE or FALSE. Using bit-fields we can declare eight similar variables in a single unsigned char (note – not true for WinAVR, which promotes them all to eight bytes).

We could define:

```
unsigned char calibrate = FALSE;
```

to control a loop:

```
while(!calibrate) {  // do something while calibrate == FALSE};
```

which runs as long as calibrate equals FALSE. We could have used:

```
struct {
        unsigned int calibrate : 1;
        unsigned int this : 1;
        unsigned int that : 1;
        unsigned int the : 1;
        unsigned int other : 1;
        unsigned int tobe: 1;
        unsigned int or!tobe : 1;
        unsigned int hello : 1;
} flags;
```

Setting aside 8 flags in the space formerly used by calibrate. Now we control the loop:

```
while(!flags.calibrate)
```

That is, we could have done this in an ideal world. In the real world, our compiler would allow us to use the above syntax, but would assign 8 bytes to do the job. K&R notes: "Almost everything about fields is implementation dependent."

Bit-fields the masking-way

This is mostly a review of stuff presented with the bitwise operator section, but reviews are good. Let's look at a bit-masking example from OSCCAL.C:

We define an alias name for the Timer/Counter 2 Interrupt Flag Register:

```
#define TIFR2  _SFR_IO8(0x17)
```

Noting that the _SFR_IO8(0x17) is itself an alias defined elsewhere, but eventually is aliased to a specific register address on our ATMEGA169.

We next define two 'bit-fields' in the TIFR2 register;

```
#define OCF2A      1
#define TOV2       0
```

Next we write a function that causes our code to wait for the timer2 compare flag, OCF2A, which is bit one of the Timer/Counter2 Interrupt Flag Register:

```
while ( !(TIFR2 && (1<<OCF2A)) );// wait for timer2 compareflag
```

So this usage will do the same as a bit-field, but with greater efficiency.

Let's look at another example where we assign Port B to a 'bit-field structure' without using bit-fields or structures. First we get the address of the Port B registers from io169.h which also has defines for each bit.

```
/* Port B */
#define PINB    _SFR_IO8(0x03)
#define DDRB    _SFR_IO8(0x04)
#define PORTB   _SFR_IO8(0x05)

#define PB7 7
#define PB6 6
#define PB5 5
#define PB4 4
#define PB3 3
#define PB2 2
#define PB1 1
#define PB0 0
```

In the Butterfly software main.c file, the initialization function has:

```
PORTB = (15<<PB0);        // Enable pullup on
```

And we ask, what's with the 15? Well, 15 in hex is 0xE which in binary is 1110, so since PB0 == 0, what we are doing is setting PORTB equal to 00001110 << 0, remembering that '<<' is the left-shift operator we know that we actually aren't doing anything, or rather we are left shifting 15 zero times, which is doing nothing if I've ever seen nothing, which I haven't but… back to our story, we are setting PORTB pins 1, 2, and 3 to 1 thus enabling the pull-ups on port B pins 2, 3, and 4. And that ends this discussion.

This alternative bit-field technique is a compromise between the K&R way of doing things in C and the machine efficient way of doing things in C for microcontrollers.

Projects

Finite State Machine

I initially thought about naming this section "Finite State Machines, Lions, Tigers, and Bears... Oh My!" because the topic seems a bit scary. And I must admit that there are graduate level Computer Science courses taught on this subject, so it can get very scary indeed. But, fortunately for us, the fundamental concepts that we will use are fairly easy to grasp, and we don't need to go to great depths to get what we need.

The basic ideas behind finite state machines are used to tame systems that seem impossibly complex. A computer is a finite state machine. At any given moment the computer state is defined by a bunch of transistor states, off or on, 0's and 1's. The computer inputs a set of 0's and 1's, from some external source, checks its current state and changes both the current state and the output state based on the current state and the input state.

Actually you and I can be seen as state machines. Right now my state is 'typing'. If my ears input the sound of a screeching tiger my state will change to 'running like hell.' And, if my 'running like hell' state isn't >= the tigers 'running like hell' state, my future state may sequence through 'being lunch', being digested', and 'being tiger poop.'

When you think about it, the Butterfly, as simple as it is, does a lot of stuff. How does the software keep track of what it is doing? How does it know to keep doing it? How does it know when to do something different? And how does it know what to do next?

Say the Butterfly is outputting a value on PORTD and you diddle the joystick, how does it respond to being diddled? You may recall this switch statement from Chapter 5.

```
switch(input){
    case KEY_PLUS :
        PORTD = ~0x01;
        break:
```

```
                   case KEY_NEXT :
                        PORTD = ~0x02;
                        break;
                   case KEY_PREV :
                        PORTD = ~0x04;
                        break;
                   case KEY_MINUS :
                        PORTD = ~0x08;
                        break;
                   case KEY_ENTER :
                        PORTD = ~0x10;
                        break;
                   default:
           }
```

This is a state machine. The current state is the value of PORTD. The input is the joystick position. The case statement for the specific joystick input sets the next state in PORTD. If this switch statement is enclosed in a for(;;){}block, the Butterfly's states and transitions are all known, so the possibilities are finite and you have yourself a finite state machine. What could be simpler? (Usually said right before things get complex.)

But, of course, the Butterfly out of the box does a lot of stuff. And it has a lot of state machines controlling its behavior. One is the menu state machine, which is really the core state machine as far as a user is concerned. Here is an illustration of the Butterfly menu structure:

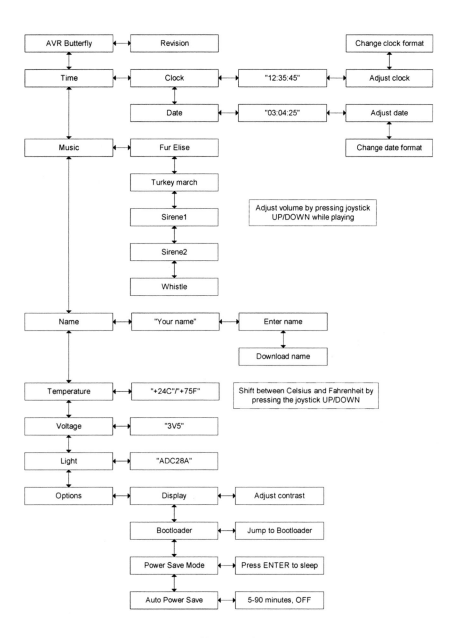

Figure 39 Butterfly Menu

At one moment the Butterfly may be scrolling the LCD with your name. Then you click the joystick down and it shows you the time. It needs to keep some sort of data set that contains what it is doing now and how to react to inputs and what to do next based on what is doing now.

We can think about input stimulated state transitions like this:

    If I am doing A_state and
            if A_input happens, then I enter Q7_state
            else if B_input happens, then I enter YM_state
            else if C_input happens, then I enter X15_state
            // and so on
            else if XXX_input happens, then I enter Mental_state
    If I am doing B_state and
            if A_input happens, then I enter B_state
            else if B_input happens, then I enter A_state
            else if C_input happens, then I enter Y_state
            // and so on
            and XXX_input happens, then I enter Pros_state
    // and so on
    If I am doing XXX_state and
            if A_input happens, then I enter Alpha_state
            else if B_input happens, then I enter Beta_state
            else if C_input happens, then I enter Gamma_state
            // and so on
            else if XXX_input happens, then I enter Tennessee_state

From the Butterfly menu we see that we can do this like:

    If I am showing "AVR Butterfly" on the LCD and
            if the joystick is clicked left, then I enter the Revision state
            else if the joystick is clicked down, then I enter the Time state
    If I am showing the "Time" on the LCD and
            if the joystick is clicked left, then I enter the Clock state
            else if the joystick is clicked down, then I enter the Music state
    // and so on
    If I am showing "Options" on the LCD and

if the joystick is clicked left, then I enter the Display state
else if the joystick is clicked down, then I enter the AVR Butterfly
state

For each state, we must know the next state that we must enter for each possible input state. That's going to be a lot of data so lets use what we've learned about structures to keep track of it. First we define two generic structures that we will later instantiate for each specific state, input, and next state data set.

[ASIDE: As mentioned before, the Butterfly software was written using an IAR compiler and ported to the Win AVR complier. There are a lot of notes in the code that begin // mt. This is a note added by Martin Thomas who did the porting. Kudo's to Martin, but I've removed his notes from the discussion as they are not relevant to what we are trying to learn here.]

In Menu.h we find the definitions of data structures for our menu state and menu next state that contains the three relevant variables:

```
typedef struct PROGMEM
{
    unsigned char state; // the current state
    PGM_P pText; // pointer to some text in FLASH memory
    char (*pFunc)(char input); // pointer to a function
} MENU_STATE;

typedef struct PROGMEM
{
    unsigned char state; // the current state
    unsigned char input; / the input stimulus
    unsigned char nextstate; // the resulting next state
} MENU_NEXTSTATE;
```

The MENU_STATE structure provides the data we need to find the function that should be run while in the specified state. The MENU_NEXTSTATE structure provides the data we need to find the next state given the present state and an input state.

Let's deal with the MENU_STATE structure first. We see that we can have 256 states, and can associate a text name and a function pointer with each. The function pointer is defined as taking a character input value and returning a

255

character to the caller. We define an array of instances of this structure in Menu.h as follows:

```
const MENU_STATE menu_state[] PROGMEM = {
//   STATE                 STATE TEXT            STATE_FUNC
    {ST_AVRBF,             MT_AVRBF,             NULL},
    {ST_AVRBF_REV,         NULL,                 Revision},
    {ST_TIME,              MT_TIME,              NULL},
    {ST_TIME_CLOCK,        MT_TIME_CLOCK,        NULL},

      // Lots more stuff

    {0,                    NULL,                 NULL},
};
```

We can use this as:

    menu_state[1].state   is defined as ST_AVRBF_REV
    menu_state[1].pText is defined as NULL
    menu_state[1].pFunc is defined as Revision

You will note in the table that each state has either a state text or a state function defined, but not both, that complication will be explained later.

For the MENU_NEXTSTATE structure we also have 256 possible states, and 256 possible inputs for each state, and 256 possible next states for all those, that's 65536 possible state transitions for each state, fortunately we won't need that many. We define an array of instances of this structure in Menu.h as follows:

```
const MENU_NEXTSTATE menu_nextstate[] PROGMEM = {
//   STATE                      INPUT        NEXT STATE
    {ST_AVRBF,                  KEY_PLUS,    ST_OPTIONS},
    {ST_AVRBF,                  KEY_NEXT,    ST_AVRBF_REV},
    {ST_AVRBF,                  KEY_MINUS,   ST_TIME},

    // Lots more states

    {0,                         0,           0}
};
```

We can use this as:

menu_nextstate[1].state   is defined as ST_AVRBF
menu_nextstate[1].input   is defined as KEY_NEXT
menu_nextstate[1].nextstate is defined as ST_AVRBF_REV

We can search this array of structures to find out what we need to do if we are in the ST_AVRBF state and the input is KEY_NEXT, we find that particular structure and see that the next state is ST_AVRBF_REV. Now all we have to do is find out what we need to do if our next state is ST_AVRBF_REV, which we can do by searching the menu_state array to find the ST_AVRBF_REV entry. We see that there is a function defined for this state, and equate the function pointer to it. Then we can call that function.

Clear so far?

The main() function slorps into an infinite loop, part of which, depending on the state, is used to search the menu_state array. The following code snippit compares the present state with the next state [if (nextstate != state)] and, being very reasonable, does nothing if they are the same. If the states differ, main() sets the global state variable to the nextstate variable and then accesses the menu_state structure array to change the current state to the next state.:

```
if (nextstate != state)
{
 state = nextstate;

 for (i=0; pgm_read_byte(&menu_state[i].state); i++)
 {
  if (pgm_read_byte(&menu_state[i].state) == state)
  {
   statetext =(PGM_P)pgm_read_word(&menu_state[i].pText);
   pStateFunc = (PGM_VOID_P)pgm_read_word(&menu_state[i].pFunc);
   break;
  }
 }
}
```

Since we took ST_AVRBF_REV to be the next state, so searching the array causes the snippet to make the function pointer, pStateFunc, point to the Revision function.

Whoa, there I was clicking right along and suddenly, I lost it; maybe its time to review what I've said so far?

- We have two data structures, one for storing the text and function associated with a state and one for finding the next state given the current state and the input.
- We have two structure arrays, one for each of the structures, which define all the states and transitions.
- We have code for searching each of these arrays. One finds the function associated with a given state and the other finds the next state to use given the current state and the inputs.

Now how should we use this? We could sit in an infinite loop checking the inputs and then looking at the current state and seeing if a transition to a new state is called for. Hey, sounds like a plan. We could write our main() function as follows, hopefully commented to crystal clarity:

```
unsigned char state; // holds the current state, according to
"menu.h"

int main(void)
{
    // Define our local copies of the state variables
    unsigned char nextstate;
    PGM_P statetext;
    char (*pStateFunc)(char);
    char input;

    // Define a loop counter
    uint8_t i; // char i;

    // Initial state variables
    state = nextstate = ST_AVRBF;
    statetext = MT_AVRBF;
    pStateFunc = NULL;

    for (;;)                // Main loop
    {
      // read the joystick buttons
      input = getkey();
```

```
    if (pStateFunc) // If a state function is pointed to
    {
        // When a state function is pointed to, we must call it
        // and get the results as the nextstate variable
        nextstate = pStateFunc(input);
    }
    else if (input != KEY_NULL) // If not, and input not NULL
    {
        // We call the StateMachine function to examine the
        // MENU_NEXTSTATE array to find the nextstate
        nextstate = StateMachine(state, input);
    }

    // Now we know what the next state is
    if (nextstate != state) // Do only if the state has changed
    {
     state = nextstate; // The state changed, so reset it

     // Read the MENU_STATE array until we find the entry
     // matching the current state
     for (i=0; pgm_read_byte(&menu_state[i].state); i++)
     {
      // If we find the entry
      if (pgm_read_byte(&menu_state[i].state) == state)
      {
        // We load the state variables from that entry
        statetext =(PGM_P)pgm_read_word(&menu_state[i].pText);
        pStateFunc
            =(PGM_VOID_P)pgm_read_word(&menu_state[i].pFunc);
        // And we exit the loop
        break;
      }
      // If we found an entry for the pStateFunc, we loop back
      // to the top were we run it.
     }
    }
   } //End Main loop

    return 0;
}
```

Of course, the actual Butterfly main() function does a lot of other stuff, but this should help you understand the menu state machine part.

I know, believe me I know. This is hard stuff, but you should be able to walk through the Butterfly menu state machine code now and fully understand how it works. If you don't... well, maybe you want to back up to the pointers section and read slowly till you are back here again. Don't feel bad, C takes a while to get used to and the guys who wrote the Butterfly software have very long, cold, and dark winters to hunker down with little else to do other than get used to C programming, well, there are the Reindeer...

Chapter 11 The Butterfly LCD

I read a book (I think it was David Brin's 'Practice Effect') where some primitive people found a digital watch with an LCD display. They were amazed that whoever made the thing was able to train all the little black bugs to run around and align themselves in such peculiar patterns. And that's the extent of the detail I'll give on the underlying technology of LCDs. We'll concentrate instead on using C to train the little black bugs to do our tricks. If you must know the magic, then Atmel has an application note: AVR065: LCD Driver for the STK502 and AVR Butterfly available from their website that will get you deep into the gory details. And the Atmega169 data book has a nice chapter 'LCD Controller' that is a sure cure for insomnia.

To keep our ignorance even more intact we will begin by using software based on the LCD-Test software available on http://www.siwawi.arubi.uni-kl.de/avr_projects/#bf_app noting that the main.c file begins with the confidence building:

> // mt - used for debugging only - may not work

However, with a few changes and some shoehorning it all into a demonstrator module, it works just fine. We use these functions without attempting to understand them. Another way to say this is that we will enhance our productivity by reusing existing code and conform to object oriented principles by not allowing ourselves to mess with perfectly good software.

Functions at our disposal in LCD_functions module:

- void LCD_putc(uint8_t digit, char character);
  - Writes a character to the LCD digit
- void LCD_puts(char *pStr, char scrollmode);
  - Writes a string to the LCD
  - *pStr is a pointer to the string
  - scrollmode is not used
- void LCD_puts_f(const char *pFlashStr, char scrollmode);
  - Writes to the LCD a string stored in flash
  - *pFlashStr is a pointer to the flash string

261

- o   scrollmode is not used
- void LCD_Clear(void);
  - o   Clears the LCD
- void LCD_Colon(char show);
  - o   If show = 0 disables Colon, otherwise enables Colon
- char SetContrast(char input);
  - o   Uses the value of input from 0 to 15 to set the contrast

PC to LCD test program

Lets modify our messenger program so that we can send strings to the Butterfly to display on the LCD. We will also add commands to set the contrast, show/hide the colon, clear the display, set the flash rate, and send strings with flashing characters.

Instead of running off willy-nilly and writing software, lets start with a short specification of what we want to test from the PC users perspective.

We will test each function by sending the following command strings to the Butterfly:

- **PUTCdigitcharacter** to test LCD_putc(uint8_t digit, char character);
  - o   Send PUTCdigitcharacter where character is a char to be displayed and digit is the LCD segment to display the input on. For example PUTC6A will cause the character A to be displayed on the 6th LCD digit.
  - o   Verify function by seeing the correct char in the correct position
- **PUTF** to test LCD_puts_f(const char *pFlashStr, char scrollmode);
  - o   Verify function by seeing the correct string on the LCD
- **PUTSstring** to test LCD_puts(char *pStr, char scrollmode);
  - o   Send PUTSstring where string is a string to be displayed. For example PUTSHello World! will cause the LCD to display 'Hello World!'.
  - o   Verify function by seeing the correct string on the LCD
- **CLEAR** to test LCD_Clear(void);

- o   Send CLEAR while displaying text on the LCD
- o   Verify function by seeing the LCD clear
- **COLON** to test LCD_Colon(char show);
  - o   Send COLON,on/off where on/off is either ON or OFF
  - o   Verify function by seeing colons on LCD turn on or off
- **SETC##** to test char SetContrast(char input);
  - o   Send SETC## where ## is from 0 to 15 and sets the contrast.

We will use this to design the functions needed on the Butterfly. We already have a command processor designed, so we will reuse that to call the functions on receipt of the correct command.

- **PUTCdigitcharacter**
  - o   Call LCD_putc(digit, character);
  - o   Send "Called LCD_putc" to PC where # are the values sent in decimal
- **PUTF**
  - o   Set a pointer, *pFlashStr, to a string in flash
  - o   Call LCD_puts_f(*pFlashStr, scrollmode);
  - o   Send "Called LCD_puts_f" to the PC.
- **PUTSstring**
  - o   Load the string and point pStr to it.
  - o   Call LCD_puts(*pStr, scrollmode);
  - o   Send "Called LCD_puts with 'string'" to the PC where string is the string sent.
- **CLEAR**
  - o   Call LCD_Clear();
  - o   Send "Called "LCD_Clear()" to the PC
- **COLON#**
  - o   If # == 1 call LCD_Colon(1);
  - o   Else if # == 0 call LCD_Colon(0);
  - o   Send "Called LCD_Colon" to the PC where # is the one sent.
- **SETC##**
  - o   Convert ## characters to a numerical value 'input'
  - o   Call SetContrast(input);

- o Send "Called SetContrast to the PC where # is the decimal number sent.

NOTE: In LCD_driver.c must comment out #include "main.h"

Now that we have our specification we can run off willy-nilly and write the software.

We write the Demonstrator.h file:

```
// Demonstrator.h LCD demo version
void initializer(void);
void parseInput(char *);
```

And the Demonstrator.c file:

```
// Demonstrator.c LCD demo version

#include "PC_Comm.h"
#include "Demonstrator.h"
#include "LCD_test.h"
#include "LCD_driver.h"
#include "LCD_functions.h"

// identify yourself specifically
const char TALKING_TO[] PROGMEM = "\r\rYou are talking to the \0";
const char WHO_DEMO[] PROGMEM = "'LCD' demo.\r\r\0";

// bad command
const char BAD_COMMAND1[] PROGMEM = "\rYou sent: '\0";
const char BAD_COMMAND2[] PROGMEM = "' - I don't understand.\r\0";

const char LCD_START_msg[] PROGMEM = "LCD demo\0";

void initializer()
{
 // Calibrate the oscillator:
 OSCCAL_calibration();

 // Initialize the USART
 USARTinit();

 // initialize the LCD
 LCD_Init();

 // Display instructions on PC
```

```
 sendFString(TALKING_TO);
 sendFString(WHO_DEMO);

 LCD_puts_f(LCD_START_msg, 1);

}

void parseInput(char s[])
{
 // parse first character
 switch (s[0])
 {
  case 'd':
   if( (s[1] == 'e') && (s[2] == 'm') && (s[3] == 'o') && (s[4] == '?') )
    sendFString(TALKING_TO);
    sendFString(WHO_DEMO);
    break;
  case 'C':
   if( (s[1] == 'L') && (s[2] == 'E') && (s[3] == 'A') && (s[4] == 'R'))
    OnCLEAR();
   else if ((s[1] == 'O')&&(s[2] == 'L')&&(s[3] == 'O')&&(s[4] == 'N'))
    OnCOLON(s);
    break;
  case 'P' :
   if( (s[1] == 'U') && (s[2] == 'T') && (s[3] == 'C'))
    OnPUTC(s);
   else if( (s[1] == 'U') && (s[2] == 'T') && (s[3] == 'F'))
    OnPUTF(s);
   else if( (s[1] == 'U') && (s[2] == 'T') && (s[3] == 'S'))
    OnPUTS(s);
    break;
  case 'S' :
   if((s[1]== C')&&(s[2 =='R')&&(s[3]=='O')&&(s[4]=='L')&&(s[5] == 'L'))
    OnSCROLL(s);
   else if( (s[1] == 'E') && (s[2] == 'T') && (s[3] == 'C') )
    OnSETC(s);
    break;
  default:
    sendFString(BAD_COMMAND1);
    sendChar(s[0]);
    sendFString(BAD_COMMAND2);
    break;

  s[0] = '\0';
  }
}
```

We write, the Messenges.h, LCD_test.h and LCD_test.c files:

```
// Messages.h
```

265

```c
// LCD test messages
const char PUTF_msg[] PROGMEM = "Called LCD_puts_f \0";
const char PUTS_msg[] PROGMEM = "Called LCD_puts with \0";
const char PUTC_msg[] PROGMEM = "Called LCD_putc\r\0";
const char CLEAR_msg[] PROGMEM = "LCD_Clear()\r\0";
const char COLON_msg[] PROGMEM = "Called LCD_Colon\r\0";
const char SETC_msg[] PROGMEM = "Called SetContrast\r\0";
const char SCROLL_msg[] PROGMEM = "Called OnScroll\r\0";


// LCD_test.h

void OnPUTF(char *PUTFstr);
void OnPUTS(char *pStr);
void OnPUTC(char *PUTCstr);
void OnCLEAR(void);
void OnCOLON(char *pOnoff);
void OnSETC(char *SETCstr);
void OnSCROLL(char *SCROLL);


// LCD_test.c
#include "LCD_driver.h"
#include "LCD_functions.h"
#include "LCD_test.h"
#include "PC_Comm.h"
#include "Messages.h"

// Start-up delay before scrolling a string over the LCD. "LCD_driver.c"
extern char gLCD_Start_Scroll_Timer;


//PUTF,#
//Verify that # represents a valid string in flash.
//Set the pFlashStr pointer to the string
//Call LCD_puts_f(*pFlashStr, scrollmode);
//Send "Called LCD_puts_f" to the PC
void OnPUTF(char *PUTFstr)
{
        sendFString(PUTF_msg);

        PGM_P text;

        text = PSTR("LCD_put_f test\0"); // won't show the _

        LCD_puts_f(text, 1);
}

//PUTS,string
//Load the string and point pStr to it.
//Call LCD_puts(*pStr, scrollmode);
```

266

```
//Send "Called LCD_puts with 'string'" to the PC.
void OnPUTS(char *pStr)
{
        sendFString(PUTS_msg);
        sendString(pStr);

        LCD_puts(&pStr[4],0); //Overlook the PUTS part of the string

}


//PUTC,digit,character
//Call LCD_putc(digit, character);
//Send "Called LCD_putc" to PC.
void OnPUTC(char *PUTCstr)
{
        uint8_t digit;

        sendFString(PUTC_msg);

        digit = (uint8_t)(PUTCstr[4] - 48);// convert to integer

        if(digit <= 6)
        {
                LCD_putc(digit,PUTCstr[5]);
                LCD_UpdateRequired(1,0);
        }

}

//CLEAR
//Call LCD_Clear();
//Send "Called "LCD_Clear()" to the PC
void OnCLEAR(void)
{
        sendFString(CLEAR_msg);
        LCD_Clear();
}

//COLON,on/off
//Verify that on/off is either "ON" or "OFF"
//If ON call LCD_Colon(1);
//Else call LCD_Colon(0);
//Send "Called LCD_Colon" to the PC.
void OnCOLON(char *pOnoff)
{
        sendFString(COLON_msg);

        if(pOnoff[5] == '1')
        {
                LCD_Colon(1);
```

267

```
        }
        else if (pOnoff[5] == '0')
        {
                LCD_Colon(0);
        }

}

//SETC
//Call SetContrast(input);
//Send "Called SetContrast(#) to the PC where # is the decimal number
//sent. Note values are from 0 to 15
void OnSETC(char *SETCstr)
{
        char temp[] = {'\0','\0','\0'};
        int input;

        sendFString(SETC_msg);

        temp[0] = SETCstr[4];
        temp[1] = SETCstr[5];

        input = atoi(temp);

        SetContrast(input);

}

// SCROLL
// Start scroll if input == 1
// Stop scroll if input == 0
// Send "Called OnScroll" to the PC
void OnSCROLL(char *scroll)
{
        sendFString(SCROLL_msg);

        if(scroll[6] == '1')
        {
         gScrollMode = 1;    // Scroll if text is longer than display size
         gScroll = 0;
         gLCD_Start_Scroll_Timer = 3;    //Start-up delay before scrolling
        }
        else if (scroll[6] == '0')
        {
         gScrollMode = 0;
         gScroll = 0;
        }

}
```

Modify the makefile with:

```
SRC += Demonstrator.c \
LCD_test.c \
LCD_driver.c \
LCD_functions.c
```

And we make sure the LCD_driver and LCD_functions .h and .c files are in the same directory as the rest. Compile and download as usual.

Open Bray's Terminal and connect to the Butterfly. You should see:

```
You are talking to the 'LCD' demo.
```

And the Butterfly LCD will be scrolling "LCD DEMO"

In the output window of Bray's Terminal type:

```
CLEAR
```

The LCD will clear. Now type:

```
PUTC0A
PUTC1B
```

And you will see AB on the LCD. Type in:

```
SCROLL1
```

And the LCD will scroll the AB. Type in:

```
SCROLL0
```

And the LCD will stop scrolling the AB. Type in:

```
PUTF
```

And the LCD will show:

```
LCD PUT F TEST
```

Notice that the message in flash was 'LCD put_f test' but the underline isn't shown on the LCD because there isn't one in the LCD character set. However, there is no good reason not to have this character sense all you have to do us use the bottom most little black bug, an exercise that, as they say, will be left to the student. (Teachers make this statement not because they want to educate the student, but because they are too lazy to do it themselves. Or maybe that's just me.)

Conclusion

You will find that much of C programming for microcontrollers uses various 'tricks' to modify C to be more efficient for a specific microcontroller and a specific compiler. These tricks are often found by reading programs written by experienced programmers. You have access to the Butterfly software as modified by the folks using WinAVR, bf_gcc_20031205.zip, and I suggest you read it since these guys are the real experts. But do be careful. One of the main reasons to use C is to write portable code, so be sure you make your tricks easily retrickable for other systems.

Now that you're familiar with C and the Butterfly software, go to the WinAVR directory and find the avr_libc user manual. At 185 pages, it provides excellent documentation for the avr_libc subset of the Standard C Library for the ATMEL's AVR. It also provides some other goodies, such as start up examples and good solid example code to learn from. Since, they did such a good job documenting this resource, I'll go no further, other than to say that this library will likely become an indispensable tool for your programming future.

Well, I hope you met your goals for using this book.

- You should have gained a basic understanding microcontroller architecture.
- You should have an intermediate understanding of the C programming language.
- You should be able to use the WinAVR and AVRStudio tools to build programs.

- You should be able to use C to develop microcontroller functions such as:
  - Port Inputs and Outputs
  - Read a joystick
  - Use timers
  - Program Real Time Clocks
  - Communicate with a PC
  - Conduct analog to digital and digital to analog conversions
  - Measure temperature, light, and voltage
  - Ccontrol motors
  - Control an LCD.

If I was successful in helping you achieve these goals, after you tell all your friends, you might want to keep tabs of my website: www.smileymicros.com to see what other good stuff is available.

Happy programming!

Appendix 1: Project Kits

Note: check the website: www.smileymicros.com to see if any of these items are available there for less (don't forget to include shipping and handling in your calculations when figuring 'less').

Parts Lists (Prices for Spring 2005):

From Digi-Key:
Note: Digi-Key charges a $5 handling charge on all orders under $25. Since the AVR Butterfly is $19.99 they add the $5 charge, but if you buy $5.01 additional items, they drop the $5 handling charge, giving you $5 worth of stuff for a penny. So add $1.84 of extra parts to the order and get $5 free. I like free, don't you?

Description	Part Number	Quan	Price/Unit	Total
AVR Butterfly	ATAVRBFLY-ND	1	19.99	19.99
D-SUB 9 female solder cup	209F-ND	1	0.63	0.63
Female header single 2 pin	S4002-ND	1	0.21	0.21
Female header single 3 pin	S4003-ND	1	0.30	0.30
Female header single 4 pin	S4004-ND	1	0.39	0.39
Female header double 10 pin	S4205-ND	2	0.82	1.64
Subtotal				23.16
MORE STUFF – see note	**Your choice - see note**			1.84
Total				25.00

From JAMECO:

Description	Part Number	Quan	Price/Unit	Total
Breadboard	20722CP	1	8.95	8.95
Wire cutter striper	127870	1	5.49	5.49
22 awg 100' white solid wire	36880	1	5.49	5.49
Battery holder – 2 size D	216389	1	0.89	0.89
Switch	204142	1	0.39	0.39

Data I/O				
LEDs red	11797	10	0.19	1.90
Resistors 150 Ohm 1/8 watt	107967	100	0.0069	0.69

Appendix 1: Project Kits

8 position DIP switch	30842	1	0.89	0.89
Potentiometer – 10 kOhm	264410	1	1.18	1.18
PWM Motor Control				
Motor	231896CA	1	0.99	0.99
Power Transistor – TIP115	288526	1	0.48	0.48
Optoisolator – 4N28	41013	1	0.46	0.46
Diode – 1N4001	35975CA	10	0.03	0.30
9V Connector	216451	1	0.34	0.34
Slotted Interrupter – H21A1	114091CL	1	0.69	0.69
2.2 k Ohm resistor	108054	100	0.0069	0.69

Solder Kit

Description	Part Number	Quan	Price/Unit	Total
Soldering iron	208987	1	2.99	2.99
Solder	170456	1	1.39	1.39
Solder wick	410801	1	1.49	1.49

Appendix 2: Soldering Tutorial

I've got a pretty good soldering station that I inherited from a company that I worked for that went belly-up. They couldn't pay me for the last month's work I did, so they let me load up on equipment which was either generous of them or saved them from paying to have it hauled off. But since this text is trying to get the most educational value for the least educational buck, I thought I'd get the cheapest soldering iron I could find and see if it would work well enough for student use. The iron in Figure 40 was less than three bucks from JAMECO and worked just fine.

First warning: these things get hot, cause fires, and char skin. If you burn yourself more than once, join the club. Some of us are just harder to train. Saying don't set up your soldering station near anything flammable, seems silly, but remember, my nickname is Smoky Joe and there are reasons for that.

Second warning: the solder has a rosin core and produces a nice trail of smoke that contains God-knows-what kind of chemicals and heavy metals. This smoke is very intelligent and will head straight for your nose. If you want to see real magic at work, try changing your position and soldering techniques to avoid the smoke: nothing works! Smart smoke will find you. Use a cheap fan to blow away from your soldering area and share the toxic crap with everybody in the room.

I've also included solder wick on the JAMECO list. This is braided copper wire and does what its name implies, it wicks solder. Just stick it to the bad glob you want to remove, heat it up and watch the power of capillary action and note that your are holding the copper between your thumb and forefinger about one inch from the tip of the soldering iron which quickly teaches you that copper is a poor insulator. Yeouch... is a common soldering term.

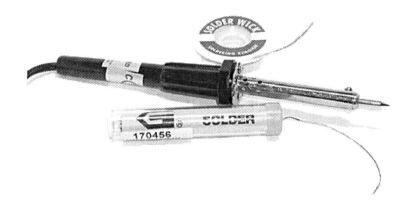

Figure 40: Cheap soldering iron, solder and wick from JAMECO

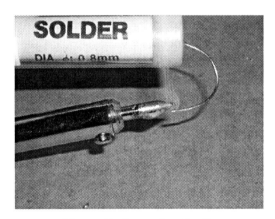

Figure 41: Seasoning the tip

When you first plug in your soldering iron stand by with the solder and as soon as the tip heats up (takes a while on a cheap iron) liberally coat it with solder as shown in Figure 41. The rest of the tip will rapidly loose its shiny newness and develop a burned look. The seasoned part will remain shiny and useful.

Get an old cellulose or natural sponge to use to clean the excess solder off the tip. Keep it moist and when the tip gets crapped up with charred resin, circuit board, and finger-burn goo, just wipe it on the sponge and … sssssttt… it's all clean and shiny again. Don't use a synthetic sponge unless you really like the stench of burning plastic.

Now go and scrounge some broken circuit boards from a dumpster somewhere. You might have to bust open some discarded electronic device, the older and cheaper the better. Now look at those solder joins. That's what a good join is supposed to look like. It looks like the solder melted, adhered, and slumped around whatever it is on. Now use the wick to clean off some joins, and then try to resolder them. Heat the join area and put the solder to it. Don't heat the solder and stick it to the join. Don't take too long, get it on and get the tip away. 'Too long' is subjective, just get the join soldered as quickly as possible. Piece of cake. If your join is bulbous or looks like it is sitting on the join and didn't slump into it, it is a bad solder. If it looks dull and crinkly rather than smooth and shiny, it is a bad solder. This isn't rocket science; you should be an expert in a couple of minutes. And be thankful that we won't be using any surface mount parts. That ain't easy to do with a cheap iron.

Appendix 3: Debugging Tale

Sometimes you have to search high and low to find out what a something really means. For instance, we often see the sbi() function, as in Butterfly main.c:

```
sbi(DDRB, 5);        // set OC1A as output
sbi(PORTB, 5);       // set OC1A high
```

We search around a while and eventually in sfr_def.h we find:

```
/** \def sbi
    \ingroup avr_sfr
    \deprecated
    \code #include <avr/io.h>\endcode
    For backwards compatibility only. This macro will eventually be removed.

    Set bit \c bit in IO register \c sfr. */
```

```
#define sbi(sfr, bit) (_SFR_BYTE(sfr) |= _BV(bit))
```

This means that sbi() is not a function, it's a macro, and a deprecated one at that. By deprecation, they mean that we shouldn't use in and eventually it may go away. To understand what it does though, we need to find the definition of _SFR_BYTE(sfr) and _BV(bit) and we can now guess these aren't functions, but macros. More searching and in the same header we find:

```
#define _SFR_BYTE(sfr) _MMIO_BYTE(_SFR_ADDR(sfr))
```

Hmmm... that's not a lot of help so more searching to find out what _MMIO_BYTE and _SFR_ADDR mean. In the same header we find:

```
#define _MMIO_BYTE(mem_addr) (*(volatile uint8_t *)(mem_addr))
```

Okay, we still don't know. So we look for uint8_t, which is tucked away in the bf_gcc directory readme.txt:

- changed some char to uint8_t to avoid compiler warnings.

279

Now we can speculate that uint8_t is a char. I say speculate because going further would require poking around in the gcc compiler stuff, and I'd rather live with my guess than suffer that. Anyway, I've already lost track of what I was trying to figure out in the first place. All theses layers of deception can be quite dense. Let's state what we found.

_MMIO_BYTE is a macro that declares mem_addr to be a pointer to a volatile char pointer. I'm getting scared, how about you?

Backing up a bit we look at the _SFR_BYTE macro and see that it provides _MMIO_BYTE with a mem_addr of the type _SFR_ADDR. Oh, bother. What is a _SFR_ADDR? Well, in sfr_defs.h we find:

#define _SFR_ADDR(sfr) _SFR_MEM_ADDR(sfr)

Which doesn't help so we look for _SFR_MEM_ADDR and find:

#define _SFR_MEM_ADDR(sfr) ((uint16_t) &(sfr))

We now know that _SFR_ADDR is an alias for _SFR_MEM_ADDR which is macro to declare sfr as a uint16_t, and we'll guess that's a 16 bit integer. What the heck is the & for? Let's do some substitutions. If you remember we were trying to understand the meaning of the sbi macro and it had _SFR_BYTE(sfr) in it so:

We had: _SFR_BYTE(sfr)
which is and alias for: _MMIO_BYTE(_SFR_ADDR(sfr))

the _ SFR_ADDR aliased   _MMIO_BYTE(_SFR_MEM_ADDR(sfr))
that aliased   _MMIO_BYTE(((uint16_t) &(sfr)))

and _MMIO_BYTE aliased   (*(volatile uint8_t *)(((uint16_t) &(sfr))   ))

which we can substitute for the _SFR_BYTE(sfr) in the sbi macro

#define sbi(sfr, bit) (_SFR_BYTE(sfr) |= _BV(bit))

280

Appendix 3: Debugging Tale

Substitution yields:

#define sbi(sfr, bit) ((*(volatile uint8_t *)(((uint16_t) &(sfr)))) |= _BV(bit))

And _BV is? In pgmspace.h it is:

#define _BV(bit) (1 << (bit))

More substitiuton yields:

#define sbi(sfr, bit) ((*(volatile uint8_t *)(((uint16_t) &(sfr)))) |= (1 << (bit)))

By the by, what's a volatile? It is an implementation specific type qualifier that tells a complier to suppress optimization that might, in our case, screw things up if we are using pointers to memory mapped registers. We don't want the compiler to help us by using some other memory address since a register is hardwired into the machine and though addressed like memory, isn't ordinary memory. Volatile also tells the compiler that that the so modified variable can change unexpectedly (like by an interrupt) so it needs to be checked each time it is used and not just stored somewhere like on the stack.

More substitution for an actual use of sbi:

    sbi(PORTB, 5);   // set OC1A high

yields:

 ((*(volatile uint8_t *)(((uint16_t) &(PORTB)))) |= (1 << (5)))

But the complier doesn't know what PORTB is. What is it?

From io169.h

#define PORTB _SFR_IO8(0x05)/* PORTB */

and _SFR_IO8 id defined in sfrdefs.h:

Appendix 3: Debugging Tale

#define _SFR_IO8(io_addr) _MMIO_BYTE((io_addr) + 0x20)

Goody, we already know what _MMIO_BYTE is so we can do substitutions:

PORTB is _SFR_IO8(0x05)
_SFR_IO8(0x05) is _MMIO_BYTE((0x05) + 0x20)

_MMIO_BYTE((0x05) + 0x20) is (*(volatile uint8_t *)((0x05) + 0x20))

yields:

((*(volatile uint8_t *)(((uint16_t) &((*(volatile uint8_t *)((0x05) + 0x20)))))) |= (1 << (5)))

What we wrote was:

sbi(PORTB, 5);   // set OC1A high

What the compiler sees is:

((*(volatile uint8_t *)(((uint16_t) &((*(volatile uint8_t *)((0x05) + 0x20)))))) |= (1 << (5)))

Aren't you glad you aren't a compiler?

Appendix 4: ASCII Table

Table 9: ASCII Table

```
Char  Dec   Hex | Char  Dec   Hex | Char  Dec   Hex | Char Dec   Hex
-------------------------------------------------------------------------
(nul)   0  0x00 | (sp)   32  0x20 | @      64  0x40 | `      96  0x60
(soh)   1  0x01 | !      33  0x21 | A      65  0x41 | a      97  0x61
(stx)   2  0x02 | "      34  0x22 | B      66  0x42 | b      98  0x62
(etx)   3  0x03 | #      35  0x23 | C      67  0x43 | c      99  0x63
(eot)   4  0x04 | $      36  0x24 | D      68  0x44 | d     100  0x64
(enq)   5  0x05 | %      37  0x25 | E      69  0x45 | e     101  0x65
(ack)   6  0x06 | &      38  0x26 | F      70  0x46 | f     102  0x66
(bel)   7  0x07 | '      39  0x27 | G      71  0x47 | g     103  0x67
(bs)    8  0x08 | (      40  0x28 | H      72  0x48 | h     104  0x68
(ht)    9  0x09 | )      41  0x29 | I      73  0x49 | i     105  0x69
(nl)   10  0x0a | *      42  0x2a | J      74  0x4a | j     106  0x6a
(vt)   11  0x0b | +      43  0x2b | K      75  0x4b | k     107  0x6b
(np)   12  0x0c | ,      44  0x2c | L      76  0x4c | l     108  0x6c
(cr)   13  0x0d | -      45  0x2d | M      77  0x4d | m     109  0x6d
(so)   14  0x0e | .      46  0x2e | N      78  0x4e | n     110  0x6e
(si)   15  0x0f | /      47  0x2f | O      79  0x4f | o     111  0x6f
(dle)  16  0x10 | 0      48  0x30 | P      80  0x50 | p     112  0x70
(dc1)  17  0x11 | 1      49  0x31 | Q      81  0x51 | q     113  0x71
(dc2)  18  0x12 | 2      50  0x32 | R      82  0x52 | r     114  0x72
(dc3)  19  0x13 | 3      51  0x33 | S      83  0x53 | s     115  0x73
(dc4)  20  0x14 | 4      52  0x34 | T      84  0x54 | t     116  0x74
(nak)  21  0x15 | 5      53  0x35 | U      85  0x55 | u     117  0x75
(syn)  22  0x16 | 6      54  0x36 | V      86  0x56 | v     118  0x76
(etb)  23  0x17 | 7      55  0x37 | W      87  0x57 | w     119  0x77
(can)  24  0x18 | 8      56  0x38 | X      88  0x58 | x     120  0x78
(em)   25  0x19 | 9      57  0x39 | Y      89  0x59 | y     121  0x79
(sub)  26  0x1a | :      58  0x3a | Z      90  0x5a | z     122  0x7a
(esc)  27  0x1b | ;      59  0x3b | [      91  0x5b | {     123  0x7b
(fs)   28  0x1c | <      60  0x3c | \      92  0x5c | |     124  0x7c
(gs)   29  0x1d | =      61  0x3d | ]      93  0x5d | }     125  0x7d
(rs)   30  0x1e | >      62  0x3e | ^      94  0x5e | ~     126  0x7e
(us)   31  0x1f | ?      63  0x3f | _      95  0x5f | (del) 127  0x7f
```

```
ASCII Name  Description    C Escape Sequence
nul    null byte              \0
bel    bell character         \a
bs     backspace              \b
ht     horizontal tab         \t
np     formfeed               \f
nl     newline                \n
cr     carriage return        \r
vt     vertical tab
esc    escape
sp     space
```

Appendix 5: Decimal, Hexadecimal, and Binary

Table 10: Decimal, Hexadecimal, and Binary Conversion

Dec	Hex	Bin	Dec	Hex	Bin	Dec	Hex	Bin	Dec	Hex	Bin
0	0	00000000	64	40	01000000	128	80	10000000	192	c0	11000000
1	1	00000001	65	41	01000001	129	81	10000001	193	c1	11000001
2	2	00000010	66	42	01000010	130	82	10000010	194	c2	11000010
3	3	00000011	67	43	01000011	131	83	10000011	195	c3	11000011
4	4	00000100	68	44	01000100	132	84	10000100	196	c4	11000100
5	5	00000101	69	45	01000101	133	85	10000101	197	c5	11000101
6	6	00000110	70	46	01000110	134	86	10000110	198	c6	11000110
7	7	00000111	71	47	01000111	135	87	10000111	199	c7	11000111
8	8	00001000	72	48	01001000	136	88	10001000	200	c8	11001000
9	9	00001001	73	49	01001001	137	89	10001001	201	c9	11001001
10	a	00001010	74	4a	01001010	138	8a	10001010	202	ca	11001010
11	b	00001011	75	4b	01001011	139	8b	10001011	203	cb	11001011
12	c	00001100	76	4c	01001100	140	8c	10001100	204	cc	11001100
13	d	00001101	77	4d	01001101	141	8d	10001101	205	cd	11001101
14	e	00001110	78	4e	01001110	142	8e	10001110	206	ce	11001110
15	f	00001111	79	4f	01001111	143	8f	10001111	207	cf	11001111
16	10	00010000	80	50	01010000	144	90	10010000	208	d0	11010000
17	11	00010001	81	51	01010001	145	91	10010001	209	d1	11010001
18	12	00010010	82	52	01010010	146	92	10010010	210	d2	11010010
19	13	00010011	83	53	01010011	147	93	10010011	211	d3	11010011
20	14	00010100	84	54	01010100	148	94	10010100	212	d4	11010100
21	15	00010101	85	55	01010101	149	95	10010101	213	d5	11010101
22	16	00010110	86	56	01010110	150	96	10010110	214	d6	11010110
23	17	00010111	87	57	01010111	151	97	10010111	215	d7	11010111
24	18	00011000	88	58	01011000	152	98	10011000	216	d8	11011000
25	19	00011001	89	59	01011001	153	99	10011001	217	d9	11011001
26	1a	00011010	90	5a	01011010	154	9a	10011010	218	da	11011010
27	1b	00011011	91	5b	01011011	155	9b	10011011	219	db	11011011
28	1c	00011100	92	5c	01011100	156	9c	10011100	220	dc	11011100
29	1d	00011101	93	5d	01011101	157	9d	10011101	221	dd	11011101
30	1e	00011110	94	5e	01011110	158	9e	10011110	222	de	11011110
31	1f	00011111	95	5f	01011111	159	9f	10011111	223	df	11011111
32	20	00100000	96	60	01100000	160	a0	10100000	224	e0	11100000
33	21	00100001	97	61	01100001	161	a1	10100001	225	e1	11100001
34	22	00100010	98	62	01100010	162	a2	10100010	226	e2	11100010
35	23	00100011	99	63	01100011	163	a3	10100011	227	e3	11100011
36	24	00100100	100	64	01100100	164	a4	10100100	228	e4	11100100
37	25	00100101	101	65	01100101	165	a5	10100101	229	e5	11100101
38	26	00100110	102	66	01100110	166	a6	10100110	230	e6	11100110
39	27	00100111	103	67	01100111	167	a7	10100111	231	e7	11100111
40	28	00101000	104	68	01101000	168	a8	10101000	232	e8	11101000
41	29	00101001	105	69	01101001	169	a9	10101001	233	e9	11101001
42	2a	00101010	106	6a	01101010	170	aa	10101010	234	ea	11101010

Appendix 5: Decimal, Hexadecimal, and Binary

43	2b	00101011	107	6b	01101011	171	ab	10101011	235	eb	11101011
44	2c	00101100	108	6c	01101100	172	ac	10101100	236	ec	11101100
45	2d	00101101	109	6d	01101101	173	ad	10101101	237	ed	11101101
46	2e	00101110	110	6e	01101110	174	ae	10101110	238	ee	11101110
47	2f	00101111	111	6f	01101111	175	af	10101111	239	ef	11101111
48	30	00110000	112	70	01110000	176	b0	10110000	240	f0	11110000
49	31	00110001	113	71	01110001	177	b1	10110001	241	f1	11110001
50	32	00110010	114	72	01110010	178	b2	10110010	242	f2	11110010
51	33	00110011	115	73	01110011	179	b3	10110011	243	f3	11110011
52	34	00110100	116	74	01110100	180	b4	10110100	244	f4	11110100
53	35	00110101	117	75	01110101	181	b5	10110101	245	f5	11110101
54	36	00110110	118	76	01110110	182	b6	10110110	246	f6	11110110
55	37	00110111	119	77	01110111	183	b7	10110111	247	f7	11110111
56	38	00111000	120	78	01111000	184	b8	10111000	248	f8	11111000
57	39	00111001	121	79	01111001	185	b9	10111001	249	f9	11111001
58	3a	00111010	122	7a	01111010	186	ba	10111010	250	fa	11111010
59	3b	00111011	123	7b	01111011	187	bb	10111011	251	fb	11111011
60	3c	00111100	124	7c	01111100	188	bc	10111100	252	fc	11111100
61	3d	00111101	125	7d	01111101	189	bd	10111101	253	fd	11111101
62	3e	00111110	126	7e	01111110	190	be	10111110	254	fe	11111110
63	3f	00111111	127	7f	01111111	191	bf	10111111	255	ff	11111111

Appendix 6: Motor Speed Control Wheel

Appendix 7: HyperTerminal

This book origianally used HyperTerminal for PC communications, but some folks were so adamant in their revulsion of HyperTerminal that I had to finally admit that maybe this wasn't just the pervasive hatred of MicroSoft, but was due to HyperTerminal itself. It is very hard to get set up and going properly and some folks said it was buggy and unreliable. I received permission from Br@y++ to use his terminal so that is the one shown in the Quick Start Section. The remaining sections still have illustrations from HyperTerminal, but you can and probably should use Bray's Terminal since it is simple and lots of folks love it. Both are free.

Test Your Connection:
The Butterfly comes with built-in code that allows you to communicate with a PC COM Port to change "Your name". This is a good way to see if your hardware is working like it should be.

- Connect an RS-232 cable between your Butterfly and your PC as in Figure 10. Open HyperTerminal
  - On you PC taskbar GOTO Start, Programs, Accessories, Communications and click on HyperTerminal, then take a deep breath, because HyperTerminal was not really designed with your use in mind, so it can be confusing (but it IS free).
  - Where it asks for a new connection name, call it Thunderfly or something equally memorable, and select the least dorky icon you can find in the list. I favor the atom next to the phone, because it makes no sense whatever.

- The 'New Connections Properties' window opens and select the COM Port you are connected to:

- If you don't know what Com Port you are connected to:
  - Your computer's manual will tell which COM Port you are using. But since you've lost your manual...
  - Click the start button
  - Click the settings button
  - Click the control panel button
  - (If you are using XP, hunt around, it's all there somewhere)
  - In the control panel, click the System button
  - Depending on your OS, hunt for the Hardware panel, and then click the Device Manager button (Why does Microsoft have to do this differently on every OS?)
  - In the Device Manager, expand the Ports(COM & LPT)
  - If fortune smiles, you'll only have one COM Port and it will be COM1.
  - If you have multiple COM Ports that aren't being used, then go find that darn manual! Or look at you connections on the back of your PC and hope one of them is labeled, or just plug it in an guess which COM Port it is connected to. If you guess wrong, just try the next one COM1, COM2, COM3... until it works, and next time you buy a PC, put the manual somewhere that you can find it.

- Set the COM Port communications parameters:
  - Bits per second to 19200, data bits to 8, parity to None, stop bits to 1, and flow control to None

- Click OK and the Properties Window appears, click the Settings tab.

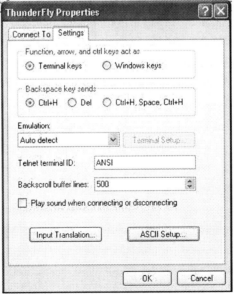

- And the ASCII Setup button, and fill out that Window as below:

- By now you are almost surely as sick of HyperTerminal as I am, but if you've done everything right (and if you are like me, you haven't) you're ready to program "Your Name" in the Butterfly.
- On the Butterfly click the joystick down until you see NAME.
- Click the joystick right to "ENTER NAME"
- Click the joystick down to "DOWNLOAD NAME"
- Center the joystick and press it. (By the way, do you know where the term 'joystick' comes from?) The message "WAITNG FOR INPUT ON RS232" appears on the LCD.
- Return to the PC and HyperTerminal. Type 'Hello world' and hit enter.

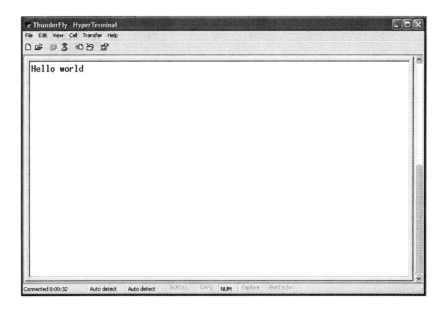

- You'll now see your message scrolling across the Butterfly LCD. If not, notice that you have three areas that you can mess up:
  - Soldering and connecting the RS232
  - Selecting the correct COM Port
  - Setting up HyperTerminal properly

So if its not working by this point go back and meticulously retry everything you can think of, including passing a dead chicken over the setup while chanting voodoo hymns. It took me a while to get all this running and I supposedly know what I'm doing, so don't feel bad if this is a little harder than you might hope. (You get what you pay for)

Index

- 51
-- 51
! 52
!= 52
#define 94
#include 94
% 51
%=...61
& 51, 53, 56
&& 52
&=..61
() 52
* 51
*=...61
, ...52
. ...51
/ 51
/=..61
?: 52
[] 51
^ 53
^=...61
| 53, 56
|| 52
|=..61
~ 53
+ 51
++...51
+=...61
< 52
<<...53
<<=...61
<=...52
= 61

-= 61
==...52
> 52
-> 51
>=...52
>> 53
>>=..61
ADC 21, 207, 208, 212, 213, 214,
    215, 216, 217, 218, 219, 220, 221,
    222, 223, 225, 227, 231, 233, 236,
    237
Addition....................................51
Address of..................................51
Addresses of variables................153
Analog to Digital Conversion 210
Arithmetic Operators....................50
Array element...............................51
array of pointers to arrays............172
Arrays 153, 159
Arrays in RAM and ROM...........171
ASCII 82, 181, 283
assembly language 12, 13, 154
Assignment Operators...................61
Associativity................................62
ATMEGA169 15, 17, 20, 31, 66, 248
atoi...81
AVRStudio.....19, 20, 31, 35, 68, 150
BCD - Binary Coded Decimal ..180
binary.. 43, 45, 46, 47, 48, 53, 54, 59,
    75, 154, 186, 212, 249
Binary Coded Decimal..............180
Bit-fields...................................247
Bits 45, 53, 60, 98, 124
Bits per second 291

Bitwise AND.................................. 53

Bitwise complement 53

Bitwise OR 53

Blocks........................ 39, 40, 73, 92

Break 79

Brightness Control 134

Bytes... 45

calibration................................... 121

case... 76

cast 52, 190

char 48

Circular Buffers................... 167, 168

CISC 12, 13

COM.................... 289, 290, 291, 293

COM0A0...............................57, 58

COM0A1...............................57, 58

comments 161

Comments 39

Conditional 52, 62, 64, 96

Conditional Inclusion.................... 96

Connections Properties 290

Constants...................................... 49

Continue 79

Control Flow 73

Counters 119

CS00.... 57, 58, 59, 60, 194, 204, 235

CS0157, 58, 128, 129, 133, 135, 143, 150, 235

CS02..................... 57, 58, 59, 235

Cylon......... 34, 35, 39, 46, 70, 94, 96

CylonEyes.c................................. 70

DAC 207

Data Types................................... 45

databook 15

Debugging...... 51, 73, 110, 207, 210, 216, 221, 279

Declarations 50

Decrement.................................... 51

Demonstrator.c 99

Demonstrator.h........................... 99

Digi-Key............. 17, 18, 66, 273

Digital Oscilloscope.................... 227

Digital to Analog Conversion 227

Division 51

Do-while................................... 78

duration 192

Encapsulation 87

Equal to 52

Escape Sequences 82

Expressions 39, 45, 61, 62, 73

External variable 90

FIFOs 167

Flow Control 40, 98

FOC0A 58, 143, 150

FOCA 57

For.. 78

frequency................................... 190

Function... 52, 87, 122, 157, 166, 169, 227, 230, 231, 232

Function Arguments.................... 157

Function Generator 227

Function Pointers 169

Functions................ 41, 87, 169, 243

Goals 14

Goto.. 80

Greater than 52

Headers.. 92

hexadecimal .. 43, 46, 47, 48, 82, 180

Hyperterminal 103, 118, 133, 136, 150, 173, 176, 188, 216, 223, 227, 230, 236, 289, 292, 293

If-Else and Else-If........................ 74

Include Files................................. 39

Increment.................................... 51

Indirection 51
int 49
interrupt 178
Interrupts 109
itoa 81
JAMECO 22, 26, 137, 225, 227, 273, 275, 276
joystick 15, 32, 33, 68, 75, 76, 98, 110, 111, 114, 116, 118, 119, 150, 151, 270, 292
Labels 80
LCD 43
LED .. 23, 26, 43, 46, 69, 70, 75, 128, 129, 134, 136, 137
LEDs .. 15, 26, 27, 34, 35, 36, 39, 43, 45, 46, 47, 48, 65, 67, 68, 70, 115, 134, 135, 147, 154, 273
Left shift 53
Less than 52
LIFOs 167
Light 219
Light Meter 219
Logical 52, 64
Logical NOT 52
long 49
Loops 78
machine language 12
Macro Substitution 95
Main() 42
masking 248
Member selection 51
messenger software 174
Modulo 51
Motor Speed Control 137
Multiplication 51
Negation 51
nitialization 92

NOT 53
Operators .. 40, 45, 50, 51, 52, 53, 61, 63
optoisolator 137, 144
Order of Evaluation 62
OSCCAL_calibration 122
oscillator ... 99, 104, 105, 115, 121, 123, 124, 125, 127, 128, 130, 132, 140, 142, 147, 149, 162, 175, 178, 183, 199, 208, 222, 232, 235
PC_Comm.c 102
PC_Comm.h 102
Piezo 192
play a tune 194
Pointers 153
pointers to arrays 189
potentiometer 225
Precedence 62
preprocessor 39, 94, 95, 97, 112, 246
Preprocessor 94
Programmers Notepad 19, 27, 36, 114, 130, 174, 182, 195
Pulse Width Modulation 134, 137
PWM 193
Queues 167, 168
Real Time Clock ... 15, 178, 182, 183, 188
Real Timer Clock Software 182
Recursion 93
Register variable 90
Returns 89
reverse 81
Right shift 53
RISC 13
RS-232 .... 21, 22, 26, 289
RXD 21, 22, 96
Sawtooth Wave 231

Scope 91
Simulation 35
simulator.......................... 27, 32, 35
Sine Wave.................................... 231
sourceforge 19, 35, 172, 189
Speedometer................................ 144
Square Wave................................ 231
Stacks 167
Statements 39, 40, 73
Statements and Blocks 73
Static variable............................. 90
strlen... 81
Structure Arrays 246
Structures 241
Structures and Functions............. 243
Subtraction.................................. 51
Successive Approximation.......... 211
Switch.. 75
Tale of a bug............................... 73
TCC0RA 59, 60, 61, 135
TCCR0A 57, 58, 59, 60, 128, 129,
    133, 135, 143, 150, 194, 204, 235
Temperature 220

Temperature Meter...................... 220
tempo... 191
Testing Bits 60
Timer0 interrupt 194
Timers 109, 119
Triangle Wave 231
TXD 21, 22, 96
Typedef.. 246
Unary Plus 51
Unions 247
unsigned 49
Variable Names 49
Variables...................................... 90
Volt Meter 221
Waveform Generator Modes 60
WGM00 57, 58, 59, 60, 61, 128, 129,
    133, 135, 143, 150, 194, 204, 235
WGM01 57, 58, 59, 60, 61, 128, 129,
    133, 135, 143, 150, 194, 204, 235
While.. 78
WinAVR . 15, 18, 19, 27, 31, 35, 113,
    171, 177, 182, 189, 195, 198, 220,
    221, 247, 270

www.SmileyMicros.com.